U.S.-RUSSIAN NAVAL COOPERATION

To the memory of
Terrence S. Shea, S.J., Ph.D.
1937–1995
Founder and 1st President of
the Institute for Global Security Studies

U.S.-RUSSIAN NAVAL COOPERATION

Charles A. Meconis and Boris N. Makeev

Westport, Connecticut
London

VA
50
M43
1996

Library of Congress Cataloging-in-Publication Data

Meconis, Charles A.
    U.S.-Russian naval cooperation / Charles A. Meconis and Boris N.
Makeev.
        p.   cm.
    Includes bibliographical references and index.
    ISBN 0–275–95387–4 (alk. paper)
    1. Sea-power—United States.   2. Sea-power—Russia (Federation)
3. United States.   Navy.   4. Russia (Federation).   Voenno-Morskoĭ
Flot.   5. United States—Military relations—Russia (Federation)
6. Russia (Federation)—Military relations—United States.
7. National security—United States.   8. National security—Russia
(Federation)   I. Makeev, Boris N. (Boris Nikolaevich)   II. Title.
VA50.M43   1996
359′.03′0973—dc20   95–30655

British Library Cataloguing in Publication Data is available.

Library of Congress Catalog Card Number: 95–30655
ISBN: 0–275–95387–4

First published in 1996

Praeger Publishers, 88 Post Road West, Westport, CT 06881
An imprint of Greenwood Publishing Group, Inc.

Printed in the United States of America

∞

The paper used in this book complies with the
Permanent Paper Standard issued by the National
Information Standards Organization (Z39.48–1984).

10 9 8 7 6 5 4 3 2 1

CONTENTS

TABLES AND FIGURES

TABLES

FIGURES

ACKNOWLEDGMENTS

The authors acknowledge the generous help they received from many quarters during this project. The project was conceived by Commander James J. Tritten, USN (Ret.), Ph.D., while he was on the faculty of the Naval Postgraduate School, and he continued to be supportive throughout. Rear Admiral F. W. Crickard, RCN (Ret.), naval analyst James L. George, Ph.D., Rear Admiral J. R. Hill, RN (Ret.), Commander Stanley Weeks, USN (Ret.), Ph.D., on the adjunct faculty of the Naval War College, and Professor Michael Wallace of the Political Science Department at the University of British Columbia reviewed the first draft. Lieutenant Gary Shiffman, USN, of the NATO, Europe, Russia Branch at the Chief of Naval Operations' Directorate for Operations, Plans, and Political-Military Affairs, provided a useful open literature summary of existing official U.S.-Russian naval contacts. Professor Ed Miles, of the School of Marine Affairs at the University of Washington, offered valuable advice on the larger issues of ocean policy. Deputy Director Eric Grove, Hull University Centre for Security Studies, offered early advice both on naval dialogue with the (then) Soviet Navy and on the topic of a possible U.N. naval force, along with Michael Pugh of the University of Plymouth in the United Kingdom. Professor Andrew Mack, Head of the International Relations Department of the Australian National University, and Pauline Kerr of that department's Publications Programme were pioneers on the topic of naval arms control in the Pacific and were early sources of inspiration.

Translation assistance for one chapter was provided by the Center for Naval Analyses. Professors Terry Johnson and Misha Tsypkin at the Naval Postgraduate School were gracious hosts during our visit there. Dr. Clay Moltz of the Monterey Institute of International Studies helped greatly to facilitate our working time together in Monterey. At the Center for Geopolitical and Military Forecasts and the Institute of World Economy and International

Relations (IMEMO) in Moscow, Dr. Alexei Arbatov and Dr. Alexander Pikayev were instrumental in launching and sustaining this effort. In particular, Dr. Pikayev's heroic efforts at real-time translation during face-to-face meetings were invaluable.

Brandon George Beams and Lynn Trepp provided valuable research and much needed secretarial and editorial assistance during the final preparation of the manuscript at the Institute for Global Security Studies in Seattle. Charles A. Meconis also wishes to thank his wife, Robbie, and daughter Dylan for their patience and support.

Any errors of fact or judgment, of course, are the authors' responsibility alone. The United States Institute of Peace provided the financial support for this project. The opinions, findings, and conclusions or recommendations expressed in this publication are those of the authors and do not necessarily reflect the views of the United States Institute of Peace.

INTRODUCTION

It seems only yesterday that U.S.-Russian naval interactions were the stuff of techno-thriller fiction and Hollywood movies such as *The Hunt for Red October*. Fortunately the spectacle of a bloody and perhaps apocalyptic Cold War confrontation on the high seas is now a matter restricted to the category of history and perhaps fantasy. This book is an effort by a retired Russian naval officer and an American naval arms control analyst to look at the future relationship of the world's two greatest navies following the end of the Cold War and the demise of the Soviet Union.

The first half of the book examines just how much has changed during the last five years in the size and, more important, the strategy, doctrine, operations, and missions of both navies, within the context of the new global security situation, and their countries' overall national security and military strategies. We have attempted, in language accessible to the nonprofessional, to offer an independent professional assessment of these matters. While both authors had access to official nonclassified documents and to active and retired naval officers, this is not in any way an "official" document. Much of the information on recent developments concerning the Russian Navy has not been previously published in English, and thus may prove especially valuable to those particularly interested in that topic. Developments concerning the U.S. Navy are widely available to naval professionals, but we have made an effort to provide a concise and accurate assessment that will prove valuable to a wider audience. We worked together on some chapters, independently on others.

The second half of the book is a series of proposals for ways to improve significantly the existing levels of U.S.-Russian naval cooperation in the volatile multipolar world we now inhabit together. Our basic premise is that, given the importance of the world's oceans, and the fact that the United States and Russia will continue to possess the two largest and most capable navies in the world, it is in everyone's interests for the two former adversaries to cooperate. We argue that, in order to complete the move from confrontation to partnership, the previously sterile and stalemated field of "naval arms control" should now be reexamined in the light of new international realities. A series of specific naval arms control proposals and an underlying methodology are spelled out. Once the last "Cold War icebergs" have been removed, we advocate a series of measures for multinational naval cooperation to address the issues of regional conflict and other threats to the global maritime environment.

We offer these proposals in the spirit of scientific inquiry and healthy debate. If this book stimulates new thought, and perhaps even new directions in policy, then it will have served the purpose we envisioned.

U.S.-RUSSIAN
NAVAL
COOPERATION

THE NAVAL DIMENSION OF GLOBAL SECURITY AFTER THE COLD WAR: A U.S.-RUSSIAN PERSPECTIVE

Charles A. Meconis

Let's face it. There isn't going to be any "Second Battle of the Atlantic."
—Admiral Leon Edney, USN (Ret.),
former Supreme Allied Commander Atlantic,
at a naval strategy symposium in Washington, D.C.

This is actually the end of a chapter in the history of the Russian Navy, in which it tried to challenge the supremacy of the U.S. Navy on the high seas.
—Sergei Rogov, Institute of USA and Canada, Moscow,
on the announcement of the mothballing of three *Kiev* class carriers

Many people in Russia and in the United States believe that everything possible has already been done. But the situation is far from that.
—Rear Admiral Valery I. Aleksin, Russian Navy

THE SEA CHANGE

For nearly forty years, the greatest threat to peace on the world's oceans was the Cold War confrontation between the North Atlantic Treaty Organization (NATO) and Warsaw pact (WTO) navies. The end of the Cold War and the political and economic collapse of the Soviet Union have greatly reduced that threat. That is a fortunate development, because had the two navies ever come to blows, the potential results ranged from global nuclear war to "conventional" carnage on all the world's oceans, with the possible exception of the Antarctic.[1]

As a result of this enormous geostrategic watershed, both the U.S. and the Russian navies (as well as the other NATO navies and those of former WTO members) are undergoing dramatic changes in their force structures and strategies. The search for a "peace dividend" to alleviate the U.S. deficit and the collapse of the centralized economy in the former Soviet Union have resulted in large reductions in both navies, with more to come. Gone are the Reagan-era dream of a "600 ship" U.S. fleet and the Brezhnev-era dream of a Soviet navy able to challenge it on the high seas. The following table gives some indication of the probable extent of these reductions over the next few years. If anything, the figures indicated may be on the high side.

Table 1.1
Current and Projected Strength of the U.S. and Russian Navies[2]

Ship Types	U.S. Navy		Russian Navy	
	1993	1999	1993	1999
Ballistic Missile Submarines, Nuclear-Powered (SSBN)	21	14	54	21
Nuclear-Powered Attack Submarines (SSN/SSGN)	87	50	95	59
Diesel Submarines (SS/G)	0	0	66	42
Aircraft Carriers (CV/N)	14	12[3]	1	2[4]
V/STOL Carriers[5]	13	11	4	1
Cruisers (CG\N)	50	29	23	1
Destroyers (DD\G)	38	63	36	28
Frigates (FF\G)	59	37	141	40
Large Amphibious	61	25	43	20?
Combat Logistics	60	50	28	14?
Auxiliary	60	55	30	15?
TOTAL	**452**	**346**	**522**	**244**

Sources: Jane's Fighting Ships 1994-95; Combat Fleets of the World 1993; IISS, *The Military Balance 1994-95;* Les Aspin, *Report on the Bottom-Up Review,* Washington, D.C., Department of Defense, October 1993; "Russia's Future Navy Plan," *Naval Forces* Vol. 14, No. 6 (1993), pp. 6-7; interviews with Capt. 1st Rank Boris N. Makeev (Ret.), Washington, D.C., Jan. 17-24, 1994 and Monterey, Calif., May 10-17, 1994; "Russia Dumping 3 Carriers," *Seattle Post Intelligencer,* February 15, 1994; Dr. Scott C. Truver, "Tomorrow's Fleet: Effective Force or 'Rotten Timber'?" Center for Security Strategies and Operations Critical Issues Paper, April, 1994; "How Many Ships?" by John Diamond, Associated Press, February 25, 1994; Department of Defense, *Nuclear Posture Review,* September 22, 1994, p. 17; Norman Polmar, "Republic Navies: A Continuing Interest . . . in Submarines," U.S. Naval Institute *Proceedings,* Vol. 124, No. 11, November 1994, p. 103; "The Jane's Interview with Adm. Boorda," *Jane's Defence Weekly,* January 7, 1995, p. 32; Office of Naval Intelligence, *Worldwide Submarine Proliferation in the Coming Decade,* p. 3. *Shaded sections indicate the most dramatic reductions.*

One should also keep in mind that, at present, many Russian ships counted as "active" may not be "operational." For example, Derek Da Cunha of the Institute of Southeast Asian Studies estimates that in 1993 only a third of the Russian Pacific Fleet's attack submarines were truly operational, along with 40% of the main surface warships and half the land-based naval aircraft.[6]

The controversial U.S. "Forward" Maritime Strategy of the 1980s centering around global war with the Soviet Union is officially "on the shelf," and has been replaced by a strategy named . . . *From the Sea*, which is entirely focused on affecting the outcome of regional conflicts.[7] This is made quite explicit in the document's introduction, which states: "Our strategy has shifted from a focus on a global threat to a focus on regional challenges and opportunities." The introduction to the November 1994 update entitled *Forward . . . From the Sea* reiterates "a shift in the Department of Defense's focus to new dangers—chief among which is aggression by regional powers."[8]

At the same time, Russia has adopted a very similar "military doctrine" which declares: "The main current source of danger is local wars and regional conflicts."[9] Its "Fleet Forward Plan" calls for a dramatic restructuring of the navy in the light of that strategic shift.[10]

Given these developments, one might be tempted to respond to questions about the future relations of these two navies with a firm "Who cares anymore?" This is especially true in light of the growing importance of the economic and environmental elements of global security in general, and the future of the world's oceans in particular.

Who Cares Anymore?

As the world's human population continues to explode, the ocean's importance as a guardian of environmental stability, a source of critical resources, and a highway for international trade is increasing. Problems of pollution and resource depletion are on the rise—and may contribute to the phenomenon of global warming. Twelve years after its publication, the U.N.'s Convention on the Law of the Sea (UNCLOS) has now come into force in a full legal sense,[11] and disputes over the "Exclusive Economic Zones" (EEZs) and other provisions established by it are on the rise.[12] It is understandable that in the light of these challenges, the relationship between the U.S. and Russian navies at this point in the history of the planet might be seen as a minor matter at best and a distraction at worst.

That view is mistaken. First of all, even keeping in mind the drastic reductions occurring in both navies, the U.S. and Russian fleets will retain their standing as the world's largest navies for the foreseeable future. Both navies will retain awesome "conventional" military power. America's fleet of huge aircraft carriers will be able to "project" enormous power, and both navies will continue to operate scores of nuclear-powered attack submarines (SSNs) capable of wreaking considerable havoc. Moreover, these forces are inherently *global* in their reach. To paraphrase the famous dictum about mountain climbing, the future interaction of the world's two greatest navies is important "because they are there."

Second, while the prospect of conflict between the United States and Russia has virtually disappeared for the near future, the democratic experiment in Russia is obviously still in an early and very fragile phase. While a return to the Soviet version of imperialism is out of the question, the rise of Russian ultranationalist forces serves as a reminder that all may not go well in the longer term. In *Russia 2010 and What It Means for the World*, Daniel Yergin and Thane Gustafson remind us that Russia's military leaders will play an important role in shaping that nation's future. Russian analyst Alexei Arbatov has made the same point in reviewing his nation's foreign policy alternatives.[13]

Of course, even assuming an unfavorable turn of political events in Russia, it will be years before Russia can substantially reconstitute its navy to a point where it could seriously challenge the U.S. Navy. For its part, the United States has demonstrated during these years of Russian weakness that it poses no aggressive threat to Russia whatsoever. Nevertheless, even if one estimates that a return to an adversarial U.S.-Russian relationship is not very likely, there is ample reason to go about resolving the "unfinished business" of making a full transition from hostility to perhaps even "partnership" between the two navies in question. At the heart of the issue is the fact that a better relationship between the two navies can contribute to a better relationship between the two nations, and thereby to global security as we approach the twenty-first century. *Now* is the time to set in place measures of cooperation that will endure.

The second answer to the "who cares?" question is the fact that Moscow remains very interested in this issue area. U.S.-Russian relations will retain their importance for a long time to come, as recent events concerning the conflict in the former Yugoslavia have shown. There have been several strong initiatives concerning naval matters put forward recently from the Russian side. In an article entitled "We're Ready When You Are," Rear Admiral Valery I. Aleksin of the Russian Navy proposed a number of measures such as mutual consultation on prevention of ships' accidents to enhance naval understanding and cooperation and stated: "The[se] opened doors and people-to-people policies will bring our two peoples together, strengthen confidence between our two governments, and make the world more reliable and stable."[14]

There has been considerable progress in this task already, but there is much more to do. Recent years have seen increased contact in the form of mutual port visits, officer visits, cadet exchanges, and even a few joint U.S.-Russian naval exercises. In addition to the annual review meeting held under the provisions of the 1972 Prevention of Incidents at Sea agreement, a supplemental navy-to-navy annual meeting has been instituted.[15]

However, from the Russian viewpoint, as Admiral Aleksin put it, there are still one or two leftover "icebergs in the Cold War sea"[16] that could wreck the hoped-for transition to naval partnership. At the top of the list is the issue of the survivability of each navy's ballistic missile submarines (SSBNs). As a result of the START I and II agreements, these submarines will constitute an ever more important element of each country's deterrent, while dramatically decreasing in numbers. In other words, each side will have more nuclear "eggs" in fewer "baskets." During the Cold War, both navies explicitly engaged in efforts at "strategic" antisubmarine warfare (ASW), that is, attempts to find, track, and, should war occur, destroy the other side's SSBNs. Some Russian sources have stated that the Russian Navy has ceased engaging in those operations, and the new U.S. Navy strategy has dropped any mention of the topic. As encouraging as those developments are, they are not sufficient from the Russian standpoint. Most Russian conservatives and some moderates complain that the START II agreement was unfair to Russia, especially in the area of SSBN numbers and security. As the United States and Russia move farther away from their Cold War standoff, some means must be found to reassure each country (and the rest of the world) that the dangerous cat-and-mouse game of "strategic ASW" is over.

The third answer is that the world community is caring more about the future of the oceans in general, and therefore the relations of the two most important navies is important. Having escaped the Scylla of World War III at sea, the world now faces the Charybdis of the "Balkanization" of the oceans under increasing environmental/economic pressure. For example, conflicting claims concerning the Exclusive Economic Zones established under the U.N. Law of the Sea are one, but not the only, source of potential maritime conflict.[17] In the vital maritime regions of Southeast Asia and the Middle East, a wide variety of efforts at preventing maritime conflict are under way, at both the "official" and the unofficial level.[18] It is in the interest of all nations that the U.S. and Russian navies put confrontation behind them and move toward cooperation and even partnership, under the rubric of "cooperative security." Naval arms control is a necessary intermediate step on the way toward partnership.

Arms Control for Its Own Sake?

During the Cold War, the very term "naval arms control" was anathema to the U.S. government and its navy. Citing the "failure" of the interwar naval arms control agreements to prevent or even mitigate World War II, and emphasizing that the United States is an "island nation" while Russia is a "continental power," the United States has steadfastly refused to engage the Russians in "naval arms control" and adopted an attitude of "Just Say No!"[19]

In the Cold War context, that was perhaps understandable. It makes much less sense now, as several American naval analysts have recently argued.[20] Critics of Cold War arms control efforts maintained that when arms control is needed, it is not achievable, and that when it is achievable, it is not needed. We intend to stand that axiom on its head. At this point in world history, U.S.-Russian naval arms control may not be "needed," but it might be achievable. And then, at some future point when it might be needed, crucial agreements and channels of communication will already be in place.

There is a precedent. The 1972 U.S.-Soviet "Prevention of Incidents at Sea" Agreement, negotiated during the early 1970s period of détente, established what turned out to be a very important enduring communications channel when U.S.-Soviet relations seriously deteriorated during the early 1980s.

At the global level, "naval arms control" is already happening. More and more countries are establishing agreements to prevent "incidents at sea." Other restrictions on naval operations are being considered or have already been enacted. This may not be naval arms control in the Cold War sense, but the U.S. and Russian navies cannot afford to ignore the phenomenon.

What's in It for the United States?

In the post-Cold War strategic context, there are several potential benefits for the United States in engaging in such negotiations, and few risks. After all, economic constraints are already reducing the size of the U.S. Navy below the levels envisioned by all but the most thorough of naval arms control advocates. The potential benefits are both political and economic in nature.

On the political side, the U.S. refusal to include naval forces in the arms control agenda plays right into the hands of Russian ultranationalists who portray the West as Russia's enemy. Conversely, by prudently engaging in appropriate forms of limiting naval operations and weapons, the United States can undercut those hard-liners and support those elements in Russia who wish to see a stable and friendly relationship develop between the two countries. It is true, of course, that Russia's future will be decided by Russians. There is *relatively* little that the United States can do to foster a democratic and peaceful Russia. But what *can* be done, *should* be done—because it is in the interest of both countries.

It is true that during the Cold War some arms control advocates argued that the very process of arms control was an intrinsic good, regardless of the outcome. The situation has changed a great deal since then. If the process of arms control can play even a minor role in sustaining the movement of Russia toward an open, democratic society, then it is worth the effort.

On the economic side, naval forces are among the most expensive to procure, operate, and maintain. It is in the interest of both countries to reduce unnecessary military spending in order to concentrate on pressing domestic priorities. By eliminating the remaining vestiges of Cold War naval confrontation, the United States and Russia will be able to reduce defense spending accordingly.

All of the above, however, falls under the category of dealing with Cold War leftovers—melting old icebergs. As we approach the twenty-first century, there will be many new opportunities for the U.S. and Russian navies to move from confrontation to cooperation, and perhaps even to "partnership" on the world's oceans.

CHARTING A NEW COURSE TOGETHER

The oceans are increasingly important to the future of the planet. The 80 million tons of seafood consumed each year represents 16% of the global animal-protein consumption. The developing world is especially dependent on food from the sea, with more than one billion Asians relying on fish as their primary source of protein. However, the world fish catch has begun to decline even as the human population continues to increase.[21] Conflict over this threatened resource is likely to intensify. The North Sea "Cod Wars" of the 1960s may have been a harbinger of things to come.

As of 1989, more than 20% of the world's production of both oil and gas came from offshore sources, and this share is rapidly growing.[22] The possibility that there are large oil deposits beneath the South China Sea is a major factor in fueling that region's dispute over the ownership of the Spratly islands, and the rapid growth and modernization of naval forces in the area.[23] Iran is building up its naval forces, apparently with a view to controlling access to the oil-rich Persian Gulf.[24]

Trade has become increasingly important to the world economy. In the early 1990s international trade amounted to approximately $3.5 trillion per year.[25] More than 90% of the world's goods are transported by sea, including virtually all of the oil. The safety of shipping is vital to the world's economic health. Piracy is on the rise.[26]

Finally, despite their vastness, the world's oceans are under increasing environmental stress. Overfishing, oil spills and other seaborne pollution, and especially damage to coastal ecosystems are taking a serious toll on the health of the oceans.

This, then, is the context in which the U.S. and Russian navies find themselves after the Cold War era. It is precisely this context that calls for a full transition from hostility to partnership in the cause of global security. No one envisions a U.S.-Russian "condominium" arrangement for policing the world's oceans. However, because the issue of maritime security is growing in importance in overall terms, it is critical that the world's two largest navies join with the international community in an effort to address the full ranges of challenges outlined above.

British naval analyst Ken Booth suggests, in *Navies and Foreign Policy*, that the tasks of navies can be divided into three basic functions: diplomatic, policing, and military (or warfighting).[27] With the prospect of World War III at sea firmly behind them, it is time for the U.S. and Russian navies to cooperate in the first two tasks.

On the "diplomatic" front, both navies have a key role to play in preventing regional conflicts. Commodore Sam Bateman, RAN (Ret.), argues that it is useful to distinguish between "cooperative" and "coercive" naval diplomacy.[28] Cooperative naval diplomacy consists primarily of multinational naval cooperation. In the European region, now that Russia is apparently accepting a "Partnership for Peace" status with NATO, it should be possible for the Russian Navy eventually to play a role in NATO's Standing Naval Force Atlantic (STANAVFORLANT). Such a move will constitute a major confidence-and-security-building measure (CSBM) in the North Atlantic, especially for Norway. An important step in this direction was taken in March 1994 when Russian naval vessels took part in a large-scale joint naval exercise off the Norwegian coast together with British, German, Dutch, Norwegian, and U.S. ships.[29]

Outside the NATO arena, however, multinational naval cooperation is a very recent development—where it exists at all. The two most troubled (and troubling) maritime regions in the world are the Middle East/Persian Gulf and East Asia. It took Iraq's invasion of Kuwait to bring together a multinational naval force in a warfighting role, under a U.N. resolution. A single Russian ship now takes part in the continuing multinational "coercive" naval diplomacy that maintains the post-Gulf War blockade of Iraq. In November 1993, Russia and Kuwait signed a bilateral defense agreement and staged a joint naval exercise in December involving three Russian ships.[30] Given the continuous U.S. naval presence in the Gulf, it is time for U.S. and Russian ships to increase their cooperation in that region, possibly as members of an international "Gulf Patrol."

In Northeast Asian waters, a serious level of tension continues to exist because of friction between Russia and Japan over possession of the southern Kurile islands, between North Korea and the international community over the nuclear issue, and between China and Taiwan. The first ever U.S.-Russian joint naval exercise in the North Pacific took place in June 1994.[31] The Russian and U.S. navies could possibly play a positive role in constructing a multilateral security system in that region by increasing their cooperative naval diplomacy.

In Southeast Asia, the U.S. withdrawal from Subic Bay in the Philippines and the near elimination of the Russian naval presence at Cam Ranh Bay in Vietnam have contributed to regional concerns over China's—and Japan's—possible desire to fill the resulting "power vacuum." According to Dr. Bakhtiyar Tuzmukhamedov, this has prompted some rather "fantastic" (i.e., unrealistic) proposals in the Russian academic community about the joint use of the Cam Ranh base by the Russian and U.S. navies as a "vacuum prevention measure."[32] That particular proposal may be unrealistic, but it is equally unrealistic for the members of the Association of Southeast Asian Nations (ASEAN) to ignore the possible contribution of both the American and Russian navies to maritime stability in the region. For their part, the Russians have put forward several recent (and more realistic) proposals in that regard.[33]

Under the general heading of "cooperative naval diplomacy," there is one other critical arena where U.S.-Russian cooperation is required: restraining the proliferation of potentially destabilizing naval weapons in regions where conflict is ongoing or likely. Of course, "navies" do not sell or otherwise transfer weapons: governments and businesses do. However, navies do have considerable influence over such decisions. For example, until recently the U.S. Navy played a major role in preventing U.S. corporations from manufacturing submarines for export.

There is an obvious mutual interest in preventing the proliferation of naval nuclear weapons, especially the "tactical" weapons recently removed from both the Russian and American navies. Also, it is not in the interest of either navy to sell or lease nuclear-powered attack submarines, as Russia once did to India. With both navies cutting their SSN fleets, there might be a temptation to get some return on the investment.

The issue of conventional naval weapons is much more complex. Naval analyst Eric Grove argues that most naval forces are "inherently stabilizing" and thus not subject to arms control. Still, Grove notes that deep-water mines and large conventional submarines might be candidates for export controls.[34] In the light of Russia's recent sale of *Kilo* class submarines to Iran and the People's Republic of China, and rumors of a possible sale of Backfire bombers with long-range antiship missiles, the issue of conventional naval weapons transfers should definitely be on the agenda for U.S.-Russian naval cooperation.

Finally, the "policing" task may offer several arenas for cooperation between these two navies as we approach what some are calling the "ocean era." The two nations certainly share a common interest in the North Pacific and Arctic oceans. As one Russian Coast Guard officer recently stated: "Russia and America have the same enemy now. We both fight illegal fishing by foreign trawlers in the Bering Sea."[35] While each nation's Coast Guard can address some of these issues within their 200 mile EEZs, only the two navies have the equipment and trained personnel to deal with long-range open ocean or under-ice operations in that region. Bureaucracies such as the U.N. International Maritime Organization are not capable of enforcing regulations concerning environmental matters. This is a very new approach to the use of navies, of course, but it is not fanciful. In *Top Guns and Toxic Whales: The Environment & Global Security*, Gwyn Prins and Robbie Stamp outlined existing governmental proposals for involving navies in the issue of "environmental security" as follows:

- *Stage 1:* Making available data from existing sensors on existing ships and aircraft following existing operational patterns.
- *Stage 2:* Using existing assets following existing operational patterns to carry additional automatic recording or sampling equipment requiring little or no attention by service personnel.
- *Stage 3:* As Stage 2 but using environmental observational requirements as a consideration in weighing the balance between training options that, from an operational point of view, are equally attractive.
- *Stage 4:* Using assets, including shore assets, to support environmental research activities in ways that would involve additional expenditure.[36]

In fact, the U.S. Navy has recently begun employing its Cold War antisubmarine surveillance systems in an effort to monitor global warming, with possible applications to marine mammal surveillance and seismic event monitoring.[37]

CONCLUSION

By removing the few remaining "Cold War icebergs" and cooperating in "diplomatic" and "policing" operations, including the aspect of environmental protection, the U.S. and Russian navies can play a significant role in improving the relationship between their two countries and in enhancing the maritime aspect of global security. As the importance of the world's oceans to the future of the planet increases, a peaceful partnership between the world's two largest navies is something worth achieving.

In the following chapters we present an up-to-date analysis of U.S. and Russian post-Cold War naval strategies and force structures. We then go on to propose an agenda of naval arms control measures and forms of naval cooperation designed to lead to a peaceful U.S.-Russian naval partnership, in the context of global security.

NOTES

1. The intense debate over the U.S. Maritime Strategy of the 1980s, and in particular the likelihood of the use of nuclear weapons at sea during the Cold War, and the possible escalation to a full-scale nuclear exchange, remains unresolved, albeit happily reduced to a largely historical exercise at this time. The best one-volume review of the debate is *Naval Strategy and National Security: An International Security Reader,* eds. Steven E. Miller and Stephen Van Evera (Princeton: Princeton University Press, 1988). The best bibliography is Captain Peter M. Swartz, USN and Jan S. Breemer, with James J. Tritten, "The Maritime Strategy Debates: A Guide to the Renaissance of U.S. Naval Strategic Thinking in the 1980s," Monterey, Calif.: Naval Postgraduate School Report NPS-56-89-019, September 30, 1989. The only debate

concerning the "conventional" cost of such a war is over how narrow NATO's margin of victory would have been. Some idea of the potential cost in lives and ships can be gained by reading Eric Grove's vivid account of the last full-scale "Teamwork" Atlantic exercise in 1988, *Battle for the Fiørds: NATO's Forward Maritime Strategy in Action* (Annapolis, Md.: Naval Institute Press, 1991).

2. Only active duty major combatants and combat support ships over 1,000 tons displacement are included. The shaded sections highlight the most dramatic reductions. According to the Vol. 16, No. 3 (1995) issue of the journal *Naval Forces*, Russian naval analysts are predicting that by 2010-2025 the Russian Naval Order of Battle will include approximately 440 combatants: 20 SSBNs, 70 SSNs, 30sss, 5-6 CVs, 5-6 escorts, 10-12 Cgs, 35 DDGs, 50FFGs, 40 landing vessels, 50-60 missile corvettes and 100 Mine Countermeasures ships. It remains to be seen whether such an ambitious forecast is accurate.

3. One aircraft carrier will operate in a "reserve/training" role. Further reductions remain possible.

4. This assumes that the second unfinished *Kuznetsov* class carrier languishing at Nikolayev is completed and put into service in the Pacific Fleet, an ever more unlikely development.

5. While neither nation lists their "amphibious assault craft" or "aircraft carrying cruisers" as "aircraft carriers," we have included here all vessels capable of deploying more than two helicopters or Vertical or Short Take Off and Landing aircraft, i.e., the (mostly erstwhile) Russian *Kiev* class, as well as the U.S. LPH/LHA/LHD. The latter do have a primary amphibious mission and related capabilities, but are also "aircraft carriers" in the basic sense employed here. E.g., an LHD can deploy twice the number of Harrier "jump" jets carried by the V/STOL carrier HMS *Invincible*.

6. Cited in Yi-Hua Shen, "The Disarmament of Naval Forces in the North Pacific," *The Korean Journal of International Studies*, Vol. 24, No. 4 (Winter 1993), p. 542.

7. The new strategy is contained in the joint Navy/Marine Corps White Paper *From the Sea: Preparing the Naval Service for the 21st Century, A New Direction for the Naval Service*, Washington, D.C., Department of the Navy, September 1992. The unclassified version of the U.S. "Maritime Strategy" of the 1980s was published under the name of then Chief of Naval Operations Admiral J. D. Watkins as a special supplement to the January 1986 issue of the U.S. Naval Institute *Proceedings*, Vol. 122, No. 1.

8. Department of the Navy, *Forward . . . From the Sea*, November, 1994, p. 1.

9. Serge Schmemann, "Moscow Outlines 'Doctrine' for Its Military of the Future," *New York Times*, November 3, 1993.

10. "Russia's Future Navy Plan," *Naval Forces*, Vol. 14, No. 6 (1993), pp. 6-7.

11. "60 Nations Celebrate Law of the Sea Treaty," *Seattle Post-Intelligencer*, November 17, 1994.

12. For a concise overview of these issues, see Peter Weber, "Safeguarding Oceans," chapter 3 in Lester R. Brown et al., *State of the World 1994* (New York: W.W. Norton, 1994), pp. 41-60. UNCLOS came into force on November 16, 1994.

13. Daniel Yergin and Thane Gustafson, *Russia 2010 and What It Means for the World* (New York: Random House, 1993), pp. 78-80, 94-96, 151-157; Alexei Arbatov, "Russia's Foreign Policy Alternatives," *International Security*, Vol. 18, No. 2 (Fall 1993), p. 14.

14. Rear Admiral Valery I. Aleksin, Russian Navy, "We Are Ready When You Are," U.S. Naval Institute *Proceedings*, Vol. 119, No. 3 (March 1993), p. 57.

15. For a report on recent U.S.-Russian naval contacts, see Lieutenant Commander Melissa Harington, USN, "Comments and Discussion," in U.S. Naval Institute *Proceedings*, Vol. 119, No. 6 (June 1993), p. 28.

16. Aleksin, "We Are Ready When You Are," p. 55.

17. Cf. *Maritime Security: The Building of Confidence*, UNIDIR Doc. 92/89 (New York: United Nations, 1992).

18. Cf. Charles A. Meconis, "Naval Arms Control in the Asia-Pacific Region after the Cold War," *Ocean Yearbook 11* (Chicago: University of Chicago Press, 1994).

19. In 1991 the Conventional Arms Control Cell of the Navy's Strategic Concepts Group (OP-603) actually printed up and distributed an informal business card with the phrase "Just Say No to Naval Arms Control!" on it, with the subheading: "It's not in U.S. interests and *we just don't like it.*" Photocopy in the author's possession.

20. See Richard C. Davis, "Future Directions for Naval Arms Control," chapter 6 in Lewis A. Dunn and Sharon A. Squassoni, eds., *Arms Control: What's Next?* (Boulder, Colo.: Westview, 1993), pp. 103-118; James L. Lacy, *A Different Equation: Naval Forces and Arms Control after 1991* (Alexandria, Va.: Institute for Defense Analyses Paper P-2768, December 1993); James J. Tritten, "A New Look at Naval Arms Control," *Security Dialogue*, Vol. 24, No. 3 (September 1993), pp. 337-348; Adam B. Siegel, "'Just Say No!' The U.S. Navy and Arms Control: A Misguided Policy?" *Naval War College Review*, Vol. 43, No. 1 (Winter 1990), pp. 73-86.

21. United Nations Food and Agriculture Organization (FAO), "Marine Fisheries and the Law of the Sea: A Decade of Change," Fisheries Circular No. 853, Rome, 1993.

22. Jan Van Ettinger, "Oceans, Climate Change, and Energy," *Ocean Yearbook 10* (Chicago: University of Chicago Press, 1993), p. 132.

23. Cf. Charles A. Meconis, "Naval Arms Control in the Asia-Pacific Region after the Cold War," *Ocean Yearbook 11* compiled by the International Ocean Institute (Chicago: University of Chicago Press, 1994).

24. Lieutenant (JG) James Kraska, USNR, "Gatekeepers of the Gulf," U.S. Naval Institute *Proceedings*, Vol. 120, No. 3 (March 1994), pp. 44-47; "Iran Builds Navy Power in the Gulf," *Seattle Times*, March 27, 1994.

25. 1990 figure from the U.S. Bureau of Economic Analysis.

26. Colin Nickerson, "Fast, Well-armed Pirates Terrorize Modern Shippers," *Boston Globe*, May 11, 1993.

27. Ken Booth, *Navies and Foreign Policy* (London: Croom Helm, 1977), pp. 15-16.

28. Sam Bateman, "Strategic Change and Naval Roles," chapter 3 in S. Bateman and D. Sherwood, eds., *Strategic Change and Naval Roles: Issues for a Medium Naval Power* (Canberra: Strategic and Defence Studies Centre Paper No. 102, 1993), p. 43.

29. Lynnley Browning, "Russia To Join Western Ships in Naval Manoeuvres," Reuter, March 17, 1994.

30. "Kuwait and Russia Start Naval Exercises in Gulf," Reuter, December 26, 1993.

31. Lieutenant Gary Shiffman, USN, NATO, Europe, Russia Branch of the Chief of Naval Operations Directorate for Operations, Plans, and Political-Military Affairs,

Summary of Former Soviet Union and Central/Eastern Europe Military Contacts, letter to the authors, August 29, 1994.

32. Dr. Bakhtiyar Tuzmukhamedov, quoted in Charles A. Meconis, ed., "Asia-Pacific Dialogue on Maritime Security and Confidence Building Measures," Transcript of Proceedings held on September 11-13, 1992 (Seattle: Institute for Global Security Studies, 1993), p. 46.

33. For example, see Capt. 1st Rank Boris N. Makeev (Ret.), "Naval Aspects of National Security and Confidence Building Measures in the Asia Pacific Region," paper presented to the United Nations Workshop on Confidence Building Measures, Katmandu, January 1993.

34. Eric Grove, "Naval Technology and Stability," chapter 16 in Wim A. Smit, John Grin, and Lev Voronkov, eds., *Military Technological Innovation and Stability in a Changing World* (Amsterdam: VU University Press, 1992), pp. 197, 213.

35. Valery Yunoshev, quoted in Bryan Hodgson, "Kamchatka: Russia's Land of Fire and Ice," *National Geographic*, Vol. 185, No. 4 (April 1994), p. 56.

36. Gwyn Prins and Robbie Stamp, *Top Guns and Toxic Whales: The Environment and Global Security* (London: Earthscan Publications, 1991), p. 149. It should be noted that then Senator Al Gore found this work to be "powerful and thought provoking."

37. Gerald M. Corrigan, "A Sound Investment Reconsidered: The Future of the U.S. Navy's Undersea Surveillance System," in *Naval Forces*, Vol. 14, No. 6 (1993), pp. 50-54; cf. also Vol. 27, No. 44 (Winter 93-94) of the *Marine Technology Society Journal* for a thorough review of these activities.

2

NAVAL ASPECTS OF U.S. NATIONAL SECURITY

Charles A. Meconis

We are a maritime nation with many interests, global economic interdependence, and a heritage inextricably tied to our geography. . . . Ensuring that the world's sea lanes remain open is not only vital to our own economic survival; it is a global necessity.

—Naval Warfare, U.S. Naval Doctrine Publication 1

For forty-five years, America's national security strategy was described by a single phrase: "containment of international communism." The end of the Cold War and the demise of the Soviet Union have changed all that. Beginning with then President George Bush's speech "In Defense of Defense" at the Aspen Institute on August 2, 1990, and continuing through the Clinton Administration's second National Security Strategy statement in February of 1995, the definition of what constitutes America's national security has changed dramatically, and continues to change as this is being written.

The enormous military threat once posed by the Soviet Union has dramatically declined, in both nature and size. By the end of August 1994, all Russian troops were withdrawn from the Baltic states and the former East Germany, ending a fifty-year occupation. If the March 3, 1994 Russian budget proposal presented by Prime Minister Viktor Chernomydrin was passed, the Russian defense budget would decline to $22 billion U.S., a more than 50% reduction from its 1993 level, and down by several orders of magnitude from its high point in the 1970s and early 1980s.[1] As part of the START I and II agreements with the United States, Russia has agreed to reduce its nuclear warheads from an estimated high of more than 20,000 to a total of 3,500 by the end of the decade, and to eliminate all of its most dangerous missiles, the huge SS-18s.[2]

In naval terms, the Cold War threat once presented by the Soviet Navy has also diminished greatly. The Russian Federation Navy is declining just as dramatically as the rest of that nation's military forces. By the end of the decade, the Russian Navy may be down to some 230 ships in all, with the most dramatic reduction occurring in the category of nuclear attack submarines, which will decline from 95 in 1993 to about 60 by 1999.[3]

In response to these dramatic changes, during the Bush Administration the United States announced a new national security strategy and a reduced military force structure to go with it. The new strategy has never been given a formal title, but its central military components are quite clear. The strategy revolves around four basic components:

- *Strategic Deterrence and Defense.* Deterring nuclear attack remains our top priority. We must still possess modern strategic nuclear forces and a reliable warning system. . . .
- *Forward Presence.* While reducing our forward-deployed forces, we are redefining our presence abroad with combined exercises, new access and storage agreements, security and humanitarian assistance, port visits, military-to-military contacts, and periodic and rotational deployments. Our forward presence forces and operations lend credibility to our alliances and ensure the perception that a collective response awaits any threat to our interests or to those of our allies.
- *Crisis Response.* We must maintain an adequate capability to project power in response to crises should our efforts to deter conflict fail. The very existence of robust crisis response capability strengthens deterrence. . . .
- *Reconstitution.* As we reduce the size of our military forces in response to the demise of the global threat, we must ensure that we continue to deter potential adversaries from militarizing and, if deterrence fails, retain the capability to recreate a global warfighting capability.[4]

In October 1993, then Secretary of Defense Les Aspin released a *Report on the Bottom-Up Review* of the U.S. Department of Defense. That document, while adding political and economic concerns to the framework of national security, emphasized "Regional Dangers" and concluded that "it is prudent for the United States to maintain sufficient military power to be able to win two major regional conflicts that occur nearly simultaneously."[5] Controversy over the adequacy of the U.S. defense budget to sustain the necessary force structure for this so-called "win-win" strategy continues, but there is little debate over the strategy itself.

The Clinton Administration, in its first national security strategy "White Paper," again placed greater emphasis on economic, diplomatic, and environmental aspects in its overall national security strategy than the Bush Administration did. However, there were no substantial changes made to the main *military* components as listed above, with the possible exception of a downgrading of the "reconstitution" component.[6] All four of these basic components have a naval dimension.

In February 1995, President Clinton released a revised *National Security Strategy of Engagement and Enlargement*, and the Joint Chiefs of Staff issued a new version of the *National Military Strategy of the United States of America*. If anything, both documents place an even greater emphasis on the importance of continued U.S. involvement "overseas," within carefully outlined limits. Given the return of many U.S. ground forces to the continental United States and the closure of many U.S. foreign military bases, it is likely that naval forces will carry the main burden of implementing this strategy, whether the mission is peacekeeping, forward presence, deterrence, or fighting and winning regional conflicts.[7]

However, it is necessary to look deeper into the issue of the national security of the United States to understand the true nature of its naval aspect. There are four main factors to be considered: (1) geography, (2) history, (3) economics, and (4) politics.

GEOGRAPHY AND THE NAVAL ASPECT
OF U.S. NATIONAL SECURITY

Geography is obviously the most enduring aspect of any nation's security. In the case of the United States, its large land mass of more than 3.5 million square miles (9 million square km) sometimes obscures the fact that the nation's *coastline* (including Alaska and Hawaii) is 12,383 miles long (19,929 km), the eighth longest inhabited coastline in the world. The State of Hawaii, in the middle of the Pacific Ocean, is more than 2,300 miles from the mainland's west coast. Alaska's Aleutian archipelago also stretches more than 1,000 miles into the North Pacific. In addition, the United States has many island "outlying areas" of various jurisdiction in both the Atlantic and Pacific oceans, among them American Samoa and Guam in the Pacific, and Puerto Rico and the U.S. Virgin Islands in the Atlantic.

Given the United States' long land borders with Canada on the north and Mexico on the south, it is an exaggeration to call the United States an "island nation." Nevertheless, it is true that from the standpoint of geography the United States *is* a "maritime nation" of the first rank. This unchanging geographic fact is a major component of the naval aspect of U.S. national security. While it is true that at this point in history no nation on earth poses a credible conventional military threat to the U.S. mainland, it is equally true that many of the nation's vital interests depend on its ability to use the world's oceans freely.

HISTORY AND THE NAVAL ASPECT
OF U.S. NATIONAL SECURITY

The most prominent scientific theory posits that humans first arrived on what we now call the North American Continent from Asia via a "land bridge" that once spanned the Bering Sea in the North Pacific, although many Native Americans question that theory. Some of the coastal "First Nations" such as the Haida and Makah of the Pacific Northwest developed amazing open-ocean fishing and hunting capabilities. In that sense the maritime history of the region goes back to prehistoric times.

However, it was the arrival of European explorers in sailing vessels beginning in the fifteenth century that ushered in the modern maritime era in the Americas. While many of the early explorers were freelancers, the navies of Holland, England, Spain, and France all played major roles in the European exploration of what is now the United States. Navies played a pioneer role in preparing the way for the vast waves of European immigration that would eventually lead to the founding of colonies and the subsequent establishment of the "United States" of America.

When those colonies decided to break away from England, their mother country across the Atlantic, they had to face the greatest naval power in the world at that time. Consequently, there was an essential, some would say central, naval dimension to the history of the very founding of the United States. That fact is every bit as important as the nation's unchanging geography.

The Continental Navy was established in 1775, a year before the colonies formally declared their independence. In the two hundred plus years of its illustrious history, the U.S. Navy has had a major impact on the nation. In his definitive two-volume *History of the U.S. Navy*, Robert W. Love, Jr. describes the Navy as the foremost "gloved fist" of American foreign policy. Love outlines three basic phases in the Navy's history:

1. The "maritime access" or nation-building phase from 1775 until the late nineteenth century, during which the Navy defended the principle of the "freedom of the seas," mostly close to the fledgling republic's own coastlines;

2. The "great power" phase from the war with Spain at the end of the nineteenth century until World War II, in which the Navy was the key foreign policy instrument in establishing the United States as a "great power" in the international arena from the globe-circling visits of "the Great White Fleet" to the final victory ceremony aboard the battleship *Missouri* in Tokyo Bay in 1945;

3. The "world bailiff" phase from the end of World War II to the end of the Cold War, during which the United States Navy played a role similar to that of the Royal Navy in the nineteenth century.[8]

An appreciation of the importance of the Navy to the nation's history can perhaps best be gained by remembering that while the U.S. Constitution authorizes Congress to "raise" an army when the need arises, that same document directs Congress to "*maintain*" a navy (emphasis added).[9] While the long lead time and great expense (even in the eighteenth century) involved in ship-building were the primary reasons for this difference, anyone who has ever visited the U.S. Naval Academy at Annapolis, Maryland cannot doubt the important role the Navy has played in the history of the United States. There is a strong argument (with the inevitable objection from the Army) that in terms of history, the United States Navy is the nation's premier military force. From that perspective, there is little doubt that the naval aspects of U.S. national security will not be neglected in the future.

ECONOMICS AND THE NAVAL ASPECT
OF U.S. NATIONAL SECURITY

Geography and history are the unchanging factors that have contributed greatly to the maritime background of the United States. Economics has also played a vital role, if an ever changing one. For, despite the country's enormous land mass and immense natural resources, from the very beginning of the European immigration to North America to the present day, overseas contact has been essential to the economy of the United States. It is well beyond the scope of this work to review the historical importance of that connection. A brief overview of the current economic situation will suffice to make the point.

In the broadest possible terms, the importance of the maritime aspect of the U.S. economy can be measured in three categories: international trade, access to energy, and access to other essential resources.

In terms of sheer volume, whether measured in dollars or tons, the amount of trade, export and import combined, that comes to or from the United States *by sea* is enormous. For example, in 1991, 830 million tons of goods, worth a total of $461.7 billion entered or left the United States by ship.[10] While there is a great deal of concern over the fact that the United States suffers from a serious trade deficit ($84.3 billion in 1992), the four leading states in terms of international trade—California, Texas, Washington, and New York—are heavily dependent on that trade and would suffer enormously from any decline.[11] Despite the complaints of the "Buy American" lobby, the global economy is now so internationalized that seaborne commerce will remain an essential and major element of the U.S. economy.

The 1990-91 Persian Gulf War left little doubt in anyone's mind about the importance of that region's oil to the world's economy, including that of the United States. While U.S. oil imports declined for a brief period of time after the 1973 OPEC oil crisis, they soon rebounded and are now at record levels. In 1991 the United States imported 2.1 billion barrels of oil.[12] While the Clinton Administration has shown more interest in alternative, and/or renewable sources of energy than its predecessors, for the foreseeable future the U. S. economy will remain heavily dependent on oil from the Persian Gulf and other OPEC sources—and that oil will come to the United States by ship. While it might be possible to bring oil from Alaska's Prudhoe Bay to the lower forty-eight states by overland pipeline, it would be enormously expensive to do so, which is why the current pipeline ends at Valdez, Alaska, where oil tankers lie in wait. To put matters in perspective, the United States maintains only a three-month emergency reserve of petroleum.[13] Some would argue that this factor is the single most important—and vulnerable—element of the U.S. economy.

But oil is not the only important resource that comes by or from the sea. Although the United States is a net food exporter, U.S. food imports rose from a value of $12.5 billion in 1985 to $17.45 billion in 1992[14]. The United States lacks adequate deposits of such critical minerals as chromium, manganese, and tungsten and must import them from overseas.[15]

When all of these economic factors are put into perspective, it becomes clear that seaborne commerce is vital to the economy of the United States. Any major disruption of that commerce, especially regarding oil, would have a devastating impact. As became clear during the "tanker war" in the Persian Gulf in 1987-88 and then again during Operations Desert Shield and Desert Storm, the U.S. Navy will be called on to respond to any threatened disruption. While the Persian Gulf oil connection is an obvious crisis scenario, there are others. For example, regional conflict between China and Taiwan, or between China and other nations claiming part of the South China Sea, would severely disrupt the vital sea-lanes and ports in Southeast Asia that now handle the largest concentration of container ship traffic in the world.[16]

By any measure, then, the fact that the United States is now so closely integrated into an international economy that relies primarily on seaborne transportation guarantees that the country's security will continue to have a very significant naval aspect.

GLOBAL POLITICS AND THE NAVAL ASPECT OF U.S. NATIONAL SECURITY

The final and perhaps most important element in the naval aspect of U.S. national security are the political factors that link the United States to many nations "overseas." First and foremost among these are formal defense treaties with overseas nations. In this century, through two world wars and the Cold War, the U.S. Navy has played a critical, perhaps paramount, role in fulfilling mutual defense treaties with a wide range of allies. In 1994, the fiftieth anniversary of the World War II D-Day invasion of France commemorated the single most important event in that long history of U.S. naval intervention and support.

The end of the Cold War has thus far not decreased the number of U.S. overseas commitments, although it has changed their nature. In theory, the United States allies itself with nations that share its deepest values: political democracy and a free market economy. During the Cold War, the sixteen-nation North Atlantic Treaty Organization (NATO) was the most important alliance of which the United States was a founding member. While NATO's former Cold War strategy and force structure have changed dramatically with the demise of the global Soviet threat, the alliance endures, and so does the U.S. commitment to it. The likelihood of a "battle of the Norwegian Sea" versus the Russian Navy has all but disappeared, but the 1991 Gulf War served as a wake-up call about future dangers. Controversy over NATO's performance in support of the United Nations in the civil war in the former Yugoslavia has indeed raised new questions about the organization's future. At this writing, however, U.S. support for NATO appears to be firm.

In November 1991, NATO released a "New Strategic Concept" which placed the emphasis on preventing and dealing with regional conflicts. It must be pointed out that NATO's official area of operations extends well beyond the North Atlantic. In maritime terms, NATO's Southern Region, (the Mediterranean), is now paramount.[17] The Mediterranean Sea is a strategic zone for the entire western world, as well as the strategic crossroads of Europe and Africa, and the Middle East and Africa. On any given day about one-quarter of all ships, worldwide, move through the Mediterranean. In addition, 70% of the world's known oil reserves are within reach of the Mediterranean. The region is unstable, with heavily armed nations, an active arms trade, and neighbors in territorial and ideological dispute with each other. For example, NATO Southern Region members Greece, Italy, and Turkey are near the ongoing war occurring in the former Yugoslavia. The heavily armed Middle East nations of Syria, Lebanon, and Israel are near NATO member Turkey.

In response, the new NATO Strategic Concept calls for "Multinational Maritime Forces" (MNMF) to form part of "Immediate Reaction Forces" and "Rapid Reaction Forces" to deal with regional conflicts. One such force will remain in the traditional operating area in the North Atlantic. Potential unrest in the Baltic states will no doubt be one focus of attention.

However, it is NATO's Southern Region that is increasingly the center of attention. In April 1992, a NATO "Standing Naval Force Mediterranean" (STANAVFORMED or SNFM) was formed to patrol that sea, and it has provided support for the U.N.-mandated blockade of Yugoslavia.[18] In addition to contributing ships to this MNMF, it is clear that the United States will maintain a substantial naval presence in the Mediterranean, according to the recently appointed Chief of U.S. Naval Operations, Admiral J. M. Boorda, who formerly commanded NATO forces in the Southern Region.[19]

The U.S. commitment to NATO alone would guarantee an enduring naval element of U.S. national security. However, while NATO remains America's most important multinational overseas alliance, the United States is a party to many mutual defense treaties with overseas nations. Some of these are indeed being reviewed in the light of post-Cold War realities, and reduced U.S. naval commitments may result. For example, the 1993 closing of the massive U.S. Subic Bay naval base in the Philippines came as a result of the virtual disappearance of the "Soviet" threat to that region, as well as domestic political considerations. Nevertheless, the United States continues to maintain a defense treaty with the Philippines.

However, in the Pacific region, by far the most important U.S. defense commitments are to Japan and South Korea. While the former Soviet threat as represented by the Russian Pacific Fleet has greatly declined, the North Pacific remains a region of potential conflict, with North Korea as the greatest destabilizing factor. The U.S. Seventh Fleet is currently headquartered in Yokosuka, Japan, and an aircraft carrier battlegroup is homeported there. Other U.S. naval forces are homeported in Sasebo, Japan. It is true that, in the light of changing economic and political realities, both Japan and South Korea are steadily shouldering more of their own defense burdens, including substantial increases in their naval capabilities. Continuing economic friction between the United States and Japan may eventually erode the U.S.-Japan Security Agreement. Some experts even predict that all U.S. forces may be gone from Japanese soil by the end of the century.[20] An eventual peaceful reunification of Korea would also reduce a major U.S. commitment.

It is unlikely, however, that the United States will completely withdraw its naval forces from the Western Pacific in the foreseeable future. Aside from the requirement to defend U.S. territories in the Pacific (the Alaskan Aleutian islands, Hawaii, Guam, and American Samoa), the United States will retain some form of alliance with free-market democracies in the Asia-Pacific region, from Japan in the north to Australia and New Zealand in the south (currently under the Australia, New Zealand, and United States, or ANZUS, treaty). Moreover, many other countries in the region remain fearful of a developing "power vacuum" and the possible rise of a new regional hegemon—such as Japan, China, or India—and several have concluded "access" agreements that will enable the U.S. 7th Fleet to continue to operate in the region without permanent bases.[21]

Closer to home, U.S. naval forces played a prominent role in restoring Haiti's democratically elected government in 1994. Because of its proximity to the United States, the Caribbean region will remain important to the nation's security.

Political reality has also dictated that the United States form alliances with nations that do not share its commitment to either democracy or a free-market economy. Saudi Arabia is perhaps the clearest current example. Because of Saudi Arabia's oil, the United States is committed to the defense of that nation, and to freedom of navigation in the Persian Gulf. This is true not only because of the substantial U.S. dependence on Persian Gulf oil, but the even greater dependence on the same by our European and Japanese allies. The U.S. Navy will therefore retain a presence near and in the Gulf.

The participation of U.S. naval forces in peacekeeping and peacemaking operations mandated by the United Nations has increased dramatically since the end of the Cold War. In addition to the Gulf War and continuing enforcement of sanctions against Iraq, U.S. naval forces have recently taken part in U.N. operations off the former Yugoslavia and in Somalia. In an era of diminishing resources, the United States will sometimes decide that contributing naval forces to U.N. operations is in its best national security interests. While dreams of a "United Nations Navy" now seem a long way off, given recent disillusionments, such U.N. operations add yet another naval dimension to U.S. national security in the post-Cold War era.

In addition to these large-scale military requirements, the protection and rescue of American citizens caught in emergency situations in foreign nations is often the responsibility of naval forces when considerable numbers of people are involved. While humanitarian missions requested by international agencies may not seem to come under the traditional notion of "national security," the prevention or amelioration of catastrophes that might otherwise result in large numbers of refugees is growing in international importance. Naval forces will play a key role in these actions when coastal states are involved.

Finally, in the realm of future political demands that would have an integral naval aspect, the growing concern about the global environment must be included. In the fiscal year 1994 report of the Department of Defense, "environmental security" is listed as a key component of overall national security.[22] Aside from improving its own environmental record in controlling pollution and the disposal of toxic and nuclear waste, the U.S. Navy may be called upon to perform various functions such as monitoring ocean environmental conditions, responding to environmental disasters, and even enforcing environmental agreements.

CONCLUSION

When all of these factors are considered together, it becomes apparent that there has always been a major naval dimension to U.S. national security, and that this dimension will remain substantial as long as the United States remains a great world power. The nation's post-Cold War naval strategy is the subject of Chapter 5. In the next two chapters we examine the naval dimension of the Russian Federation's national security.

NOTES

1. Arthur G. Atkins, "Budget Cuts, Troop Withdrawals Shake, Reshape Russian Military," *Arms Control Today*, Vol. 24, No. 3 (April 1994), p. 25.

2. *The Military Balance 1993-1994* (IISS: Brassey's, 1994), pp. 230-236, includes current numbers.

3. "Russia's Future Navy Plan," *Naval Forces*, Vol. 14, No. 6 (1993), pp. 6-7.

4. *National Security Strategy of the United States*, The White House, January 1993, pp. 14-15. This was the last official strategy statement issued by the Bush Administration.

5. Les Aspin, *Report on the Bottom-Up Review* (Washington, D.C.: Department of Defense, October 1993), p. 7.

6. *A National Security Strategy of Engagement and Enlargement*, The White House, July 1994, pp. 8-15. It could be argued that the fourth military element of "reconstitution" has been virtually dropped in this first Clinton national security strategy statement. There was a great deal of controversy reported during the drafting of this first Clinton statement. Cf. John Lancaster and Barton Gellman, "National Security Strategy Paper Arouses Pentagon, State Department Debate," *Washington Post*, March 3, 1994.

7. President Bill Clinton, *A National Security Strategy of Enlargement and Engagement* (Washington, D.C.: The White House, February 1995), esp. pp. 8-10; Joint Chiefs of Staff, *National Military Strategy of the United States of America: A Strategy of Flexible and Selective Engagement* (Washington, D.C.: The Pentagon, February 1995). There is, of course, an intense debate within the U.S. military over "Roles and Missions" in an era of declining defense budgets. For example, the "Air Force bombers vs. Navy carriers" argument of the late 1940s is currently being revisited. The fact remains that only naval forces are capable of sustained overseas presence in the absence of land bases.

8. Robert W. Love, Jr., *History of the U.S. Navy*, Vol. One: 1775-1941 (Harrisburg, Pa.: Stackpole Books, 1992), pp. ix-xix.

9. U.S. Constitution, Article One, "Powers Granted to Congress," Section 8, paragraph 13: "to provide and maintain a navy."

10. *U.S. Waterborne Exports and General Imports* (Washington, D.C.: U.S. Bureau of the Census, TM985), updated monthly.

11. *Statistical Abstract of the United States 1993: National Data Book* (Washington, D.C.: U.S. Department of Commerce, 1994), p. 808, tables 1344-55.

12. *Statistical Abstract of the U.S. 1993*, p. 692.

13. *Statistical Abstract of the U.S. 1993*, p. 693.

14. *Statistical Abstract of the U.S. 1993*, p. 819, table 1354.

15. *Statistical Abstract of the U.S. 1993*, p. 702, table 1193.

16. Dr. Ross Robinson, "The Changing Patterns of Commercial Shipping and Port Concentration in Asia," chapter 6 in Ross Babbage and Sam Bateman, eds., *Maritime Change: Issues for Asia* (Sydney: Allen & Unwin, 1993), pp. 69-88.

17. Cf. Admiral Leon Edney, USN, "Future Alliance Maritime Posture," *NATO's Sixteen Nations*, Vol. 37, No. 1 (1992), pp. 4-6; Admiral Paul David Miller, USN, "Adapting Alliance Forces to Meet Needs," *NATO's Sixteen Nations*, Vol. 39, No. 1 (1994), pp. 4-6. Admiral Miller is the current Supreme Allied Commander Atlantic.

18. Admiral J. M. Boorda, USN, "The Southern Region—U.S. Forces in Action," *NATO's Sixteen Nations*, Vol. 38, No. 2 (1993), pp. 5-9 and "Loyal Partner—NATO's Forces in Support of the United Nations," *NATO's Sixteen Nations*, Vol. 39, No. 1 (1994), pp. 8-12. Admiral Boorda is currently the U.S. Chief of Naval Operations.

19. Quoted in Guy A. H. Toremans, "NATO's New Standing Naval Force Mediterranean," *Naval Forces*, Vol. 14, No. 3 (1993), p. 8.

20. Richard Holbrooke, "Japan and the United States: Ending the Unequal Partnership," *Foreign Affairs*, Vol. 70, No. 5 (Winter 1991-92), p. 50.

21. Among those nations providing such "access" are the Philippines, Singapore, Thailand, Malaysia, and Brunei.

22. Les Aspin, *Annual Report to the President and the Congress* (Washington, D.C.: Department of Defense, January 1994), pp. 82-90.

3

NAVAL ASPECTS OF
RUSSIA'S NATIONAL SECURITY

Boris N. Makeev

> The Russian Federation is a major naval power in the world, and has both
> global and regional interests in purely military, as well as in economic and
> political, spheres connected with the world's oceans.
> —Admiral Felix Gromov, Commander-in-Chief of the Russian Navy

Russia was and remains a great maritime power. It has more maritime frontier
(38,000 km) than land frontier. It has direct access to three oceans: the Atlantic, Pacific, and Arctic. Thirteen seas wash its shores. Russia's navy always
played an important role in support of its national security. This was the case
throughout both the Russian Imperial period and the Soviet era. Formed in
1696 as a regular force, its navy has, in the course of three hundred years, participated in twenty-two wars and conducted eighty-seven major naval battles.
The disintegration of the Soviet Union, the end of the Cold War, and the aban-
donment of confrontational policies with regard to the West have led to a
significant foreign policy reorientation and dictate development of a new concept of national security for Russia. The Russian Federation's Military Doctrine does not now consider any state to be Russia's enemy. Of course that does
not mean that potential military dangers no longer exist.

POTENTIAL THREATS TO RUSSIA'S SECURITY

The Russian Federation is the legal heir of the Soviet Union. It has taken
the latter's place as a permanent member of the U.N. Security Council. Democratic changes in Russia have been accompanied by changes in its relations
with the United States. Both countries no longer see each other as enemies. In

---

All comments in this chapter on the issues of the use of the Russian Navy are the
author's opinions and do not necessarily correspond to the official point of view.

that sense the threat of nuclear war is significantly lessened, a fact that must be taken into account.

Today Russia's primary objects of concern in the area of security are the instabilities and conflicts occurring in several of the republics of the former Soviet Union, in the Asia-Pacific region, and in other areas of the world, including territorial disputes, and the proliferation of weapons. These regional problems will be described in later sections of this chapter.

While not comparable in scale to the global "East-West" confrontation that was characteristic of the Cold War, the United States and its NATO allies still conduct large exercises of the type seen during the Cold War, including dangerous antisubmarine activity related to the search for nuclear-powered ballistic missile submarines (SSBNs).

However, in the issue of maintaining Russia's naval potential at the level of "defensive sufficiency," one cannot be captive to the political confluence of only the current day. The international situation has changed for the better, but one must not accept current trends as enduring ones. Therefore, it follows that Russia must consider objective *potential* threats in order to ensure reliable national security from the maritime axes on both the global and the regional scale.

On the global plane, the only nation in the world that has the physical ability to destroy the Russian Federation remains the United States, which, after the disintegration of the Soviet Union, has become the only superpower having enormous maritime power. Notwithstanding the softening of the military-political situation in the world and the normalization of relations between Russia and the United States, it seems that the activity levels of the West's navies basically will be preserved. A reduction is possible only by means of concluding and realizing treaties on naval arms limitations. Despite the already achieved agreements in the areas of arms limitations, the maritime component of these negotiations has thus far been almost completely neglected.

It is true that the unilateral reduction of the U.S. Navy's order of battle is occurring, mainly because of the writing off of outdated ships and aircraft. However, the *quantitative* limitations in the programs of building new means for combat at sea are being accompanied by an increase in their effectiveness due to the *qualitative* composition of U.S. naval forces. According to our estimate, the United States plans to increase the combat power of its naval forces by 1.5 to 2 times, by the application of future weapons systems and means of supporting their combat activity.

THE OVERALL MISSION OF THE RUSSIAN NAVY

These potential threats to Russia's national security must be taken into account in formulating the overall mission for the Russian Navy. In a recent interview, Admiral Felix Gromov, Commander-in-Chief of the Russian Navy, described its tasks in the following terms:

- deterring, jointly and with other branches of the Armed Forces, any aggressor from attempting to use military means to coerce Russia and its allies . . .
- protecting Russian independence, sovereignty, territorial integrity and national interests from any threat coming from the seas and oceans, protecting merchant shipping and guaranteeing access to world ocean resources, as well as protecting sea regions of industrial activity from unsanctioned use by other states . . .
- repelling jointly with the rest of the Armed Forces, any aggression against Russia or its allies, inflicting damage on the military-industrial potential of the aggressor and destroying him by a naval offensive . . .
- ensuring the implementation of foreign policy and of Russian commitments to the world community in maintaining peace and stability.[1]

In our view, the mission of the Navy comprises the prevention—together with other armed forces components—of the unleashing of war, and—in case of aggression—its repulsion, the protection of military facilities and troops from sea assault, by denying the enemy the ability to conduct offensive operations and by creating conditions for the reestablishment of peace.

An important mission for the Russian Navy will be the defense of the nation's economic interests at sea: defending the extremely rich natural resources of adjacent waters and the continental shelf, assuring the security of Russian shipping and fishing vessels, and combating smuggling, terrorism, and sea piracy. In this way, the Russian Navy is intended exclusively for the protection of Russia's independence and territorial integrity and the fulfillment of the nation's international obligations, including those on behalf of the Commonwealth of Independent States (C.I.S.).

For executing these missions, and considering Russia's geostrategic situation, it will be necessary to maintain naval forces in the North Atlantic, the Baltic, the Black Sea, the Caspian Sea, and the Pacific. The changed international and internal situation and the economic position of Russia have halted the previous trend toward increasing the forces of each of these fleets to the level of the most powerful of the world's navies, that of the United States. It is now sufficient that the fleet force in each of these regions be capable of adequately confronting only the real and specific threats to Russian national security. This chapter offers an assessment of the situation in each of the regions mentioned.

THE REGIONAL MISSIONS OF THE RUSSIAN NAVY

The North Atlantic and Baltic Region

Russia cannot dismiss the possibility of the resurrection of traditional historic desires "toward the East" on the part of a Germany that is growing stronger. The strengthening of Germany's influence on the countries of Eastern Europe and the appearance of revanchist feelings and territorial claims against the lands lost during World War II are troubling. Another alarming symptom are NATO's attempts to include Lithuania, Latvia, and Estonia within the sphere of its activity. In December 1991 the NATO Council adopted a decision to create a standing operational force in the Baltic which, during a period of increased tension, will use the ports and naval bases of the Baltic states. There could be territorial claims against Russia from these countries and also from Finland, which is gradually moving away from its traditional position of neutrality toward Russia.

In the naval sense, this region has great significance. It is directly adjacent to the Arctic basin and includes, together with the continental and island territories, the Baltic, White, Barents, North, and Norwegian seas, the strait of LaManch, and the Skagerak and Kattegat straits.

Reviewing the region from the point of view of Russia's national security, it contains the following states: Poland, Germany, Norway, Denmark, Great Britain, France, Belgium, the Netherlands, Iceland, Sweden, and Finland. In assessing the correlation of naval force and threats from the sea, the naval forces of the United States and Canada, which operate in these regions, must also be included. With the exception of Poland, Finland, and Sweden, all of the countries are part of NATO.

Of the NATO member states, the United States, Great Britain, and France are nuclear powers, even though the latter left the bloc's military organization in 1966. Norway maintains a non-nuclear status and does not permit permanent foreign military presence on its territory. Denmark has stated a demand to not have nuclear weapons located on its territory, and Iceland has practically no armed forces.

These and other factors related to the various political structures of these states, the level of their economic development, their military potential, and their differing interests could have a substantial influence on the military-political situation in the region and on the level and form of a potential military confrontation there. The peculiarity of this potential confrontation is that it would basically be determined not by the comparison of ground troops but by the composition of naval forces, which all the countries in this region possess.

In assessing the naval balance in a given region, it is necessary first of all to take into account its nuclear component. Of the 48 strategic nuclear missile carrying submarines (SSBNs) of the Russian Navy, 30 are based on the Kola

Peninsula, including the newest *Typhoon* and *Del'fin* (*Delta-IV*) classes with 20 and 16 missiles onboard, respectively. The range of these missiles is 8,000-9,000 km.

These SSBNs, depending upon the nuclear deterrence missions assigned, can be used from combat patrol regions located in the Barents Sea. Part of the SSBNs are armed with missiles of shorter range and require deployment into the North Atlantic in order to achieve target reachability for their weapons. In so doing, on the way to their combat patrol area they must pass through a powerful NATO antisubmarine zone, which has been created between Greenland, Iceland, and the Faeroe and Shetland islands.

Most of the SSBNs of the U.S. naval forces (10 out of 17) are likewise concentrated in the Atlantic region, including the newest *Ohio* class with 24 ballistic missiles aboard and a range of up to 12,000 km. They are based at the Norfolk Naval Base and at King's Bay and can patrol in waters adjacent to the coast of the United States well covered by antisubmarine forces and means.

The comparison of general purpose naval forces in the North Atlantic and Baltic region is such that in overall numbers of ships and in their qualitative composition it is Russia and the United States that have the basic forces. In the Russian Navy order of battle within this region in 1994, the Northern Fleet included about 70 submarines (26 of which are diesel), more than 50 major surface ships (including 2 aircraft carriers, 8 cruisers, 9 destroyers, 32 large ASW ships [frigates]), 12 assault ships, about 260 aircraft, and 70 helicopters belonging to naval aviation.

Turning to the Baltic Fleet, it consists of 10 diesel submarines, 32 major surface ships (including 3 cruisers, 3 destroyers, 26 large ASW ships), and 20 assault ships. The fleet has 214 aircraft and 50 helicopters belonging to naval aviation. In this way in the region under review there are concentrated 114 submarines (75 of which are nuclear-powered), up to 80 major surface ships, and about 600 naval aviation aircraft and helicopters. The U.S. forces in the Atlantic have in their order of battle more than 60 nuclear-powered submarines, more than 70 major surface ships (including 6 aircraft carriers, 23 cruisers, 22 destroyers, and about 30 frigates), 25 assault ships, and about 900 aircraft and 200 helicopters belonging to naval aviation.

In addition, the fleets of both countries have a large quantity of small displacement ships (patrol ships, minesweepers, missile and torpedo boats, and so on) and auxiliary vessels. An analysis of the comparison of Russian and U.S. forces at sea in this region shows that, given some quantitative superiority, Russian submarines and surface ships fall significantly behind the U.S. ones in their qualitative characteristics, particularly in the area of radioelectronic equipment and aviation armament. This fact, as well as the existence within the order of battle of the Atlantic Fleet of nuclear-powered aircraft carriers and the quantitative advantage in naval aviation lead one to conclude that at this time the U.S. fleet has a significant advantage over the Russian fleet. This advantage is even greater if we take into account the order of battle of the other NATO countries' naval forces in this region: Norway, Denmark, Belgium, Germany, Great Britain, and France (a de facto U.S. ally), which together have 18 nuclear attack submarines, 71 diesel submarines, and 117 major surface ships. True, the naval forces of Great Britain and France are used in many regions around the world, but a significant number are assigned in the interests of NATO's maritime strategy in the North Atlantic region.

For this reason, during the Cold War the Soviet Navy was built and was trained to fulfill in this region the major missions of defending SSBN patrol areas, to do combat with the enemy's strategic SSBNs, to support their own ground troops in defense and offense, to destroy enemy shipping in the Atlantic, and to defend their own sea lines of communication.

The change in the international situation—the disintegration of the Soviet Union and the Warsaw Pact, Russia's economic difficulties, and the demise of communist ideology—has led the former enemies to review the concept of the use of their navies overall and especially in this region. Chapters 2 and 5 present a detailed analysis of the changes in the naval concepts of the United States and NATO. This chapter presents current views and trends in the use of the Russian Navy for the support of national security in the framework of defense sufficiency for this region.

With the adoption of Russia's new defense doctrine, and given her economic and internal difficulties, it is not likely to be possible to fulfill a number of the missions for which the Soviet-era navy in this region was built and trained. The dominant location of these missions has now changed from the broad regions of the Atlantic to Russia's own shores. The achievement of superiority in ocean and sea regions not contiguous to those shores is becoming unrealistic. It is likely that the mission of interdicting Atlantic sea lines of communication and the anti-SSBNs mission in the northeastern Atlantic and near the U.S. coast will be canceled.

In our view, the basic efforts of the Northern Fleet should be concentrated on covering and supporting the combat endurance of Russian SSBNs in their firing areas; repulsing the strikes of the first operational echelon of an enemy's naval forces; and supporting the flanks of ground forces and covering them from attack from the sea.

A part of the fleet forces must be used to interdict enemy maritime transport, to defend the navy's communications in coastal regions, and to conduct warfare with the enemy's submarines and antisubmarine forces. In the case of a counterattack by Russian troops, the fleet should, to the maximum degree, support this mission by providing fire and aviation strikes against the enemy's defensive positions and by landing tactical assaults on the Norwegian coast.

No doubt this discussion may seem outdated in light of the new geopolitical situation. However, there are more contemporary security concerns for Russia in this region. Russia's economic and military interests in the Arctic are growing. In the 1980s several major gas and oil fields were discovered on the shelf. These will require actions by naval forces for their cover and protection. Military interests in this region are determined by the seas of the Arctic Ocean contiguous to Russia's territory, since they have favorable conditions for the location of its SSBNs, which form a vital part of deterrence forces.

The military and economic significance of the Northern Sea Route, which supports the shortest path from Europe to Southeast Asia and the intertheater maneuver of naval forces, is also growing.

In reviewing the problems of Russia's national security in this region, it is obviously necessary to take into account new political realities and the increased level of trust between the Russian Navy on the one hand, and the naval forces of the United States, Great Britain, France, Germany, and Norway on the other. Russia's participation in the NATO "Partnership for Peace" agreement, including some joint exercises, is obviously a very important positive step.

However, one should not ignore the other realities in the situation at sea: the continuing exercises near Russia's shores (e.g., Teamwork-92); the active reconnaissance activity by ships of Great Britain, France, and Norway;[2] and the maneuvering of American submarines near the entrance to the Kola Gulf, among others, which require negotiations on this type of naval activity in the Atlantic and the Arctic.

The situation in the Baltic Sea is coming together in such a way that apparently the previously existing possibility of Baltic Fleet forces operating beyond the straits zone and establishing a blockade to prevent an enemy navy from entering the Baltic Sea will not be realistic. The loss of naval bases in Lithuania, Latvia, and Estonia will make it difficult to counteract the deployment of an aggressor's forces. In these circumstances it is realistic to consider only the mission of control over the central part of the Baltic Sea and the creation of a strong defense against attacking enemy naval forces not farther away than the Bornholm Island barrier.

In our view, these scenarios of the possible development of combat operations at sea in the region reviewed should become the basis for developing and training the Northern and Baltic Fleets with the aim of supporting Russia's national security within the bounds of defense sufficiency should the international situation become unfavorable. However, this does not at all mean that we continue to view the naval forces of the United States and NATO as the likely enemy.

The negotiations under way on naval problems and the conclusion of an agreement on confidence building measures and the prevention of incidents at sea, though far from real processes for the reduction of naval armaments, still support the hope for developing friendly relations between NATO forces and the Russian Navy. This in itself makes the possibility of a military collision less likely. An exchange of warship visits and of officer training experience has begun, and unofficial meetings of representative delegations of the navies of NATO and Russia are continuing. An agreement is near on the joint conduct of an exercise for naval fleets providing humanitarian assistance in case of natural disasters. The issue of joint actions by our navies against a local aggressor in the Atlantic region, similar to the actions of the multinational forces in the Persian Gulf, is being considered.

However, it should be kept in mind that stability at sea within the region requires further steps toward the real limitation of naval armaments up to their inclusion in the overall process of balanced arms reduction. The first step on this path might be an agreement on the limitation of fleet operations zones, stemming from interests of mutual security and economic benefit. This would provide strong stimulation for unilateral reduction of the order of battle for Russia's Baltic and Northern fleets, which in turn would significantly stabilize the military situation in this region.

The Black, Caspian, and Mediterranean Seas

A very complex situation is occurring along Russia's southwest flank in the Black, Caspian, and Mediterranean sea zones. An important factor in this region is the emerging issue of relations between the industrial development of the north and the lagging south. A confrontation between them could reach a level of acuteness similar to that which existed between the East and the West.

The Islamic factor plays an important role in the problem of the north-south relations. At this time Islam is on the rise. The Arab-Israeli conflict, the Iranian Revolution, the victory of the Mujahedin in Afghanistan, the growing influence of Islam on some previous Soviet republics and autonomous areas, the strength of Islamic fundamentalism—all these factors make the situation on Russia's southern flank both unpredictable and explosive.

The military actions between Georgia and Abkhazia, between Azerbaijan and Armenia, the political instability in the northern Caucasus (e.g., Chechnya), Turkey's increased interest in these regions, and the proliferation of its economic and, subsequently, its military-political influence on these areas can have negative consequences for Russia's geostrategic positions. This could entail the neutralization of Russia's naval presence in the Black and Mediterranean seas, and the destruction of maritime communications in southern waters. The inclusion of the Black Sea and the reorientation of former Warsaw Pact allies Rumania and Bulgaria into NATO's zone of interest are also not beneficial factors for Russia. These countries have turned the direction of their previous military ties toward the West, and at the invitation of their naval staffs, a joint NATO squadron has operated in the Black Sea.

These factors engender instability in this region and require, in the interest of the national security of Russia and those C.I.S. countries pulling for collective security, maintaining sufficiently strong ground and naval forces. The foundation of the ground forces grouping are the troops of the North Caucasus Military District. The core of the naval grouping are the forces of the Black Sea Fleet. Its order of battle currently consists of 18 submarines, 31 major surface ships (missile cruisers, destroyers, large ASW ships, assault and other ships), more than 60 smaller ships and combat boats, about 140 auxiliary fleet vessels and 400 naval aviation aircraft (220 in reserve). From the point of view of the balance of naval forces, the remaining Black Sea states do not pose a serious threat to such a fleet.

The Bulgarian fleet is comprised almost entirely of Soviet-built ships, which Russia is gradually taking off line (2 diesel submarines, 9 small displacement ASW ships, and about 20 combat boats). The Rumanian naval forces are in a slightly better situation. They include 1 destroyer, 1 submarine, and about 90 small ships and boats with some missile types bought not only in the Soviet Union but also in Germany and the People's Republic of China (P.R.C.) and some built on their own wharves.

Within the Turkish naval forces order of battle are 15 diesel submarines, 5 destroyers, 16 relatively new frigates, 16 missile boats, and also an essential coastal operations fleet. Not more than one-third of these forces are in the Black Sea; the rest are in the Marmara, Aegean, and Mediterranean seas. This small order of battle notwithstanding, these forces hold the "key" to the Black Sea. It is sufficient for them to blockade the Bosphorus in order to lock any fleet within the waters of this closed sea.

One cannot omit including the U.S. Sixth Fleet in the balance of naval forces of the southern region. As a rule, it is comprised of 1–2 aircraft carriers, about 10 other surface ships, 3–4 assault ships, 3–4 submarines, and several auxiliary vessels. To these should be added part of the NATO forces used in this region.

The Mediterranean Sea held and continues to hold an important place in the issue of using the Black Sea Fleet along the southern operational-strategic axis. In the Cold War years, the requirement for the presence of the Soviet Navy in the Mediterranean was determined by the necessity of denying the ships of the U.S. Sixth Fleet and the ships of NATO an unlimited control of the sea, which it had until the formation of the Soviet Navy's Fifth Squadron, and also to limit the possibility of using the Sixth Fleet in foreign policy goals, including against regimes then friendly toward the Soviet Union.

Although the international situation has changed, the necessity for a Russian naval presence in the Mediterranean has not completely fallen by the wayside. It is through the Mediterranean that the shortest link is maintained with the countries of southern Europe, Asia, and Africa, which requires corresponding actions by the Russian Navy in both peacetime and wartime. In addition, one must recall that, notwithstanding the greatly reduced likelihood of a global war and large-scale military operations, the threat of local conflicts in this region remains.

For the neutralization of this type of local conflict, the Military Doctrine of the Russian Federation envisions the creation of highly mobile general purpose forces comprised of ground and naval groupings. The basic naval grouping in Russia's southern flank obviously must be the forces of the Black Sea Fleet, which have powerful missile-artillery, antiaircraft and ASW armaments, and the necessary cruising range and endurance which permit them to operationally reach and localize the sources of tension that would threaten the work of peace and Russia's national security. Russia continues to have its own interest on the southern flank related to maritime problems on both the economic and the military-political level.

However, the fundamental changes in the international and internal political situation do force the review of the scope and level of the operational-strategic missions of the Black Sea Fleet. There must be a narrowing of the military-political goals these forces are intended to achieve. In so doing it is necessary to take into account the military-economic capabilities of Russia should there ever be an unfavorable scenario in the development of events.

First of all, Russia probably cannot count on active participation by the fleet in operations in the Mediterranean Sea at the start of combat activities. In conjunction with this, Russia should limit the composition and missions of its ship groupings to a level that supports the defense of communications, reconnaissance, and maintaining information in zones adjacent to the Black Sea. However, notwithstanding such a substantive adjustment of the Navy's missions, it cannot completely close down the operations of the fleet in this region. One cannot exclude the participation of Russia in the operations of multinational naval forces for stabilizing peace and security in the countries of the Mediterranean basin. Such missions could have a strategic character, but they would not require the resources and efforts once expended on the maintenance of a full-size, combat-ready squadron in this region. The resources needed would be significantly smaller.

Within the Black Sea itself, one may suppose that the Black Sea Fleet will fulfill the basic spectrum of operational-strategic missions, mostly with the aim of gaining superiority at sea by blockading the straits zone and by destroying enemy naval forces equipped with precision weapons. The Navy's cover and support of ground troops will require fleet operations not only in the coastal regions but throughout the waters of the Black Sea.

These missions for the achievement of even limited-scope goals in the interest of Russia's national security and the defense capability of the C.I.S. require a full-blooded structure and corresponding order of battle for the Black Sea Fleet. The Russian fleet in the Black Sea should thus preserve in its order of battle missile cruisers, destroyers, ASW and patrol ships, multipurpose submarines, antimine forces, naval aviation and protection forces for fleet basing areas in an adequate quantity for supporting these missions. For this reason, the division of the Black Sea Fleet between Russia and Ukraine, in accordance with some proportional quotas and by territorial means, without taking into account real operational-strategic missions, is completely unacceptable.

There can be various options for the division, command, and control of the forces of the Black Sea Fleet, but its preservation as strong and unified, and coordinated in operational-strategic missions with the entire shore-based infrastructure and the main naval base at Sevastopol, is not subject to doubt. But even with the division of the Black Sea Fleet and a divided command for the Russian Navy and the Ukrainian Naval Forces in the Black Sea, there must be preserved a commonality of maritime borders, one system of basing and mission coordination for the protection of common interests of security and stability on the southern flank of Russia and Ukraine. Such an objective necessity for resolving the issue of the Black Sea Fleet was confirmed during two meetings of the presidents of Russia and Ukraine in 1993 which were aimed at stabilizing relations between these countries on this acute military-political issue. Preserving the basic backbone of the Black Sea Fleet as a unified combat force in the southwest operational axis is a priority task for political and military leaders in order to guarantee the national security of Russia and other countries of the C.I.S.

The order of battle of the Southern Operational Axis also includes the Caspian Flotilla, whose main base prior to the disintegration of the Soviet Union was Baku. Today the flotilla is forced to be satisfied with weaker basing points at the mouth of the Volga, in the area of Astrakhan and the coast of Dagestan. These areas freeze in the winter and are capable of supporting only 20% of the flotilla's normal basing and logistics needs. It will be necessary to create a new navy base at Astrakhan and a minimum of 1–2 maneuver basing points. Today the order of battle of the flotilla is represented by 2 ASW ships, 12 patrol ships and coastal patrol boats, 18 minesweepers, 10 assault ships, and 10 auxiliary vessels. The flotilla has been divided among the republics of Russia, Azerbaijan, Kazakhstan, and Turkmenistan, but operates jointly under Russian command.

The Pacific

The means of supporting military security in the Asia-Pacific region (APR) greatly depend on achieving a balance in the interests of Russia, the United States, the People's Republic of China (P.R.C.), and Japan and on their individual approaches to the assessment of the strategic situation in the region. In recent years the geopolitical location of forces in the APR has quickly changed. Russia is not colliding with the powerful coalition of the United States, Japan, and the P.R.C. which once confronted the U.S.S.R. A serious improvement in relations between Russia, the United States, the P.R.C., and the Republic of Korea has been achieved. U.S. military presence in the western part of the

Pacific Ocean is steadily declining. The P.R.C. is demonstrating a high level of economic and military strengthening and is conducting a more active foreign policy. Japan is beginning to play an independent political role.

The possible appearance of geopolitical striving by the P.R.C. or Japan is capable of creating a threat to the Russian Far East. The significant potential of an increasingly strong P.R.C., and even more so of Japan, does not facilitate a stabilization of the regional situation.

In the APR today there are no clearly defined confrontational alliances with a large number of members. The interrelations of the region's leading countries are complicated, variable, and depend on many circumstances. Potential military confrontation now has a multipolar configuration. This means that in developing one or another option for guaranteeing security it is necessary to take into account the position of a large number of countries, whose influence tangibly affects the regional situation. It should be noted that the center of gravity in confrontation is moving toward naval forces. Ground forces could play only a substantive role in the case of a conflict between the C.I.S. and the P.R.C. and on the Korean peninsula. But even in these conflicts, the navies' support of the troops' maritime flanks would play a substantive role.

To ensure the security of Russia from the Pacific axis the character of its relations with the United States has great significance. Notwithstanding the partnership relations that are evolving between Russia and the United States, the *potential* confrontation of Pacific fleets—full of nuclear and precision conventional weapons—remains. Moreover, the naval component of the armed forces of Russia and the United States, with the exception of nuclear deterrent forces and tactical nuclear weapons, has not yet been included in the negotiations leading to the reduction of military treats from maritime axes. Such a danger from the Pacific axis remains real for Russia.

As is obvious from official U.S. documents such as *Directives in the area of Defense for FY 1994-1998* and *The U.S. National Military Doctrine*, Washington strives to preserve the forward presence of U.S. armed forces in key areas of the world, including the APR. The U.S. military doctrine envisions a naval presence in the APR sectors that are distant from the United States, shows of force, and participation in regional conflicts with the use of naval groupings already deployed there in peacetime.

As of 1994, U.S. naval strategic forces in the APR had in their order of battle 7 SSBNs of the *Ohio* class with 24 ballistic missiles each and with a range of 7,000 to 12,000 km, which enables their use from internal and coastal waters. General purpose forces include 32 nuclear submarines, 68 major surface ships including 6 aircraft carriers, 29 missile cruisers, 17 destroyers, 16 frigates, 28 assault ships, and more than 800 naval aviation combat aircraft. As pointed out in Chapters 1 and 4, some of these numbers will decline significantly by the end of this decade.

Russia's naval strategic forces in the Pacific in 1994 had 16 SSBNs of the *Navaga* class (*Yankee-I*) and *Kal'mar* class (*Delta-III*) with 16 ballistic missiles each and of the *Murena* class (*Delta-I*) with 12 missiles aboard each. Russian Pacific Fleet general purpose forces have in their order of battle 34 submarines (16 of them diesel), about 50 major surface ships comprised of 11 cruisers, 6 destroyers, 33 large ASW ships (frigates), and more than 300 naval aviation aircraft. On July 19, 1994, Commander of the Russian Navy Felix Gromov announced that Russia's Pacific Fleet will be "seriously trimmed," with outdated ships being the first to be cut.[3] Some sources say this cut will amount to a third of the Pacific Fleet. According to ITAR-Tass, Russias Pacific Fleet was forced to cancel plans to visit Australia in July of 1995 because of a severe shortage of fuel oil. It is reported that the fleet even lacks enough fuel to celebrate Navy Day. The fleet also owes more than $33 million to shipyards for repairs.[4]

Although it is behind Russia in submarines, the United States has significant superiority over the Russian Navy in this region in major warships. It should also be noted that the U.S. submarine fleet, unlike the Russian one, is completely equipped with nuclear propulsion and has, as a rule, more improved sonar and other radioelectronic gear, and longer range and more accurate missiles, while the effectiveness of their aircraft carriers is many times superior to any of Russia's surface ships.

In addition, the U.S. forces in the APR are supplemented by the naval forces of their basic allies. Thus, just within the order of battle of the Japanese naval forces there are more than 60 major ships (frigates and destroyers), 17 submarines, and as many as 300 aircraft and helicopters. The Republic of Korea has 38 major ships and 4 submarines. All of these forces are based directly near the Far Eastern coast of Russia and could be quickly redeployed there in a crisis situation.

However remote the prospect of actual military attack may be at this time, the foreign naval forces operating near Russia in the APR *objectively* create a potential threat of strikes from the sea against its Far East and fleet forces, including against its SSBNs—the most important element of nuclear strategic parity and stability.

The main axes of the operation of the Russian Pacific Fleet, in our view, should support the preservation of this grouping of naval strategic nuclear forces and their effective use, should cover from the sea the troops in the Far East by way of combating enemy naval forces in the region of Kamchatka, in the Sea of Okhotsk, and in the northern part of the Sea of Japan, and should not allow the landing of enemy assault forces on the Russian coast. At the same time, under changing conditions, the traditional missions of interdicting oceanic lines of communication and warfare against enemy SSBNs should obviously be considered unrealistic and economically inappropriate.

In light of the major changes in the international situation, the important mission of the Pacific Fleet should be considered to be the protection of the economic interests of Russia in the Far East, with its unique reserves of natural resources, and also to serve as a deterrent factor against the territorial claims of other states of the Asia-Pacific Region. A very important part of the fleet's significance consists of the protection of the shelf economic zone and Russia's sea frontiers, and also the sea lines of communications in this enormous region which stretches for many thousands of kilometers, from the eastern sector of the Arctic to the Indian Ocean. This mission includes the protection of merchant and fishing vessels from maritime piracy in peacetime, which has wide scope in the southern seas of the region.

While preserving the naval power essential for counteracting the potential threats from the maritime axes, Russia, in the current international situation under the new geopolitical status of forces in the APR, strives to ensure its national security and overall regional stability to a great degree by way of skillful diplomacy, the policy of a balance of forces, negotiations, the achievement of regional agreements, joint action to settle conflicts, adoption by states of limits on military operations, and so on.

Recently an agreement was reached to establish direct communications between the Russian Pacific Fleet and the command of the U.S. Seventh Fleet. This is an important first step in preserving peace in the region. Going beyond this, it is appropriate to develop Russia's initiatives concerning other maritime confidence-building measures and naval arms control measures in the region, including:

- creation of an international system to guarantee the security of navigation in the Pacific Ocean;
- a widening of the exchange of information between the staffs and scientific research organizations on the naval aspects of the national security concerns of the United States, Russia, and other countries of the APR;
- notification and limitation of the number and scale of planned naval exercises;
- the creation of zones within the Pacific Ocean in which antisubmarine warfare operations of sufficient "strategic mass" to threaten SSBNs would be limited.

These and other measures are discussed in greater detail in Chapters 6 to 9.

Progress in these directions would substantively raise the level of trust and security in the Pacific region and could enable a transition in the next stage to measures on the limitation of naval presence in zones of common interest agreed upon by both parties. Under these conditions the question could be raised of reducing the composition of the Russian Pacific Fleet and balancing it in its effectiveness to fulfill missions together with that part of the U.S. naval forces which by agreement can be present in Russia's interest zones at sea.

Of course, the *unilateral* steps taken in recent years by the United States to reduce their armed forces, including those of the Navy, are very significant. The Pentagon's 1993 *Report on the Bottom-Up Review* called for a reduction of the U.S. Navy to 346 ships, and the U.S. Navy's *1994 Posture Statement* has reduced that number still lower to 331. This trend can be strengthened by corresponding unilateral steps on Russia's side, such as the one-third reduction of the Pacific Fleet mentioned above.

Given a stage-by-stage, integrated approach to the reduction of maritime armaments along the Pacific Ocean axis, there can be realized a transition from the Russian Pacific Fleet order of battle created for the fulfillment of *global* missions at sea, to a composition limited by the bounds of defense sufficiency.

Of course, Russia's security interests in the northwestern part of the Pacific Ocean are greatly influenced by its relations with Japan and the P.R.C. Relations with Japan are strained by the absence of a peace treaty and by the argument about the four islands of the southern Kurile chain, which Japan considers its "northern territories." The term "northern territories" means the islands of Iturup, Kunashir, Shikotan, and the Habomai chain. An increase in the intensity of this argument could have a substantive effect on the situation along Russia's eastern frontier and on its economic and strategic interests. In our view, a compromise resolution of these territorial questions between Russian and Japan is possible.

Relations with the P.R.C., notwithstanding ideological contradictions, are getting better on the whole. For this reason, and also as a result of the current weakness of the P.R.C.'s naval forces in comparison to the Russian Pacific Fleet, it cannot significantly influence Russia's national security in this region. The relative weight of the navy within the P.R.C. armed forces is not great. It has a little more than 50 ships of medium displacement (destroyers, patrol ships, etc.). The P.R.C. has mainly minor coastal combatants and boats (about 860 units) and a relatively large number of diesel submarines with limited endurance and cruising range (about 40 units). Several nuclear submarines, assault ships, a missile patrol ship, and a frigate with an onboard helicopter have entered the P.R.C.'s order of battle only in recent years.

However, the P.R.C. is putting much of its new resources into military production and is increasing its expenditures for these goals. It is preparing for a confrontation in the area of the Taiwan strait. A disagreement between the P.R.C. and a number of ASEAN countries and Vietnam over the control of the Spratly islands in the South China Sea, and the P.R.C.'s claims to the enormous maritime space that stretches more than 1,000 miles south from Hong Kong, could become sources of armed confrontation at sea. (In 1992 the P.R.C. adopted a law that extended its sovereignty over the entire South China Sea.) Even though the argument around the status of Taiwan, the Spratly islands, the oil shelf, and the lines of communication of the South China Sea do not

directly touch upon Russia's national security, their escalation and the participation in them of the major powers in the context of a struggle to rearrange
economic and political spheres of influence can violate the currently existing
regional and subregional balance of forces and could pull Russia into a conflict
situation.

In the newly evolving system of interrelationships in the APR, Russia is
interested in maintaining overall regional stability, preventing the rise of regional hegemonist powers, warning of local armed conflicts, and reducing
their dangers. Realizing the measures listed earlier on the limitation of naval
forces in the APR and their activity would greatly help to achieve these goals
and strengthen trust at sea.

The developing military-political situation, Russia's requirement for a defensive naval potential, and its ability to maintain and develop its Navy show
that there is no necessity to strive to retain that quantitative Pacific Fleet order
of battle that existed before and that was aimed at counteracting U.S. forces in
the Pacific Ocean. This is no longer justified from either the political or the
economic point of view.

However, it should be noted that reducing the quantitative makeup of
Pacific Fleet forces will be accompanied by a qualitative improvement in the
order of battle, in armaments and military equipment, and in the optimal expenditure of the appropriations and reserves given to the Pacific Fleet. Such an
approach will require concentrating efforts on developing more standardized
types of fleet forces that are capable of effectively fulfilling these defensive
missions in the Pacific theater of military operations, taking into account the
peculiarities of this region and the military-political situations there. We discuss ongoing reduction in the Russian Navy (and its future shipbuilding plans)
in detail in the next chapter.

Such unilateral reductions, both from the Russian and the U.S. side, con-
firming the peace-loving intentions and goals of these countries in the APR,
will without a doubt facilitate positive changes in the military policy of other
powers, the beginning of multilateral regional consultations on issues of
strengthening stability, and the establishment of more firm bases for security
in this region of the world.

CONCLUSION

This review of the naval aspects of Russia's national security by regions
allows us to conclude that the development of the Russian Navy will be directed toward the fulfillment of the following basic missions:

- the fulfillment, jointly with other armed forces components, of the function
  of deterring any aggressor from attempting to unleash war against Russia
  and its allies;

- the defense of Russia's independence, sovereignty, territorial integrity, and state interests from threats from maritime axes;
- the repulsion of strikes from maritime axes in case of aggression or armed conflict, attacks against groupings of the naval forces of a possible enemy, denying them the capability of conducting offensive operations;
- joint operations with Russia's ground troops in combat actions along maritime axes;
- ensuring the protection and defense of Russia's maritime lines of communications and of maritime regions of domestic economic activity from their unsanctioned use by other states;
- supporting foreign policy actions and fulfillment of Russia's world community obligations in the maintenance of peace and stability, including participation in peacemaking actions as part of multinational forces under the U.N. flag, and combating piracy and terrorism at sea;
- demonstrating goodwill and reinforcing diplomatic relations by making warship visits to friendly countries.

In order to fulfill these missions within the framework of the military reform that is under way, a qualitatively new and more modern Russian Navy that will be less economically burdensome, but sufficiently capable, will have to be created. That is the subject of the next chapter.

NOTES

1. Admiral Felix Gromov, "Reforming the Russian Navy," in *Naval Forces,* Vol. 14, No. 4 (1993), pp. 6-7. For another overview, cf. Captain 1st Rank Victor Potvorov, RFN, "National Interests, National Security, and the Russian Navy," *Naval War College Review*, Vol. 47, No. 4 (Autumn 1994), pp. 53-67. Concerning the Russian Baltic Fleet, cf. Admiral Valentin Y. Selivanov, "The Baltic Fleet—Safeguarding National Interests", *Naval Forces*, Vol. 16, No. 3 (1995), pp. 8-11.

2. For example, the British Navy frigate *Sheffield* and Norwegian navy ships closely monitored a Russian naval exercise in proximity to Russian territorial waters in the Barents Sea in July 1994, according to a July 19 report in the *ITAR-TASS World Service* in Moscow.

3. "Gromov: Serious Cutbacks To Affect Pacific Fleet," Moscow, *INTERFAX*, in English, July 19, 1994. According to the Vol. 16, No. 3 (1995) issue of the journal *Naval Forces*, it was reported in the *Moscow Tribune* that Russia is to sell as many as 259 ships from the Pacific fleet to South Korea to be melted into scrap-iron: 220 surface vessels including two aircraft carriers, and 39 submarines including two nuclear submarines.

4. As summarized by the Associated Press, July 21, 1995, in a report from Vladivostok. The one-third figure is cited on p. 35 of the July 23, 1994 issue of *The Economist*.

4

NAVAL ASPECTS OF RUSSIA'S MILITARY REFORMS: THE DEVELOPMENT PROGRAM OF THE RUSSIAN NAVY

Boris N. Makeev

A new building program has been worked out and submitted to the government.
—Admiral Felix Gromov, Commander-in-Chief, Russian Federation Navy

The development of the Russian Navy will be carried out within the overall framework of military reform. The principle aim of this reform is the formation of qualitatively new armed forces. The naval aspect of this reform will differ significantly from the reorganization of formerly Soviet land forces.[1] The Soviet military command based large portions of its land forces outside the Russian Republic. However, Soviet naval forces, were based mainly within Russia. (Only 10 to 12% of these forces were placed elsewhere.) Thus the structure and composition of the new Russian Navy will only partially change. The Russian Navy as a whole will retain its existing branches: surface ships, submarines, maritime patrol aviation, and marines.[2]

CHANGES IN FORCE CLASSIFICATION

Surface forces will be composed of the following vessel classes: aircraft carriers, missile-artillery ships, submarines, minesweepers, landing craft, missile-and-torpedo boats, special purpose ships (flagships, training vessels, and reconnaissance ships), and auxiliary ships (rescue and hospital, supply, floating repair bases, etc.). Ships of the same class will differ in terms of tonnage and designation, thereby forming subclasses. For instance, cruisers, minelayers, minesweepers, escort vessels, and so on would all belong to the same class.

The views expressed in this chapter are those of the author alone, and are not in any way an expression of official views of the Russian Navy or government.

Submarines are subclassified according to their mode of propulsion—nuclear- or diesel-powered—and their armament—missile-, torpedo-, or missile-and-torpedo carrying. Missile-carrying submarines may be armed with cruise or strategic missiles. Submarines with nuclear-armed strategic missiles form part of Russia's strategic nuclear forces. Submarines will be further organized into brigades, divisions, squadrons, and flotillas.

Maritime patrol aviation (MPA) forces are composed of missile-carrying, antisubmarine, reconnaissance, assault, fighter, and transport aviation. MPA aircraft fall under shore-based and ship-based designations as well as various supply designations. These aircraft will, with all probability, be formed into divisions and individual squadrons. Ship-based aviation will be formed into individual regiments, squadrons, and links. There will also be single aircraft assigned to certain ships.

Shore-based forces (marines) will be formed into regiments, divisions, and brigades, shore missile-artillery forces, and shore defense forces.

CHANGES IN FORCE COMPOSITION

Bearing in mind the geostrategic position of Russia and possible ocean and sea theaters of operations, as described in Chapter 3, Russian interests demand that fleets and forces remain in the Pacific and in the North Atlantic oceans, and in the Baltic, Black, and Caspian seas. The reduced number of bases in the Baltic, Black, and Caspian seas means that new bases will have to be built in the St. Petersburg and Astrakhan districts and possibly in the Krasnodar region.

Though the Navy's reformation will not require *fundamental* restructuring, its composition and mission will be subject to considerable change. Recent developments in Russia's military-political and military-strategic situation, as well as a reevaluation of both the nation's requirements for naval defense and its capacity to meet those requirements, show that there is no need at this time to retain as large a force as that possessed during the Cold War. The maintenance of such large forces is becoming a heavy burden given Russia's present economic situation. As a result of changes in the military-political situation, the Navy's missions will be reduced. Specifically, the struggle for sea communications, the search for SSBNs in the world's oceans, the support of land forces in European theaters of operations, and a number of other missions current during the Cold War have been eliminated. All of this makes it possible for Russia to reduce its forces substantially.

Allocations for building and operating ships and other armaments have been drastically cut since 1992. A halt in military shipbuilding is planned for many shipyards within the next two or three years in order to devote resources toward nonmilitary construction. Reduced defense production is scheduled for other yards.

The Russian Navy will focus on the *quality* of new ships—greater precision of their weapons and improvement of their command and control systems, for example. At the same time, obsolete and insufficiently effective combat ships will be decommissioned. This process has already started and continues at a rapid pace.

Ninety-one submarines, 88 surface ships, and 34 motor boats were decommissioned in 1990; 33 submarines, 50 surface vessels, and 27 motor boats followed in 1991; and 21 submarines, 62 surface ships, and 33 motor boats were decommissioned in 1992. In all, 40% of Russian naval forces were cut between 1988 and 1992.

The 670 project (pr) *Charlie* class missile-carrying submarines, the 675 pr missile-and-torpedo carrying *Echo II* and 659 pr *Echo I* boats, the 671 pr *Victor I* attack submarines, the diesel-powered missile-carrying 651 pr *Juliett* class, and the diesel-powered torpedo-carrying 641 pr *Tango* and 633 pr *Romeo* classes were among those vessels decommissioned.

Among the decommissioned surface ships were the 1123 pr antisubmarine cruiser *Leningrad*; the 68A pr light artillery cruiser *Murmansk*; the large anti-submarine vessels or *Kresta* class cruisers *Admiral Makarov*, *Admiral Jumashev*, *Admiral Ysachenkov*, and *Marshall Timoshenko*; the large anti-submarine vessels or *Kara* class 1134B pr ships *Khabarovsk*, *Nikolayev*, and *Tashkent*; and the large *Kashin* class antisubmarine vessels 61 pr *Soobrazitelny* and *Sposobny*. The heavy aircraft-carrying 1134 pr cruisers *Kiev*, *Minsk*, and *Novorossiisk* were decommissioned in 1993.

In addition, 10 escort vessels, 1 destroyer, 1 large landing ship, 2 small missile ships, 13 sea minesweepers, 3 port minesweepers, 12 bay mine-sweepers, 5 small antisubmarine ships, 15 landing craft, and 8 artillery, torpedo, or landing motor boats have been decommissioned.

The Russian Navy intends to reduce the number of its ships further by approximately 22% by 1995 and another 16% by the year 2000. There will also be drastic reductions in the number of MPA aircraft.

As of mid-1994, 195 submarines—125 of which are nuclear-powered and 48 of which carry strategic missiles—470 combat surface ships, 320 motor boats of various designations, about 700 auxiliary ships, and about 2,000 air-craft and helicopters remained in Russian naval service.

Soviet shipbuilding met world-class standards at the time of the union's break up. This enabled the U.S.S.R. to have a navy of an aggregate 4 million tons, that is, about equal to that of the United States. But the current number of industrial enterprises engaged in naval shipbuilding has fallen, followed by a sharp fall in production capacities. This situation is further exacerbated by a loss of test ranges for naval armaments and equipment, the disruption of coop-eration between the defense industry's various branches, an acute shortage of funds, and the subsequent halt in shipbuilding programs.

About two-thirds of the former U.S.S.R.'s shipbuilding capacity remains in Russia. This includes factories producing sheet and profile metal for ships; gas turbines; radar and hydro-acoustic assets; and mines, torpedoes, missiles, and other types of naval armament.

The disruption of cooperation with "near abroad" countries and allocation limits have threatened the completion of a number of vessels in midproduction. Calculations show that should this work be abandoned, the cost of scrapping those vessels will far exceed that of their completion.

Within the framework of the new military doctrine and the new missions entrusted to the Russian Navy, Russia is trying to restore disrupted links between industries working for the Russian Navy in separate C.I.S. countries by concluding bilateral and multilateral agreements, regulating mutual supplies and joint projects, increasing imports from third countries, and further developing Russia's own production capacities. Russian experts say it may take five to seven years to solve these problems. Scientific research, experimental design, and other work determining the direction of naval construction over the next ten to fifteen years are expected to continue at a steady pace.

Twenty-eight new ships and auxiliary vessels were added to the Russian Navy in 1992 in spite of considerable difficulties after the breakup of the Soviet Union. The strict limits imposed by budget allocations will determine the further existence, operation, and development of the Navy. The Northern and Pacific fleets will receive special attention in developing and maintaining combat capability.

FUTURE DIRECTIONS

Four main directions in shipbuilding will be to: (1) render Russian naval vessels universal according to class and mission; (2) reduce the number of ship types within any one class to one or two, thereby facilitating greater production and repair capacities at any one yard; (3) design new ships with greater adaptability vis-à-vis weapons innovation, subsequently increasing the life expectancy of those vessels; and (4) pursue optimal development and use of dual-purpose technologies in naval shipbuilding, thus yielding side benefits to Russia's civilian-economic sector.

Bearing in mind the reduction of allocations for weapons procurement and shipbuilding, naval construction programs envision the continued serial production and commissioning of advanced-design submarines and surface vessels. It is important to note that submarines will remain the principal arm of the Russian Navy, and priority will undoubtedly be placed on their construction. The submarine projects 677 pr *Delta IV* and 941 pr *Typhoon* will continue. At the same time, submarine numbers will be reduced in accordance with START by more than 50%. Sixteen SSBNs, mostly built in the 1970s, have already been decommissioned. A fourth generation of SSBNs is envisioned, armed with new missile complexes for the destruction of land targets.

Apart from this, the main direction in Russian nuclear-powered submarine development will be toward multipurpose vessels armed with anti-submarine/antiship missiles and torpedoes. This development follows from the 971 pr *Akula*, 945V pr *Sierra*, 671RTM pr *Victor III* and 949 pr *Oscar*. Diesel-powered submarines will retain their role in antisubmarine and other missions in closed naval theaters of operations and in the coastal waters of the North Atlantic Sea and the Pacific Ocean. The 877 pr *Kilo* class will be the main focus in this respect.

The construction of surface ships will undergo considerable changes. An enhancement of the 1155 pr *Udaloy/Balkom-3* large antisubmarine ships and the 956 pr *Sovremny/Balkom-2* destroyers is planned. The combination of missile-artillery and antisubmarine designs into a single cruiser or destroyer configuration could be a most promising project. Such a new design would have equally powerful antiaircraft, antisubmarine, missile, and artillery capacities.

Projects for the 1135 pr *Krivak* and the 1154 pr *Neustrashimy/Balcom-8* escort vessels, the 1241 pr *Tarantul* missile motor boats, and the 1124 pr *Grisha* small antisubmarine vessels represent developments in light naval forces.

These ships will in all probability develop toward greater universality of specialized single-design construction, making the flexible use of small combat deployments possible. Priority along this line will be given to small escort vessels armed with those antiship and antisubmarine weapons now used on destroyers. These new ships will be equipped with radioelectronic assets and various auxiliary systems. The shipbuilding program also envisions the further development of minesweepers. Emphasis will be placed on the introduction of promising antimine assets: self-propelled search assets, mine destroyers, hydro-acoustic stations, automated guidance systems, and so on.

The building of landing ships will probably give way to the construction of dual-purpose ships designed for both military missions and transport in the civilian sector. These vessels would be especially useful in the Far North and Far East. A fleet of icebreakers will be similarly deployed to carry out civilian, military, and lifesaving missions.

In spite of an ambiguous attitude toward them, the limited production of aircraft-carrying ships should, in my opinion, become a priority in the renewal of Russia's naval combat forces. Cost-effectiveness analyses and experience using the *Kuznetsov*-class aircraft carrier show that their continued use makes it possible to carry out missions with smaller forces than could be done without them.[3] From the perspective of keeping a minimal defense sufficiency within the limits of current allocations, it is necessary to provide the Northern and Pacific "high-seas" fleets with two aircraft carriers each. Air cover heightens the combat stability of battlegroups. Its absence requires considerably greater expenditures for the building of ships to compensate for overall force losses and for providing air cover from coastal airfields only. Moreover, MPA will lose part of its combat capability, especially in antiship warfare, as a result of considerable force reductions and a halt in the delivery of missile-carrying, assault, and reconnaissance aircraft.

It is expected that MPA will be augmented by limited deliveries of fighters, antisubmarine aircraft, and helicopters. Also planned is the building of shore-based multipurpose aircraft to carry out reconnaissance, targeting, antiship, and antisubmarine missions. Serious attention will be paid to enhancing the mobile and assault capabilities of amphibious forces, including marines, in order to impress upon them those qualities necessary for of mobile forces.

The future distribution of ships and aircraft throughout the fleets should be decided by taking into account the length of any given theater of operation's sea boundaries and that area's importance to the national security of Russia. An analysis from this standpoint of the fleets' future missions was presented in the previous chapter. This analysis determined that the main concentration of Russian naval forces should be deployed in the Pacific and Northern regions. Provision should be made for naval forces' movement between these theaters via inland waters and the Northern Sea route. This enables reinforcement in accordance with the concept of mobile defense. It follows that a great effort must be made to develop the necessary shore infrastructure and enhanced repair facilities and command systems.

It is essential throughout the reform process to take into account the insufficient development of base systems, fleet service and repair facilities, and auxiliary ships, piers, quays, and anchorages. Many large ships cannot be berthed alongside quays and must remain in roads, wasting fuel and deteriorating more rapidly than necessary. The combat capability of the fleet suffers from a lack of repair facilities. This is especially true of the Northern and Pacific fleets.

In order to create "normal" conditions for the naval forces, it is planned in the course of reforms to:

- enhance and develop the basing system, especially for nuclear-powered submarines and large surface ships;
- increase the total length of piers to enable normal berthing;
- enhance the naval logistics system;
- build, repair, and modernize hydrotechnical installations;
- maintain railways and roads leading to ports and naval bases;
- considerably improve the energy supply from shore-based power plants to surface ships, submarines, and shore establishments;
- establish the dispersal of naval forces;
- provide timely repair for ships.

Continued proper administration of Russian naval forces in light of present arms reductions demands that the command system not lag behind those of other great naval powers. If the arms race belongs to the past, the race for ever more advanced command and logistics systems continues. It even gathers pace with each new scientific and technical achievement. The enhancement of these systems enables greater assault potential for naval forces, an important factor when overall numbers are reduced as a result of reform.

CONCLUSION

Russia is now reforming its armed forces. Existing naval groups and formations are being reduced. New groups of forces, together with corresponding logistics and command systems, are being developed. The creation of a qualitatively new and more modern navy is the final aim of this reform. This navy will remain capable of defending Russia's national interests on the high seas within the limits of defense sufficiency and despite the considerable reductions made in order to relieve the nation's economic burden. The development program of the Russian naval forces for the next ten to fifteen years has been worked out within the framework of overall military reform and in close connection with it.

NOTES

1. There has been considerable reporting in the western press on the reduction of formerly Soviet land forces. For example, see the six part series on "Russia's Military: A Shriveled and Volatile Legacy," the *New York Times*, November 28-December 3, 1993. There is almost no mention, however, of the Russian Navy in that series.

2. Recently, some information concerning the future of the Russian Navy has been published in the West in English. Cf. Admiral Valentin Yegorovich Selivanov, Chief of the Main Staff of the Russian Navy, "A Navy's Job: The Role of the Russian Navy in the System of International Security and Cooperation in the Field of Naval Armaments," *Naval Forces*, Vol. 15, No. 2 (1994), pp. 22-24, 29-31; Admiral Felix Gromov, Commander-in-Chief of the Russian Navy, "Reforming the Russian Navy," *Naval Forces*, Vol. 14, No. 4 (1993), pp. 6-12.

3. For a report on the performance of the MiG-29 operating on the *Admiral Kuznetsov*, cf. Igor A. Vlasov, "MiGs over the Sea," *Naval Forces*, Vol. 15, No. 1 (1994), pp. 16-23.

5

THE MAIN ASPECTS OF THE "NEW U.S. NAVAL STRATEGY"

Charles A. Meconis

... the threat posed by a blue-water Soviet navy has disappeared ...
—*Report on the Bottom-Up Review*, Department of Defense, 1993

Our strategy has shifted from a focus on a global threat to a focus on regional challenges and opportunities.
— ... *From the Sea: Preparing the Naval Service for the 21st Century*,
Department of the Navy, 1992

The end of the Cold War and the demise of the Soviet Union have led to a sea change in U.S. naval strategy and the force structure meant to implement it. Under the basic guidelines of the new U.S. national security strategy first developed during the Bush Administration and later amended by President Clinton's defense team, in September 1992 the U.S. Navy, together with the Marine Corps, published a White Paper entitled ... *From the Sea: Preparing the Naval Service for the 21st Century*. This seminal document, and its 1994 update *Forward ... From the Sea*, summarize the Navy's post-Cold War strategy. The *Report on the Bottom-Up Review* of the U.S. defense posture published by the Department of Defense in October 1993, the *Report to the President and the Congress* by the Secretary of Defense released in January 1994, and the 1994 Posture Statement by the Department of the Navy entitled "Revolutionizing Our Naval Forces" provide additional official information on U.S. naval strategy and force structure. In this chapter, the basic elements of the new strategy and force structure will be outlined, with an emphasis on the impact of the profound changes that have occurred in the former Soviet Union and in the Russian Navy.

THE "MARITIME STRATEGY" OF THE 1980S—ONE LAST LOOK

In order to appreciate fully the magnitude of the recent change in U.S. naval strategy, it is necessary to briefly review its predecessor, the "Maritime Strategy" of the 1980s. The most succinct review can be found in the unpublished August 27, 1992 draft of the new U.S. naval strategy.

> As our focus has shifted from global war to regional conflicts, we have recognized that the Maritime Strategy (published in 1986 to articulate the contribution of Naval forces to the Cold War effort which dominated training, acquisition and tactics), can no longer guide the Navy. The assumptions established under the Maritime Strategy envisioned a global war which would be at the initiative of the Soviet Union. The strategy called for Naval forces to *indirectly influence* events on the Central [European] Front by establishing and *defending the fleet's battlespace* in sea areas on the Soviet flanks, thereby threatening the Soviet homeland, and containing the Soviet fleet which otherwise would threaten our sea lines of communications. Under the old National Military Strategy, the task was *war at sea* through sea control. Naval operations on the Soviet flanks were *coordinated* with Army and Air Force operations on the Central Front.[1]

In other words, the old Maritime Strategy envisioned a "forward defense" of NATO (and to a lesser extent, Japan and South Korea) against Soviet attack, by U.S. naval forces operating at sea on the "Soviet flanks," that is, the Norwegian Sea and the North Pacific. Another way to describe these "forward" defense operations is "the best defense is a good offense."

In order to "defend the fleet's battlespace," early naval air and missile attacks against Soviet land bases, especially on the Kola peninsula in the Barents Sea, but also against bases in the Soviet Far East, were planned in order to catch Soviet strike aircraft and ships before they could launch attacks against the U.S. fleet or the cargo ships bringing supplies and reinforcements to western Europe. However, the Soviet Union's large submarine force posed the greatest threat to U.S. naval forces and the reinforcements. In order to "contain" or pin down these submarines (and other Soviet naval forces), U.S. attack submarines were tasked to conduct early attacks on Soviet ballistic missile submarines (SSBNs) in their so-called "bastions" near the Soviet North Atlantic and Pacific coasts, thereby forcing the Soviets to use their attack submarines (SSNs) and other forces to guard their SSBNs. This mission was described as a "strategic antisubmarine warfare" campaign, and antisubmarine warfare was officially described as the top priority mission of the U.S. Navy, despite doubts about its feasibility expressed by some naval analysts.[2]

In the early 1980s the Navy successfully argued that a force structure centered around at least 15 deployable aircraft carrier battlegroups, four battleship battlegroups, and 100 nuclear attack submarines was essential. A "600 ship" combat fleet became the declared goal.[3]

The "Maritime Strategy" was much more than a statement and an acquisition program, however. It was tested and fleshed out in a series of Global War Games conducted at the Naval War College every summer beginning in 1979.[4] Moreover, it was intensely *rehearsed* and refined in a series of supposedly realistic, and often provocative, live exercises in the North Atlantic and the North Pacific throughout the 1980s.[5]

By 1989 the U.S. Navy had essentially fulfilled the vision contained in the "Maritime Strategy" and reached a strength of about 570 ships—just as the threat it was designed to counter collapsed with a suddenness that surprised even the most seasoned analysts.

SEARCHING FOR "THE WAY AHEAD": THE IMPACT OF THE END OF THE COLD WAR

The fall of the Berlin Wall in 1989 symbolized the end of the Cold War. What began as a modest program of reform in the Soviet Union under President Gorbachev soon gained an irresistible momentum that ultimately led to his downfall and the breakup of the Soviet Union in December 1991.

The impact of these events on U.S. naval strategy and force structure was swiftly felt. President Bush's August 2, 1990 speech "In Defense of Defense" publicly outlined a "new national security strategy" which recognized the end of the Cold War and focused on "regional threats." Iraq's invasion of Kuwait on that very same day at once overshadowed the speech and validated its central theme.

The Joint Chiefs of Staff issued their *1991 Joint Military Net Assessment* in March of that year. It outlined five possible scenarios of future post-Cold War conventional conflict. In escalating order of significance, they were: (1) a relatively low-level counterinsurgency or counternarcotics contingency; (2) a "lesser" regional contingency such as Panama (2,000 miles) or the Philippines (6,000 miles); (3) a "major" regional conflict [MRC] in either Korea or Southwest Asia; (4) two simultaneous major regional contingencies (Korea and Southwest Asia); and (5) an invasion of Poland and Lithuania by Russia and Belarus.

Despite the buildup for Operations Desert Shield and Desert Storm, by the spring of 1991 spokespeople for the Bush Administration had outlined a 25% reduction in U.S. defense spending based on these new geopolitical realities. The new "Base Force" envisioned the Navy reduced to 452 ships and 11 or 12 carrier battlegroups.[6]

The first public attempts to reformulate American naval strategy appeared in two articles published in April 1991. In an article entitled "The Way Ahead," the Secretary of the Navy, Chief of Naval Operations, and Commandant of the Marine Corps stated: "Events since the summer of 1989 have brought a fundamental shift in the post-World War II balance of power. . . .

We must reshape naval force structure, strategy, tactics, and operating patterns that are *wedded too closely to the concept of an Armageddon at sea with the Soviet Union.*"[7]

At this stage, these naval leaders recognized a *reduced* "Soviet threat" but were unwilling to dismiss it altogether: "[we] must take into account the uncertainty surrounding the ongoing upheaval in the Soviet Union . . . and the capabilities of the Soviet military threat that we expect to remain in place during the foreseeable future."[8] What they *did* acknowledge was both the reduced likelihood of any Soviet aggression in Europe and a much longer "warning time" prior to any such aggression. But they cautioned that the "Maritime Strategy" of the 1980s remained "on the shelf, . . . ready to be retrieved if a global threat should reemerge."[9]

Having hedged their bets, they went on to indicate some major shifts that were beginning to occur in light of the growing importance of regional threats to U.S. security. The most important change they noted was a shift in the Navy's top warfighting priority from antisubmarine warfare to "power projection" against land targets. Throughout the Cold War, the Soviet Union's massive nuclear submarine fleet was seen as the greatest naval threat to the security of the United States and its overseas allies. As late as April 1990, the Antisubmarine Warfare Division of the Office of the Deputy Chief of Naval Operations (Naval Warfare) publicly pronounced that "antisubmarine warfare must be the primary warfare area in which the U.S. Navy maintains a robust capability. It must remain, of necessity, the Navy's top warfare priority."[10]

In the April 1991 issue of *Seapower* magazine, the new Chief of Naval Operations still believed that "we must hedge against the Soviet submarine force."[11] In "The Way Ahead," after again stating the need to retain America's technological edge in ASW forces as a hedge against a renewed Soviet threat, the leaders stated that preserving that edge would *not* require a massive submarine building program, and that "freed from a nearly full-time requirement to train for ASW in far forward areas, this [submarine] force can now be available for more *regional power projection* and support missions."[12] This shift would eventually have a profound impact, far beyond that forecast in early 1991. At the time, the only immediate impact was the consignment of all forty of the Navy's *Knox* (FF-1052) class frigates, which were primarily designed for the ASW convoy mission, to the reserves.

A *geographic* shift in the Navy's warfighting priorities also became apparent in "The Way Ahead." After noting that the new national defense strategy is geared primarily to answering regional threats to U.S. interests, and that most of the world's population lives within fifty miles of the sea, the authors stated that "Having the capability to project sea-based power is essential to the defense of these interests, *most of which are found in littoral areas.*"[13]

With regard to force structure, the naval leadership reluctantly accepted the 450 ship, 12 carrier Base Force level associated with the new national security strategy, and indicated that "smaller battlegroups" might be used in the future.

While these articles clearly showed that U.S. naval leaders were beginning to react to the momentous changes that had occurred since 1989, they fell far short of a "new" naval strategy. In his January 1992 article entitled "Crafting a New Maritime Strategy," Commander Stanley Weeks USN (Ret.), co-author of the first draft of the 1980s Maritime Strategy, pointed out that "regional crisis response" had *always* been the Navy's "bread and butter" even at the height of the Cold War, when such regional interventions were considered "lesser included cases of the U.S. Soviet naval competition."[14] But the new strategic environment would give a *new meaning* to such basic concepts as Deterrence, Forward Presence (not Forward *Defense*), and Crisis Response.

The failure of the attempted coup in Moscow in August 1991, the dissolution of the Soviet Union in December of that year, and the election of Bill Clinton to the U.S. presidency in 1992 were the pivotal events that finally shaped the "new U.S. naval strategy" and force structure of the 1990s.[15]

"... FROM THE SEA" TO THE "BOTTOM-UP REVIEW" AND "FORWARD"

On September 29, 1992, the Department of the Navy released its long-awaited White Paper entitled . . . *From the Sea: Preparing the Naval Service for the 21st Century, A New Direction for the Naval Service* under the signatures of the Secretary of the Navy, Chief of Naval Operations, and Commandant of the Marine Corps. Here at last was the official new U.S. naval strategy. Or was it?

The brief (twelve pages) White Paper was clearly a watershed document. First of all, unlike the transitional 1991 statements, . . . *From the Sea* is unequivocal in its declaration about the end of the "Soviet" threat: "With the demise of the Soviet Union, the free nations of the world claim preeminent control of the seas. . . . As a result, our maritime policies can afford to deemphasize efforts in some naval warfare areas."[16]

Second, the document clearly states that as a result of the end of the Cold War, U.S. national security strategy—and therefore its naval strategy and associated force structure—are undergoing a "fundamental" shift: "We must structure a fundamentally different naval force to respond to strategic demands. . . . The *new* [strategic] direction of the Navy and Marine Corps team . . . represents a *fundamental* shift away from open-ocean warfighting *on* the sea toward joint operations conducted *from* the sea."[17]

Finally, . . . *From the Sea* spells out the new direction for the Navy-Marine Corps team. It is "to provide the nation: *Naval Forces—Shaped for Joint Operations/Operating Forward From the Sea—Tailored for National Needs.*"[18]

After noting that the Navy also has "a continuing obligation to maintain a robust strategic deterrence by sending ballistic missile submarines to sea," the document fleshes out all four components of the new direction summarized above:

1. "Naval Expeditionary Forces" are:

- Swift to respond, on short notice, to crises in distant lands.
- Structured to build power from the sea when required by national demands.
- Able to sustain support for long-term operations.
- Unrestricted by the need for transit or overflight approval from foreign governments in order to enter the scene of action.[19]

2. Naval forces will be *Shaped for Joint Operations* because "the battlefield of the future will demand that everyone on the field be teammates." Three examples are offered:

- A naval force commander can command the joint task force while the operation is primarily maritime, and shift the command ashore later.
- The Navy and Marine Corps can seize and defend an adversary's port, naval base, or coastal air base to allow the entry of heavy Army or Air Force forces.
- Sealift will provide the maritime bridge for the arrival of heavy forces.[20]

3. The Navy and Marine Corps will be *Operating Forward, From the Sea* in order to "project a positive American image, build foundations for viable coalitions, enhance diplomatic contacts, reassure friends, and demonstrate U.S. power and resolve," in other words, "to demonstrate United States commitment overseas and protect American interests."[21] In times of tension, these forces will attempt to "contain crises," and if diplomacy fails, "project United States combat power."

. . . *From the Sea* then gives a new meaning to the term "forward." Under the Cold War Maritime Strategy, "forward defense" meant operating forward *on the high seas on the flanks of the Soviet Union*: for example, the Norwegian and the Bering seas. Now:

Operating forward means operating in the littoral or "near land" areas of the world. As a general *concept* we can define the littoral as comprising two segments of battlespace:

- Seaward: The area from the open ocean to the shore which must be controlled to support operations ashore.
- Landward: The area inland from the shore that can be supported and defended directly from the sea.[22]

. . . *From the Sea* does not try to predict *which* "near land" areas of the world are likely sites for future action. However, all the examples mentioned in the text are "regional" or "third world" locations: Iraq, Iran, Kuwait, Bangladesh, Liberia, Somalia.

It is important to note that, beginning in 1989, the annual "Global War Games" conducted at the Naval War College have shifted from conflict with the (former) Soviet Union to such topics as Yugoslavia, Panama, Iraq, "catastrophic natural disaster," the relationship between economic and security agendas, arms proliferation and technology transfer, and "the regionalization" of security strategy.[23] In December 1992 the Marine Corps conducted a major war game entitled "Operational Maneuver From the Sea" which focused on four scenarios: Cuba, Libya, Iran, and Korea.[24] Moreover, . . . *From the Sea* specifically tasks the Navy to "continue to *reorient naval intelligence resources from the former Soviet Navy to regional, littoral threats.*"[25] In other words, whatever is meant by "regional, littoral" areas, it clearly does *not* mean the former Soviet Union.

4. Under the new strategy, naval forces will be "*tailored for national needs.*" The term "package" is applied to the "Naval Expeditionary Force" concept to indicate that a "mix-and-match" approach to force composition will be taken, depending on the precise nature of each situation. One obvious conclusion is that "The answer to every situation may *not* be a carrier battlegroup."[26] Every element from maritime patrol aircraft, to submarines, surface combatants, amphibious craft, mine warfare forces, and Navy Special Warfare Forces will be considered.

In an even greater departure from past practice up to and including the war with Iraq, . . . *From the Sea* explicitly acknowledges that future Expeditionary Force "packages" will include "joint" forces from the U.S. Air Force, Army, Coast Guard, Reserves, and Allied forces and assets. This has proven to be a very controversial development.

Does . . . *From the Sea* articulate a "*new* naval (or maritime) strategy"? One thing *is* clear. Conflict with the former Soviet Union has been *eliminated* as the strategic focus of U.S. naval forces. In May 1993 the Chief of U.S. Naval Operations and the Commandant of the Marine Corps wrote:

> . . . *From the Sea*, the new strategic concept of the naval service, . . . is a dramatic departure from the Maritime Strategy, which dominated naval strategic planning during the Cold War. *The global naval threat is gone.* Instead of preparing for independent blue-water operations to defeat a powerful Soviet navy, our Navy and Marine Corps will focus on projecting military might in littoral regions of the world. . . . *The Soviet blue-water threat is gone.* The United States holds the capability in our Navy to command the seas anywhere in the world.[27]

This outlook has been reiterated in the first major Navy publication in a series designed to translate the vision and strategy of . . . *From the Sea* into doctrinal reality, which explicitly confirms the U.S. Navy's "shift from the global struggle envisioned under the Cold War maritime strategy—which called for independent blue-water, open ocean naval operations on the flanks of the Soviet Union—to preparation for regional challenges."[28]

If by "naval strategy" is meant "the use of military forces for the purpose of winning—or denying—command of the sea," that is, "the struggle for the sea lines of communication," then it follows that "if command of the sea is not in dispute, perhaps because one side has lost or won it, or because there is no opponent to contest it," in the words of British naval author Sir Julian S. Corbett, "pure naval strategy comes to an end" or, as Jan Breemer of the Naval Postgraduate School put it, "naval strategy is dead."[29] To put it yet another way, "Sea control by default means, by definition, the end of naval strategy."[30] A similar situation occurred immediately after World War II, when the U.S. Navy ruled the ocean unchallenged, and from 1815 to 1853, when the Royal Navy ruled the waves.

Of course, this does not mean that every potential for "open ocean" warfare has ceased to exist. Any regional adversary capable of competently deploying diesel submarines or modern maritime strike aircraft, for example, could pose a substantial threat beyond "the littoral." What *has* disappeared is the specter of full-scale fleet-vs.-fleet battles taking place thousands of kilometers from the nearest shore.

From this perspective, then, . . . *From the Sea* does *not* contain, in the pure sense, a new *naval* strategy. What it does articulate is a genuinely new strategic framework for linking U.S. naval capabilities with national military goals in an era when the ability of the fleet to influence events *on land* is paramount. For some who have devoted their lives to preparing for blue-water fleet-vs.-fleet engagements with the Soviet Navy for "command of the sea" in the tradition of American naval strategist Alfred Thayer Mahan, this new strategic framework may seem disappointing at best and dangerously premature at worst.[31] Developments since the publication of . . . *From the Sea* leave no doubt about the irreversible change in the strategic direction and force structure of the nation's naval forces.

The 1992 election of Bill Clinton as President of the United States resulted in a new emphasis on addressing the domestic issues facing the country in the last decade of the century. The national deficit, health care crisis, economic shortfalls, and environmental issues were seen as the priority items on the Clinton agenda, with foreign affairs and defense taking a secondary role. It became apparent early in the Clinton Administration that additional cuts would be made in the defense budget beyond the 25% called for under President Bush. Under Secretary of Defense Les Aspin, in 1993 the Department of Defense conducted an across-the-board *Bottom-Up Review* of U.S. Defense

Policy and Programs, the results of which were published in October of that year. The impact of this review on naval forces was significant.

The *Bottom-Up Review* reiterated the basic premise of the new strategic framework for the naval forces: " the threat posed by a blue-water Soviet navy has disappeared."[32] Instead, the overriding requirement for U.S. military forces, in addition to nuclear deterrence, is stated to be the ability "to fight and win two major regional conflicts (MRCs) that occur nearly simultaneously."[33] Two illustrative scenarios are mentioned: a rerun of the invasion of Kuwait by Iraq, and an invasion of South Korea by the North.

When it came to outlining the naval forces necessary to meet this requirement, the *Bottom-Up Review* stated that "Sizing our naval forces for two nearly simultaneous MRCs provides a fairly large and robust force structure that can easily support other, smaller regional operations. However, our overseas presence needs can impose requirements for naval forces, especially aircraft carriers, that exceed those needed to win two MRCs."[34] The U.S. Naval Force Structure for 1999 was set at 11 aircraft carriers (active), 1 aircraft carrier (reserve/training), 45-55 attack submarines, and 346 ships.[35]

Subsequent documents have detailed the substantial reductions implied by this force structure. Table 5.1 shows a comparison of the U.S. Navy at the height of its Maritime Strategy, Cold War strength in the late 1980s to the . . . *From the Sea*, regional conflict size envisioned by the end of the 1990s.

Table 5.1
Changes in U.S. Naval Force Structure

U.S. Naval Strength	1989	1999
Aircraft Carriers (CV/N)	15	12
Battle Force Ships	566	346
Aircraft	5,400	3,700
Personnel in Uniform	782,000	568,000

Sources: Scott C. Truver, "Tomorrow's Fleet: Effective Force or 'Rotten Timber?'" Center for Security Strategies and Operations, Techmatics, Inc. Arlington, Va., April 1994, p. 7.; Department of the Navy, "Revolutionizing Our Naval Forces," 1994 Posture Statement, p. 20.

An examination of exactly *what* is being cut is much more revealing than aggregate figures. A close look reveals that the fundamental strategic shift away from the old Maritime Strategy's vision of open ocean conflict with the Soviet Navy is being rigorously implemented in the new force structure. In Chapter 2 we noted that the *Knox* class frigates designed to protect Europe-bound convoys from Soviet submarines were cut. Now, additional large cuts are being made in two ship categories (and future building plans) whose mission profiles were defined by the Cold War: nuclear attack submarines (SSNs), and nuclear-powered and older conventional guided missile cruisers.

The announced primary mission of nuclear attack submarines is anti-submarine warfare—sinking other submarines, although it should be stated that some naval officers and analysts continue to doubt the feasibility of that mission.[36] The old Maritime Strategy called for a force of 100 SSNs, ostensibly to counter the Soviet submarine threat. According to the latest reports, the U.S. nuclear attack submarine force will ultimately be reduced *by more than half* to perhaps 45 boats.[37] The program director for the Chief of Naval Operations' Strategic Studies Group has put it succinctly: "We are in a time of great change. Among naval forces, this change will most affect the U.S. attack submarine force . . . submarines have dropped from the extraordinary position they had in war plans against the Soviets, to filling narrow niches."[38] The Navy is decommissioning many submarines that have considerable life left in them. For example, in 1994 the Navy began decommissioning *Los Angeles* class SSNs thirteen years earlier than originally planned and with half of their service life remaining.[39] Production of the next-generation *Seawolf* class SSN will be terminated after the third unit is completed, and long-lead funding for a follow-on "New Attack Submarine" will not be sought until 1998 at the earliest, with some doubts being raised about the very existence of the project.[40]

At the same time, it must be noted that, in operational terms, the submarine force has given the impression that it is clinging to a Cold War tradition of shadowing Russian submarines so closely as to invite actual collision, as occurred in 1992 and 1993.[41]

The Navy's 9 nuclear-powered and 18 older conventional guided missile cruisers were designed primarily to accompany its aircraft carriers in order to provide them with defense on the high seas against regiments of Soviet Backfire bombers carrying supersonic antiship missiles. By 1999 *all* of these cruisers will be gone, some after having recently received nuclear refueling or expensive upgrades to their defensive systems. For example, in 1993 the nuclear cruiser *USS Texas* was retired only halfway into her planned service life of thirty years.[42] These ships are not optimally equipped to operate "in the compressed battlespace of the littoral warfare environment" and were thus deemed expendable.

The only major warship category to survive the transition to the post-Cold War security environment relatively unscathed is the aircraft carrier. At one point during the intense (and ongoing) debate about the future of the carrier force, a low figure of 6 carriers was considered,[43] but the *Bottom-Up Review* concluded that in order to adequately fulfill the Navy's "presence" requirements, plus the requirement to fight and win two nearly simultaneous MRCs, a force of 11 active and 1 reserve carrier is essential. To date, this figure is holding, although funding for future nuclear aircraft carrier construction beyond the 3 ships already in progress is by no means assured.

Cuts of this magnitude have caused considerable controversy. The Republican election landslide in the November 1994 midterm Congressional elections may result in somewhat smaller reductions or a longer time scale. But the basic trend toward a smaller Navy will not change.

It is true, that in the face of these significant reductions, the U.S. Navy continues to *improve qualitatively,* especially in such categories as the high-tech air defense of the Aegis system, a vertical launch system (VLS) with "cells" to accommodate a variety of missiles, and advanced propulsion. Some Russian analysts, for example, have concluded that in terms of "combat efficiency" the smaller U.S. Navy is 1.5 times better. Table 5.2 outlines some of the improvements from 1987 projected through 1997.

Table 5.2
Qualitative Improvements in the U.S. Navy

Type of Improvement	1987	1997
Ships with Aegis defense	9	48
Old steam-powered ships	115	0
New gas turbine ships	79	107
VLS cells	480	6,100
Tomahawk cruise missiles	280	3,162

Source: Scott C. Truver, "Tomorrow's Fleet," p. 17.

Still, however capable a ship is, it can only be in one place at a time. The U.S. Navy of the future will be well equipped to operate within the new regionally oriented strategic framework set out in . . . *From the Sea.* But it will be a great deal *less* capable than the massive 600 ship fleet envisioned at the height of the Cold War. In terms of the basic "levels of warfare," the Navy-Marine Corps team of the future will be able to conduct *unilateral* interventions only at the "tactical" level, that is, something along the lines of the 1989 Operation Just Cause in Panama: deploying approximately one Marine Expeditionary Brigade (MEB) of 16,000 personnel with thirty days combat sustainment. To carry out missions at the "operational" or campaign level, such as Operation Desert Storm, additional Army/Air Force and "host nation" support would be required. If the "strategic" level, such as the massive Allied invasion of Normandy in World War II, is the benchmark, then it would require years of "reconstitution" to reconstruct and assemble the necessary force, which would include major Allied contributions.[44]

However, the Department of the Navy's November 1994 strategy update and expansion document *Forward . . . From the Sea* emphasized the importance of maintaining forward deployed naval forces, based on the premise that in a situation short of war, naval forces are best suited "to be *engaged* in forward areas, with the objectives of *preventing* conflicts and *controlling* crises."[45] While remaining committed to the concept of "joint" operations with the U.S. Air Force and Army, *Forward . . . From the Sea* makes it clear that the U.S. Navy and its brother service, the U.S. Marine Corps, intend to remain the premier element of American forward presence and to retain the necessary force structure to fulfill that role.

CONCLUSION

It is clear from our examination of both the new regional strategic framework outlined in . . . *From the Sea* and *Forward . . . From the Sea,* and the force structure outlined in the *Bottom-Up Review* and other sources that the U.S. Navy has definitively left behind its Cold War anti-Soviet Navy outlook and makeup. Whether or not the U.S. and Russian navies can move all the way from confrontation to active cooperation in the post-Cold War environment remains to be seen.

NOTES

1. "Power from the Sea," unpublished draft, Department of the Navy, August 27, 1992, pp. 13-14. Copy in the authors' possession. This passage was dropped from the final document.

2. The nonclassified version of the "Maritime Strategy," under the name of then Chief of Naval Operations Admiral James D. Watkins, was first published as a special supplement to the January 1986 issue of the U.S. Naval Institute *Proceedings.* There have been several valuable commentaries, among them are Norman Friedman, *The U.S. Maritime Strategy* (London: Jane's, 1988); Frederick H. Hartmann, *Naval Renaissance: The U.S. Navy in the 1980s* (Annapolis, Md.: Naval Institute Press, 1990); John F. Lehman, Jr., *Command of the Seas: Building the 600 Ship Navy* (New York,: Scribner's, 1988); Steven E. Miller and Stephen Van Evera, eds., *Naval Strategy and National Security: An International Security Reader* (Princeton: Princeton University Press, 1988).

3. Cf. *The 600 Ship Navy and the Maritime Strategy: Hearings before the Seapower and Strategic Materials Subcommittee of the House Armed Services Committee* (Washington, D.C.: U.S. Government Printing Office, 1986). The final presentation of the 600 ship force structure was contained in U.S. Department of the Navy, *Report to Congress, Fiscal Year 1988* (Washington, D.C.: U.S. Government Printing Office, 1987).

4. Cf. Peter P. Perla, *The Art of Wargaming* (Annapolis, Md.: Naval Institute Press: 1990), pp. 97-102, 186, 299, 300, 320 for a concise description of these important games. The official history of the first five Global War Games is contained in Bud Hay and Captain Bob Gile, USNR (Ret.), *Global War Game: The First Five Years* (Newport, R.I.: Naval War College, n.d.), 68 pp., released to Charles A. Meconis under the Freedom of Information Act.

5. Many of these exercises were recounted annually in the "Naval Review" issues of the U.S. Naval Institute *Proceedings* which appear every May. Two other valuable sources are William M. Arkin, *The Nuclear Arms Race at Sea* (Washington, D.C.: Greenpeace and the Institute for Policy Studies, Neptune Papers No. 1, October 1987)

and Pauline Kerr, *Eyeball to Eyeball: U.S. & Soviet Naval & Air Operations in the North Pacific 1981-1990* (Canberra: Peace Research Centre, Australian National University, 1991). The veil of secrecy over Cold War submarine operations was lifted by the *Chicago Tribune* in a six-part series entitled "Enemies Below" January 6-11, 1991. The most detailed account of a single exercise is contained in Eric Grove, with Graham Thompson, *Battle for the Fiørds: NATO's Forward Maritime Strategy in Action* (Annapolis, Md.: Naval Institute Press, 1991), which covers "Teamwork '88" in the Norwegian Sea. The most complete annotated bibliography on the Maritime Strategy is Peter M. Swartz and Jan S. Breemer, bibliographers, with James J. Tritten, principal investigator, "The Maritime Strategy Debates: A Guide to the Renaissance of U.S. Naval Strategic Thought in the 1980s," rev. ed., Naval Postgraduate School, Monterey, Calif., Report NPS-56-89-019, September 30, 1989.

6. For a thorough analysis of the origins of the new national security strategy and the "Base Force," see James J. Tritten, *Our New National Security Strategy: America Promises To Come Back* (Westport, Conn.: Praeger, 1992), chapters 1-3.

7. The Honorable H. Lawrence Garrett III, Secretary of the Navy, Admiral Frank B. Kelso II, Chief of Naval Operations, General A. M. Gray, Commandant of the Marine Corps, "The Way Ahead," U.S. Naval Institute *Proceedings*, Vol. 117, No. 4 (April 1991), p. 36 (emphasis added).

8. Garrett, Kelso, and Gray, "The Way Ahead," pp. 38-9.

9. "The Way Ahead," p. 38.

10. *Antisubmarine Warfare: Meeting the Challenge*, U.S. Navy, Office of the Chief of Naval Operations, April 1990, introduction.

11. Admiral Frank B. Kelso II, "Charting a Course for the Future," *Seapower*, Vol. 34, No. 4 (April 1991).

12. "The Way Ahead," p. 42.

13. "The Way Ahead," p. 38 (emphasis added).

14. Dr. Stanley Weeks, "Crafting a New Maritime Strategy," U.S. Naval Institute *Proceedings*, Vol. 117, No. 1 (January 1992), p. 31.

15. Two excellent insider accounts of the internal process whereby the U.S. Navy reached a new consensus on strategy and force structure are now available. Cf. Captain Edward A. Smith, Jr., U.S. Navy, "What '. . . From the Sea' Didn't Say," *Naval War College Review*, Vol. 48, No. 1 (Winter 1995), pp. 9-33, and Admiral William A. Owens, U.S. Navy, *High Seas: The Naval Passage to an Uncharted World* (Annapolis, Md.: Naval Institute Press, 1995) esp. pp. 121-137.

16. ". . . *From the Sea: Preparing the Naval Service for the 21st Century*," Washington, D.C.: Department of the Navy, September 29, 1992, p. 2. This document was also published in Vol. 118, No. 11 (November 1992) of the U.S. Naval Institute *Proceedings*, pp. 93-96. To date, this document has not spawned nearly the volume of commentary inspired by its predecessor. The most pertinent commentaries are, in chronological order: Lieutenant General John H. Cushman, U.S. Army (Ret.), "Maneuver from the Sea," U.S. Naval Institute *Proceedings*, Vol. 119, No. 4 (April 1993), pp. 47-49; Admiral Frank B. Kelso II, U.S. Navy, and General Carl E. Mundy, Jr., U.S. Marine Corps, "The Naval Service Is Joint," U.S. Naval Institute *Proceedings*, Vol. 119, No. 5 (May 1993), pp. 44-48; Commander Tom Katana, USN, " . . . From the Sea: SEALS to the Carriers," U.S. Naval Institute *Proceedings*, Vol. 119, No. 6 (June 1993), pp. 61-63; Captain Scott A. Fedorchak, U.S. Army, "It Must Be Joint," U.S.

Naval Institute *Proceedings*, Vol 119, No. 6 (June 1993), pp. 64-65; Majors William T. DeCamp III and Kenneth F. McKenzie, Jr., USMC, "A Hollow Force?" U.S. Naval Institute *Proceedings*, Vol. 119, No. 6 (June 1993), pp. 66-70; Rear Admiral Daniel T. Oliver, USN, "A Force Molecule," U.S. Naval Institute *Proceedings*, Vol. 119, No. 6 (June 1993), pp. 71-73; Commander Terry C. Pierce, USN, "Not a 'CVN Gator,'" U.S. Naval Institute *Proceedings*, Vol. 119, No. 6 (June 1993), pp. 74-76; Lieutenant Commander P. Kevin Peppe, USN, "Submarines in the Littorals," U.S. Naval Institute *Proceedings*, Vol. 119, No. 7 (July 1993), pp. 46-48; Commander C. P. Mott, USN, "Naval Forces after '. . . From the Sea,'" U.S. Naval Institute *Proceedings*, Vol. 119, No. 9 (September 1993), pp. 44-46; General Carl E. Mundy, Jr., USMC, "Getting It Right '. . . From the Sea,'" U.S. Naval Institute *Proceedings*, Vol. 120, No. 1 (January 1994), pp. 69-71; Commander James A. Winnefeld, Jr., USN, "Staying the Course," U.S. Naval Institute *Proceedings*, Vol. 120, No. 5 (May 1994), pp. 32-39; Rear Admiral Philip A. Dur, USN, "Presence: Forward, Ready, Engaged," U.S. Naval Institute *Proceedings*, Vol. 120, No. 6 (June 1994), pp. 41-44. It is interesting to note that five of the twelve articles were written in whole or in part by Marine and Army authors.

17. ". . . From the Sea," p. 2.

18. ". . . From the Sea," p. 2.

19. ". . . From the Sea," p. 3.

20. ". . . From the Sea," p. 4.

21. ". . . From the Sea," p. 5.

22. ". . . From the Sea," p. 5.

23. Rear Admiral Joseph C. Strasser, USN, "President's Notes," *Naval War College Review*, Vol. 46, No. 3 (Summer 1993), p. 5.

24. Lieutenant General John H. Cushman, U.S. Army (Ret.), "Maneuver . . . From the Sea," U.S. Naval Institute *Proceedings*, Vol. 119, No. 4 (April 1993), p. 47.

25. ". . . From the Sea," p. 12.

26. ". . . From the Sea," p. 6.

27. Admiral Frank B. Kelso, USN, and General Carl E. Mundy, Jr., U.S. Marine Corps, "The Naval Service Is Joint," U.S. Naval Institute *Proceedings*, Vol. 119, No. 5 (May 1993), pp. 45-46 (emphasis added).

28. *Naval Warfare: Naval Doctrine Publication 1* (Washington, D.C.: Department of the Navy, March 28, 1994), p. 60.

29. Jan S. Breemer, "Naval Strategy Is Dead," U.S. Naval Institute *Proceedings*, Vol. 120, No. 2 (February 1994), pp. 49-53. Breemer uses the Corbett quote which is from Julian S. Corbett, *Some Principles of Maritime Strategy* (1911) (Annapolis, Md.: Naval Institute Press, 1972), p. 87.

30. Breemer, "Naval Strategy Is Dead," p. 52.

31. Cf., for example, Commander James A. Winnefeld, Jr., USN, "Staying the Course," U.S. Naval Institute *Proceedings*, Vol. 120, No. 5 (May 1994), pp. 32-39. He raises the specter of Russian resurgence and the possible emergence of the People's Republic of China (P.R.C.) as a "blue water" threat.

32. Les Aspin, *Report on the Bottom-Up Review* (Washington, D.C.: Department of Defense, October, 1993), p. 92.

33. Aspin, Bottom-Up Review, p. 7.

34. Aspin, Bottom-Up Review, p. 24.

35. Aspin, Bottom-Up Review, p. 28.

36. Concerning the feasibility of this mission, cf. Commander Richard Compton-Hall, RN (Ret.), *Sub vs. Sub: The Tactics and Technology of Underwater Warfare* (New York: Orion Books, 1988). Compton was a submarine commander. Rear Admiral J. R. Hill, RN (Ret.), *Anti-Submarine Warfare* (Annapolis, Md.: Naval Institute Press, 2nd ed., 1989); Mark Sakitt, *Submarine Warfare Under the Arctic: Option or Illusion?* (Stanford: Center for International Security and Arms Control, 1988). Admiral Hill states "I think submariners still regard surface ships as their prime targets. SS vs. SS (and SSN vs. SS) was not remotely a runner in the Falklands, even though the Argentines had submarines deployed." Letter to the authors, November 2, 1994.

37. Les Aspin, Secretary of Defense, *Annual Report to the President and the Congress* (Washington, D.C.: U.S. Government Printing Office, January 1994), p. 167.

38. Dr. John T. Hanley, "Implications of the Changing Nature of Conflict for the Submarine Force," *Naval War College Review*, Vol. 46, No. 4 (Autumn 1993), pp. 9, 26.

39. Scott C. Truver, "Tomorrow's Fleet: Effective Force or 'Rotten Timber'"? Center for Security Strategies and Operations, Techmatics, Inc., Arlington, Va., April 1994. This monograph has been published in abbreviated form in the June and July 1994 issues of the U.S. Naval Institute *Proceedings*.

40. Truver, "Tomorrow's Fleet," pp. 32-33.

41. Hanley, "Implications of the Changing Nature of Conflict for the Submarine Force," p. 23 and note 19.

42. Truver, "Tomorrow's Fleet," p. 47.

43. Cf. U.S. General Accounting Office, Report to the Congress, *Navy Carrier Battlegroups: The Structure and Affordability of the Future Force* (GAO/NSIAD-93-74), February 1993, 148 pp. The most recent challenge to the future of the U.S. Navy's nuclear carrier fleet has come from Greenpeace. Cf. Hans Kristensen, William M. Arkin, and Joshua Handler, *Aircraft Carriers: The Limits of Nuclear Power* (Washington, D.C.: Greenpeace, June 1994). This position paper was given a mostly favorable review by prominent naval analyst Norman Polmar in "The U.S. Navy: Nuclear Carrier Questions," U.S. Naval Institute *Proceedings*, Vol. 120, No. 9 (September 1994), pp. 121-122.

44. Tritten, *Our New National Security Strategy*, pp. 45-46.

45. Department of the Navy, *Forward . . . From the Sea* (Washington, D.C.: U.S. Navy Department Office of Information, November 1994), p. 1.

6

NAVAL ARMS CONTROL: A STEP TOWARD U.S.-RUSSIAN COOPERATION?

Boris N. Makeev and Charles A. Meconis

Our countries have a good record of dialogue concerning naval problems . . . it is time for all such problems to be solved by professionals.
> —Rear Admiral Valery I. Aleksin, Russian Navy

Instead of merely dampening competition, arms control now plays a major role in creating the framework for cooperation.
> —*National Security Strategy of the United States*, January 1993

With the end of the Cold War, some analysts have concluded that arms control has lost all relevance. This view is held by traditional critics of arms control such as Colin S. Gray, as well as by some former proponents of arms control as Kosta Tsipis.[1] With regard to "naval" arms control, throughout the Cold War the U.S. Navy maintained a highly visible "Just Say No" attitude toward naval arms agreements with the Soviet Union,[2] and the demise of the U.S.S.R. is seen by some as evidence of the wisdom of that policy—and the end of further talk on the subject. Naval arms control is, in this view, simply another item in a long list of dubious political processes that have been "overtaken by events."

If by "naval arms control" one means only formal, bilateral, negotiated agreements between the United States and the "Soviet Union" resulting in unfavorably lopsided major ship reductions or unrealistic operational restraints that affect one party unfairly—the U.S. Navy's preferred Cold War definition—then of course it *is* dead, along with the Soviet Union and the Cold War itself.

However, the issue of preventing or containing maritime conflict in the post-Cold War era is not dead. We are convinced that naval arms control in the *broad* sense can play an important role in that effort—and in creating a framework for U.S.-Russian naval cooperation and possibly even partnership.

We define "naval arms control" as any action, agreement, or statement, whether unilateral, bilateral, or multilateral in form, that reveals, restricts, restrains, or reduces the operations, capability, composition, structure, or size of any nation's naval forces for the purposes of preventing conflict, reducing damage should conflict occur, and reducing the cost of procuring and maintaining naval forces. By "naval" forces is meant both sea-based forces and those land-based forces that have sufficient reach to significantly affect naval activities, for example, strike aircraft and antiship missiles.

CONFRONTING THE OBSTACLES TO NAVAL ARMS CONTROL

Of course we recognize that, despite the end of the Cold War and the demise of the Soviet Union, there are serious obstacles to any progress in the field of naval arms control. These obstacles fall into three categories: (1) historical; (2) politico-economic; and (3) technical.

The Ghosts of "Naval Arms Control" Past

The United States took part in the series of naval arms control conferences and agreements that marked the period between the two world wars. Until recently, the judgment of many western analysts was that these negotiations were at best a waste of time and at worst a serious mistake that failed to prevent and even led to World War II.[3] That judgment has come under serious scrutiny in the past few years. Robert Kaufman concludes his thorough study of the interwar naval agreements by stating:

> Then was the experiment with naval limitations during the interwar years a total mistake? No . . . it made sense to experiment with naval arms control from 1922 to 1930, when détente prevailed among the United States, Great Britain, and Japan. Perhaps the Washington Naval Treaty even contributed to the détente of the 1920s, which it symptomized. Naval limitation became folly only when the United States and Great Britain persisted in their efforts even after world conditions changed manifestly for the worse.[4]

Caroline Ziemke of the Institute for Defense Analyses writes:

> Whatever their flaws in terms of strategic prescience, the interwar treaties did succeed in one very important respect: they provided a framework within which to reorder defense priorities and plan postwar disarmament in a manner that allowed military establishments to adjust to difficult economic times without potentially destabilizing strategic uncertainty.[5]

Retired U.S. naval officer Richard C. Davis puts it more bluntly:

... the naval arms control treaties of 1922 and 1930, although often maligned after World War II for not preventing war, did what they were intended to do: they saved money. Had that money been spent, many of the ships purchased would have been outdated by the time World War II broke out.[6]

While each historical epoch is unique, we would argue that the situation today is much like it was in 1918 after the end of World War I, and that another "experiment" in naval arms control is worthwhile. Few now recall that the interwar naval arms control agreements marked the end of naval rivalry and a certain degree of hostility between the United States and Great Britain. Perhaps the same could become true for the United States and Russia.

Still, we must overcome the more recent history of the failed Cold War efforts at naval arms control. Throughout the 1980s, the Soviet Union put forward a long list of naval arms control proposals—and the United States rejected the vast majority of them. Nearly all of these proposals had a disproportionate effect on the U.S. Navy and were therefore doomed to failure.[7] As Admiral Aleksin of the Russian Navy recently put it: "The main hindrance to starting such negotiations may have been the fact that only the upper strata of the Soviet Communist Party conducted them. The 'successes' of those would-be ideological-front fighters can now be seen by anybody as failures in Soviet domestic and foreign policy."[8] Russian analyst Alexei Arbatov offers these additional evaluations for the professional inadequacies that contributed to the failure of naval arms control efforts in that era:

1. Soviet naval professionals who understood how naval power operates nevertheless lacked knowledge or experience of arms control and how it works conventionally.
2. Soviet arms control experts did not understand the peculiarities of naval power and its differences from strategic weapons or conventional land and air forces.
3. Both the former and the latter usually failed to comprehend the role of naval power in NATO alliance politics and strategy.[9]

It must also be pointed out that many western arms control advocates harshly criticized the U.S. Navy's Maritime Strategy and its "Just Say No" attitude toward naval arms control during those years.[10] That attitude was in evidence as late as February 1993, when the Pentagon put a six-month hold on the release of a report on naval arms control written by James L. Lacy of the Institute for Defense Analyses.[11] By involving naval professional and arms control experts from both the United States and Russia in the preparation of this study, we have attempted to rectify some of those past mistakes.

Despite the many difficulties during those years, the United States and the Soviet Union *did* engage in several successful efforts at "naval arms control" broadly defined. The Strategic Arms Limitation Talks (SALT I and II) included submarine-launched ballistic missile launchers and warheads in their scope. However, the three most important agreements having to do with naval forces were the very successful 1972 agreement on the Prevention of Incidents on and Over the High Seas (INCSEA), the 1988 agreement on Notifications of Launches of Intercontinental Ballistic Missiles and Submarine-Launched Ballistic Missiles, and the 1989 agreement on the Prevention of Dangerous Military Activities (PDMA).[12]

Given the fundamental strategic shift that has occurred with the end of the Cold War and the demise of the Soviet Union, much greater progress now seems possible. Indeed the recently concluded START I and II agreements have put greater limits on submarine-launched ballistic missiles and warheads, and the mutual agreement between Presidents Bush and Gorbachev in 1991 resulted in the removal of all tactical nuclear weapons from both navies.[13] On the international level, on June 22, 1994, Russia formally signed the Partnership for Peace agreement with NATO, opening a "new chapter" in European history.[14]

Why, then, should there be any further interest in naval arms control? Has it not been "overtaken by events?"

In his late 1992 study, Lacy enumerated four likely developments that would serve to keep interests in and concerns about naval arms control active:

1. Moscow will not abandon the subject entirely;
2. Interest in some better regulation of the spread of "destabilizing" conventional weaponry is likely to persist;
3. Changing regional dynamics will lead to indigenous naval confidence-building that decouples the process from either or both the United States and Russia, even while jurisdictional disputes over sea areas are likely to increase;
4. Increased pressures to revisit, reinterpret, and/or substantially reformulate the legal regime of the seas are likely.

Lacy concludes by stating: "Little of this will be 'naval arms control' *in the Cold War sense.* Yet, in a number of respects, the underlying issues will not be all that different."[15] From the vantage point of late 1995, this estimate remains valid.

Indeed, naval arms control in the broad sense appears to be gaining momentum in such vital maritime regions as Southeast Asia and the Middle East, as the authors of this study have seen firsthand.[16] It will not do for the world's two largest navies and their governments to "miss the boat" on this issue.

If the full transition from Cold War confrontation to a genuine strategic partnership between the United States and Russia is to take place, we believe that some aspects of naval arms control are necessary to remove the last vestiges of the long confrontation between our two navies—and we believe it can be achieved without too much difficulty.

Unresolved Nuclear Issues

There is a great deal of leftover business in the area of naval nuclear weapons. Even assuming that everything goes well with the ratification of the START II agreement, the actual dismantling and disposal or storage of submarine-launched ballistic missile (SLBM) warheads under treaty is a very great challenge, especially for Russia during this time of economic hardship. Some complain that Russia is not carrying out existing agreements, and therefore no new ones should be made. The Clinton Administration's recently completed *Nuclear Posture Review* calls for no new warhead cuts beyond START II. Deputy Defense Secretary John Deutch has offered this explanation: "Given the pace at which the Russians are bringing down their actual warheads, we . . . believe that it would not be prudent to commit now to a reduction below START II levels."[17]

In Russia this task *is* being carried out by the Center for the Implementation of the Treaties on the Reduction of Naval Armaments. Apart from accounting for and constant control of the dismantling and conversion of naval armaments subject to the treaties, the center is very active in organizing and actually doing this work.

In spite of the fact that the center was only formed in May 1993, it has already accomplished a great deal. The center has entered into a number of contracts with industry to carry out preliminary work on the destruction of SLBMs and also to supply the Russian Navy with additional technological equipment for the elimination of the armaments subject to the treaties.

With the assistance and participation of the center, projects are being negotiated for the refit and construction of new installations at the SLBM utilization base near Novosibirsk. Construction has started on additional facilities for the Northern and Pacific fleets. The center controls sites for conversion or dismantling of SLBM launchers, located at Severodinsk, Pashino, and the Bolshoi Kamen Bay. It has provided work for U.S. on-site inspection groups at SLBM storage and loading sites.

However, considerable difficulties have arisen in organizing control of compliance with the treaty provisions, and with the storage and destruction of naval tactical nuclear missiles. In the Russian Navy all naval tactical nuclear weapons are being removed from surface vessels, submarines, and land-based aviation. Part of them is being stored at centralized storage sites and part is being eliminated. In controlling the elimination of naval tactical nuclear weapons, Russia is using the experience acquired during the preparation and implementation of the INF treaty, including direct borrowing of the formulas, methods, procedures, and measures with respect to these weapons.

In the next few years, the Russian Navy will have to eliminate more than a thousand ballistic missiles, hundreds of aircraft, air-launched cruise missiles (ALCMs), antisubmarine torpedoes, and scores of SSBNs. An environmentally friendly disposal technology will have to be developed, verified in practice, and then introduced into the elimination process. Special equipment will have to be developed to implement this technology. It will also be necessary to reequip existing utilization bases and to build new facilities for the elimination of liquid-fuel SLBMs and the disposal of nuclear reactors from submarines. According to preliminary estimates, work connected with compliance with the START treaty will cost the Russian Navy about 15-17 billion rubles (in 1992 prices).

However, the tempo at which naval nuclear weapons are being disposed of does not correspond to the rate of their deactivation. The disposal of nuclear submarines is a particularly difficult problem. Technically obsolete vessels built in the 1950s and 1960s are being written off at a rapid rate. The Russian Navy has worked out a timeline for their decommissioning, but because of the lack of money and sufficient shipbuilding and ship repair facilities, timely preparation for their consignment to the scrap heap is not being carried out. The difficulties connected with the disposal of submarines are aggravated further by an acute shortage of special storage depots and equipment for the disposal of nuclear fuel from reactors and other radioactive waste. A program adopted in 1992 by the government of the Russian Federation envisions the building of underground storage sites for submarines, transit depots for expended nuclear fuel, complementary equipment for naval shipyards, shore facilities for refueling reactors, and the collection and burial of radioactive waste. This program, however, is not being implemented because of lack of money. Thus, in the first half of 1993, only 1% of the allocations called for in the program have been made available.

For all these reasons, decommissioned nuclear submarines remain at their moorings for a long time while awaiting their turn to be disposed of. These "laid-up" vessels require labor-intensive service in order to assure that they do not sink, that their nuclear reactors remain in satisfactory condition, and that a normal level of radiation is maintained.

The reduced crews of specialists, left behind on those vessels, cost a great deal of money but are essential to provide for the necessary environmental safety. It is, however, not possible to guarantee absolute environmental safety in a situation where a large number of vessels with nuclear reactors are laid-up for a long time.[18] That is why it is urgent that the disposal process be accelerated to correspond to the rate at which Russian nuclear submarines are being decommissioned.

It is impossible for the Russian Navy to cope with these problems on its own. They should be included in the state program for the disposal of radioactive waste and financed accordingly. A special branch should be created for this purpose under the auspices of the State Atomic Monitoring Service. This branch should be provided with all the resources necessary for processing nuclear waste as well as regional "gravediggers" to bury the residual substances. The experience of the Russian Navy has shown that these problems cannot be effectively dealt with at the purely departmental level. From an environmental standpoint, Russia needs a centralized, state-sponsored approach to link all the aspects of the problem into a single whole.

Russia would do well to borrow from the experience of the United States, although that system is by no means perfect. In the United States, all the enterprises of the military nuclear complex come under the Department of Energy (DOE). Under the direction of the DOE and with the participation of the Federal Environmental Protection Agency (EPA), and state authorities, an ecological program is being implemented for the storage and handling of radioactive waste. More than $30 billion has been allocated for this purpose under the Federal budget. This example of an adequate approach by the state to ecological problems caused by the military-industrial complex should be studied by the Russian State Atomic Monitoring Service, especially with regard to the problem of disposing of nuclear-powered ships.

In the end, it is in the interest of the United States and the international community to help Russia address this serious problem. Perhaps, as some have proposed, a joint U.S.-Russian project for naval nuclear power cleanup and dismantling, with additional funding from the European community and Japan, would be the best answer.[19]

The issue of naval tactical nuclear weapons has not been fully resolved, either. The mutual, unilateral removal of all naval tactical nuclear weapons from the Russian and U.S. navies was a welcome development in the field of naval arms control, and one long advocated by many experts in both countries. However, in both countries it is reported that only about one-half of these weapons are being destroyed, while the rest are being put in storage—keeping open the possibility, however slight, of their reintroduction to the fleets. The recently released U.S. *Nuclear Posture Review* explicitly states that the U.S. Navy will retain the capability to deploy nuclear sea-launched cruise missiles (SLCMs) on its SSNs.[20] Moreover, because of the lack of any formal agreement, there is no verification or compliance mechanism in place. Finally, while the Royal Navy has joined the United States and Russia in voluntarily removing its naval tactical nuclear weapons, the French Navy has not, and the Chinese Navy may develop such weapons.

We believe that it is in the interest of both Russia and the United States to formalize a treaty verifying the removal and destruction of *all* their tactical naval nuclear weapons, and to attempt to bring the other actual and potential nuclear navies into such an agreement. Perhaps a first stage might entail the verified destruction of the first half of the stockpile. A second stage would then consider their complete elimination plus the involvement of other parties.[21]

Politico-economic Asymmetry: the "Island Nation" vs. the "Continental Power"

It is true that during the Cold War the U.S.S.R. strove to achieve a "mirror image" of naval forces proceeding from the desire to give the disarmament process a systematic and balanced character. The United States opposed any attempt to achieve a "balance" of naval forces, arguing that they did not play the same role for the U.S.S.R. as they do for the United States in its global and regional context. U.S. naval experts held the view that the needs of various states in regard to naval forces were asymmetrical, and that for the United States this need depended not only on the confrontation with the Soviet bloc but also on other missions on the world ocean which should not be taken into account at negotiations.[22] In our view, this difference of opinion concerning the purpose of naval forces, their number, and their composition, led to a situation where the naval component of the armed forces was largely excluded from negotiations and therefore the disarmament process.

Now, however, the situation has changed substantially. Following the end of the Cold War and the fall of the U.S.S.R., the Russian Navy no longer aspires to full parity with the naval forces of the United States and NATO. Russia is now ready to have a navy that corresponds to its *specific defensive missions* at sea—in the context of the new international environment. The Russian Navy now clearly understands that the geographical, political, strategic, and other military interests of the United States lead to naval requirements that are different from Russia's. Consequently, the Russian Navy no longer aspires to limit the naval power of the United States in areas that do not affect Russian interests.

For its part, the United States should understand the new situation in which Russia finds itself. In the present conditions of economic and internal political turmoil, the continuing withdrawal of troops from the countries of Eastern Europe and the Baltic states, and the incomplete process of political reform, Russia's defense potential has been considerably weakened. Going by former standards, the damage done to the maritime security of Russia is undeniable in spite of improved relations with the United States and other NATO states. As retired U.S. Navy Commander George F. Kraus, Jr. recently put it: "the Russian Navy is adrift in a storm of economic troubles, with much shoal water still ahead."[23]

This situation is very disturbing for Russian leadership within the context of Russia's historical concern for the "defense of the homeland." They realize that this situation will not necessarily invite direct military action against Russia—such a development is of course highly unlikely given the present circumstances. But the fact remains that the unilateral reduction of the military and naval potential of Russia and the C.I.S. creates for the West the possibility of dictating military-political conditions from a position of strength. This would not contribute to the strengthening of stability in the world.

There is also an important domestic Russian political dimension to this issue. In his 1994 report to Congress, the U.S. Secretary of Defense stated: "Pursuing cooperative defense efforts with the Russian military is important.... As Russian President Yeltsin's recent confrontation with the conservative Parliament demonstrated, *the military is a key player in Russia's ongoing efforts to consolidate its democratic transformation.*"[24] This dimension is already having an impact on the disarmament process. One unnamed U.S. defense official, commenting on the recently released U.S. *Nuclear Posture Review*'s commitment to the START II status quo and rejection of deeper cuts, offered this explanation: "What if democratic reforms are reversed and those weapons are turned against us?" U.S. Deputy Secretary of Defense John Deutch voiced similar concerns at a press conference, indicating that "I think there is certainly some possibility of a reversal in Russia. We're not predicting that, but it is certainly possible."[25]

There are, on the other hand, some in the Russian military and conservative political factions who view U.S. reluctance to engage in naval arms control as a confirmation of their opposition to democracy and economic reform, and their hostility toward the United States. For these reasons, we are of the opinion that any effective steps toward naval arms control negotiations will further improve U.S.-Russian relations and strategic stability.

Verification and Compliance Issues

In the past, issues of verification and compliance have greatly contributed to the skepticism about naval arms control. There are many examples of undetected—and even when detected, unchallenged—cheating with regard to the interwar naval arms control agreements ranging from the Versailles treaty to the final 1936 London conference.[26] To that troubling history must be added the dreary list of accusations, violations, and polemics that marked the Cold War nuclear and strategic arms control negotiations and debates.[27] There is little point in rehashing these old arguments in light of the current international situation.

Verification of, and compliance with arms control agreements are indeed important issues. But we must make a fresh start because of the new situation that has been brought about by political change and scientific progress. To begin with, there is now a strong consensus in both the United States and Russia that the *verification of arms control agreements is no longer an insurmountable problem*. There are both scientific and political aspects to this consensus.

From the scientific standpoint, the enormous technological advances of the last fifteen years have vastly improved the ability to monitor agreements and detect violations. These advances have enhanced the "National Technical Means" (NTMs) such as satellites and naval and air surveillance forces so often highlighted in arms control discussions. In addition, among the important advances have been the development of tamper-proof seals and tags, motion sensors, video surveillance systems, x-rays and infra-red detection systems, and remote sensors for detecting radiation and chemical trace elements.[28] As a result, scientists are convinced that we can now have a much greater confidence in our ability to verify arms control agreements than in the past.[29]

An equally important advance has been the political change begun in the Soviet Union under Gorbachev and continuing in the Russian Federation under President Yeltsin. Of course, the most fundamental change, is that Russia is now a democratic country. In specific terms, these changes have led to the acceptance by both sides of on-site monitoring of such agreements as INF and START. In addition to detailed data exchanges and notifications, these agreements provide arrangements for continuous monitoring of activities at key facilities and challenge-type procedures in provisions governing "special access" visits and suspect site inspections.[30]

The deeper truth is that the most basic U.S. objection to arms control in general and naval arms control in particular has centered on the disadvantage that democracies face when up against "closed" totalitarian or authoritarian countries. From this perspective, the failures of the interwar years have more to do with the fact that the Allies did not face up to the political changes occurring in Japan and Germany until it was too late.

In the current circumstances, some would argue that Russia's transition to democracy and an open market economy is too fragile to engage in something as risky as naval arms control. In our view, such a position is very short-sighted. At this critical stage, it is very important that the United States fully support the transition to democracy. Russian democracy's vulnerability is precisely the reason actions countering reactionary sentiment must be taken. Full support must embrace the trust embodied in comprehensive arms control, including naval arms control.

Beyond the question of verification lies the issue of compliance: what to do if a violation is detected. The Standing Consultative Commission established in the 1970s under the SALT I agreement enjoyed a certain measure of success in this regard. Many alleged violations were either explained or corrected. However, the process also became so politicized that all objectivity was lost.

A much better precedent is the annual meeting between U.S. and Russian naval professionals established under the 1972 INCSEA agreement. The INCSEA agreement has been quite effective precisely because of this professional oversight.[31] We need to involve current or former members of the sea services in this process—individuals "with salt water in their veins," who understand both the arms control issues and the maritime environment. Given the increased level of contact between just such Russian and U.S. naval professionals in the past several years, we are confident that an effective "compliance team" can be assembled as part of any well-conceived naval arms control negotiations.

LAYING OUT A PLAUSIBLE NAVAL ARMS CONTROL AGENDA

Bearing in mind the complexity and number of different approaches to the problems of naval arms control, and the long list of possible steps to be taken, we will limit our consideration to those measures that are particularly important and that we feel have a reasonable chance of being implemented. It took forty years to build the naval rivalry between the United States and Russia. It will take time to overcome it thoroughly. We envision a possible three-stage process.

Stage One: Maritime Confidence-Building Measures

The *first* stage, which is already in progress, involves the strengthening of existing *confidence-building measures at sea* and the initiating of new ones. Building on the legacy of the INCSEA, PDMA, and Ballistic Missile Launch Notification agreements, we urge further efforts to reduce tension and to ease the danger of military confrontation resulting from incorrect evaluations of the other side's intentions, and to improve the possibilities for cooperation.

One particularly salient area concerns the question of *incidents between submarines*. Despite the easing of tensions between the United States and Russia, dangerous incidents, including a total of at least ten collisions since 1950[32] between the two nations' submarines have continued through 1993. In March 1994, Admiral Igor Kasatonov, First Deputy Commander of the Russian Navy, claimed that although the former "adversaries now are our partners, their activity near Russian shores has not diminished."[33] According to U.S. Navy officials, in June 1995 a Russian nuclear attack submarine was detected while following an American SSBN near U.S. coastal waters in the Atlantic for the first time since 1987.[34] This type of activity is all too reminiscent of the darkest days of the Cold War, when underwater clashes had tragic consequences.[35]

The June 1993 announcement by Secretary of Defense Aspin following the most recent collision that the United States would make "major"—but unspecified—changes in its submarine operations was encouraging but insufficient.[36] Obviously there are many difficulties involved in verifying and ensuring compliance with any agreements concerning submarine operations. However, in light of the increasing dangers of collision between ever-quieter nuclear submarines,[37] and the proliferation of modern submarine technology, we should explore possibilities for an agreement to prevent "incidents *under the sea*." It has been suggested that such an agreement might involve "specification of a safety course for submarines to steer if they thought themselves in danger of collision; the obligation to transmit on active sonar if they thought a close-quarter situation was developing; and perhaps agreed frequencies for underwater telephones (though these are well known in all navies as 'the say again machine')." Alternating depth operating zones for undersea transits and the elimination of especially dangerous maneuvers have also been suggested.[38]

Several measures to improve *transparency* between the two navies can be undertaken. A full and formal exchange of data concerning the makeup, location, missions, building and decommissioning plans for the ships and aircraft of both navies should be instituted, rather than relying on secondhand sources or exotic and expensive intelligence-gathering efforts. Admiral Aleksin has suggested a direct connection between the U.S. Navy's Chief of Information and the Russian Navy press service as one avenue for such an exchange.[39] In addition to this bilateral data exchange, we support existing and proposed efforts toward multilateral and regional data sharing. For example, the recently established U.N. Register of Conventional Arms called upon member states, including Russia and the United States, to provide data annually on imports and exports of arms. The list of arms to be reported includes "vessels or submarines armed and equipped for military use with a standard displacement of 750 metric tonnes or above, and those with a standard displacement of less than 750 metric tonnes, equipped for launching missiles with a range of at least 25 km or torpedoes with a similar range."[40] Regional agreements may well expand upon this effort, especially with regard to naval forces.

In addition to ongoing communication through the established nonofficial and official U.S.-Russian naval contacts, there should be an increased exchange of ideas concerning strategy, doctrine, and operations through direct personal contacts such as naval staff meetings, and naval school faculty and student exchanges, including formal conferences and seminars, as well as ship and port visits. Such exchanges are already occurring, but they need to be increased.[41]

Modern navies possess high-precision conventional weapons with enormous firepower. In addition, they have great mobility, autonomy, and considerable survivability. As a consequence, they constitute an important means for conducting offensive operations, including against installations on land. This capability was clearly demonstrated during the Gulf War. Consequently, the sudden, unannounced arrival of formidable foreign naval forces off a nation's coast can cause concern on the part of that state.

For that reason, we recommend negotiations to establish the *prenotification and observation of naval exercises* in order to reduce suspicion about such movements and to encourage cooperation. The question of what to include in this agreement could be difficult. One analyst has suggested that each participating nation indicate the number of ships, aircraft, and submarines operating within its two hundred mile Exclusive Economic Zone (EEZ) established for coastal states under the Law of the Sea that would serve as the threshold of concern for such prenotification and observation.[42] However, others point out that this may tend to strengthen the unwelcome notions that EEZs are in effect "security zones" and that the naval operations of a coastal state should properly be confined to it.[43] In order to allay fears about damaging the "freedom of the seas," such an agreement must make it clear that simple "innocent passage" of ships would be exempt, that formal "territoriality" remains limited to the twelve mile rule, and that such an agreement would obviously be suspended during a crisis or actual conflict. Such agreements could be verified by NTMs as well as on-board observers.

Stage Two: Operational Constraints

The second stage should comprise negotiations on the limitation of particularly dangerous naval activities. These negotiations would include measures to constrain where ships operate, how they operate, and in what numbers they operate.

It must be noted that existing international law already regulates some operations, such as those concerning the right of "innocent passage" for warships through the territorial waters of another state. Both Russia and the United States recognize this right—but also its limitations concerning use of weapons, intelligence gathering, and submerged passage.[44] Furthermore the U.N. Convention on the Law of the Sea, which formally entered into effect on November 16, 1994, also contains some regulations that limit operations.[45] In addition, several coastal states are seeking, or have already implemented, other limitations, stemming from a wide variety of concerns ranging from economic, to environmental, to political issues.

The principle of the "freedom of the seas" has long been central to U.S. maritime strategy. The fact of the matter is that, as we approach what some are calling the "Century of the Ocean," that principle is coming under increasing international scrutiny and even criticism. In the past, the United States has invested enormous resources in asserting this principle through its "Freedom of Navigation" program.[46] The political, economic, and military costs of that policy are increasing. The time has come for the United States to recognize that it must be willing to consider some operational constraints that are in its basic interest, lest a frustrated world community enact even more stringent restrictions.

In the U.S.-Russian context, during the Cold War the Soviet Union sought to completely ban strategic antisubmarine warfare operations by U.S. forces in the ocean areas where its ballistic missile submarines operated. The United States rejected these proposals because they violated the principle of the freedom of the seas. In the new strategic context, however, we advocate a significantly revised version of this concept. After all, for many years the United States urged the Soviet Union to base more of its strategic deterrent at sea in "survivable"—and therefore more "stable"—SSBNs and to reduce "first strike" land-based missiles. Under the START agreements, Russia is doing exactly that. In addition, Russia asserts that it has unilaterally ceased all ASW operations directed against U.S. SSBNs.[47] In these circumstances it is understandable that as part of achieving a new partnership with Russia, the United States should make some effort at assuring the survivability of Russia's SSBNs.

Some have suggested that the United States should also "simply and quietly unilaterally cease antisubmarine operations aimed at Russian SSBNs."[48] That would be a welcome development, but it would not be sufficient because it could be quickly reversed. A declaratory statement by the U.S. Navy that it has dropped the "strategic antisubmarine warfare" mission would also be a step forward from the current state of ambiguity on the matter[49] but would also be insufficient.

Instead, we call for negotiations aimed at limiting the size and activities of U.S. naval antisubmarine forces in certain sensitive ocean areas near the Russian coast in such a way as to preclude effective "strategic" ASW but not hamper other "normal" naval activities, even including "tactical" ASW. We recognize that a complete *ban* on naval operations in entire ocean areas is not acceptable from the standpoint of the principle of the freedom of the seas. Instead, we propose to prevent the clearly identifiable gathering of forces and conducting of operations whose unmistakable purpose is the destruction of each side's SSBNs, that is, the "strategic mass" of equipment and activities uniquely suited to that purpose.

We are convinced that such an agreement is negotiable, verifiable, and can be so constructed that it would be in *each* country's interest. Clearly, establishing a *quid pro quo* that will satisfy the United States is vital to this effort. This is obviously a matter of considerable complexity and controversy, so we will devote the entire next chapter to explaining this proposal in great detail.

Going beyond the realm of operational constraints on strategic ASW, it must be acknowledged that proposals to impose complete bans or partial restraints on the operations of general purpose naval forces on the high seas are unlikely to be accepted by some western strategic analysts and most western naval officers. Even a limited agreement to prohibit operational level (but not tactical level) deployments of amphibious forces and long-range strike forces in ocean areas that might be regarded as most "sensitive" to the presence of foreign naval forces (e.g., the Black Sea, Mediterranean, Northwestern Pacific and Sea of Japan, the Barents and Baltic seas, the Sea of

Okhotsk, the Caribbean and Gulf of Mexico, etc.) is probably not feasible. There are at least three reasons for this.

First, creating such "zones of restriction" may seem beneficial in periods of normal relations and might even lead to a reduction of naval forces. However, should relations between the treaty signatories sour, those same zones can suddenly become "lines in the sand" or rungs in the ladder of risk-taking leading to unexpected escalation in a crisis. The underlying maxim here is that the more maritime boundaries there are, the less the ambiguity—and the greater the chance of losing face. When it comes to either cooperative or coercive maritime diplomacy, ambiguity is essential to achieving harmony with other instruments of foreign policy within the geopolitical context of the situation.

Second, in the new international situation, regional states in the likely "sensitive" ocean areas will have a say and set the maritime security agenda to an extent far beyond their role in the Cold War era. For example, in the Northwest Pacific neither Japan, South Korea, nor the People's Republic of China (P.R.C.) are likely to remain on the sidelines while the United States and Russia attempt to impose operational constraints on naval forces operating in the Sea of Japan.

Finally, "no go" areas for operational level deployments of general purpose naval forces may well inhibit future U.N. sanctioned or U.N. flagged maritime interventions, in which U.S. and Russian naval forces might cooperate.[50]

There may, however, be valid *environmental* reasons for limiting some types of naval operations in certain ecologically sensitive waters. Such limitations would not be bilateral in nature, however, and should come under the auspices of the relevant international bodies.

Finally, there are two other aspects of operational restraint that should at least be investigated in the current international situation: submarine warfare and the use of naval mines. The relevant international agreements concerning these types of naval warfare were formulated decades ago and are in need of updating.[51] The proliferation of modern mine warfare systems and submarines is continuing at a steady pace. Submarine warfare during the Spanish Civil War, and the more recent mining incidents in the Persian Gulf stand out as examples of threats to stability in areas of regional conflict. It is in the interests of the entire world community to address these issues. Perhaps the United Nations could take the lead on these topics.

Stage Three: Negotiated Limitations and Reduction of Naval Forces and Weapons

Now that both Russia and its western partners are striving to reduce expenditures on armaments, unilateral limitation of naval activities is of advantage to both parties. The building and maintenance of superfluous naval forces is not in the interest of either party.

In the case of the Russian Navy, it is no longer faced with the task of carrying out strategic offensives on continental theaters of operations. In addition, it has abandoned operations to search out SSBNs, limited its mission against sea communications, virtually abandoned surveillance of NATO naval forces in the Mediterranean and Indian Oceans, and stopped a number of other activities connected with the rivalry of our navies on the world ocean. As we have seen, the reduction of these missions has been accompanied by cutbacks in the Navy's components.

Similarly, the U.S. Navy has downgraded the importance of "open-ocean" antisubmarine warfare and antiaircraft warfare, and is cutting back on the forces dedicated to those missions: *Knox* class frigates, nuclear-powered cruisers, and nuclear attack submarines.

However, these unilateral reductions of naval armaments cannot be adequately verified and can be reversed. They could play a positive role if they are mutual and will be confirmed in subsequent accords on lower levels of naval armaments A reliable guarantee for the prevention of a renewed naval arms race would best consist of agreements reached in the process of normal negotiations and ensuring a balance of mutual interests and a satisfactory verification system. Moreover, the possibility of a dangerous naval arms buildup in regions of conflict is another incentive for moving on to a third stage of naval arms control.

We are not advocating a resurrection of Cold War attempts at "structural" naval arms control. Those efforts failed because at the time the Soviet Union was attempting to achieve by negotiation what it could not obtain otherwise: a naval "balance" in all aspects with the U.S. and NATO navies. However, there are two areas where a negotiated naval "balance" is desirable in the current circumstances. The first area, concerning naval strategic nuclear weapons covered under the START I and II treaties, and tactical nuclear weapons withdrawn unilaterally, was covered earlier in this chapter under "Unresolved Nuclear Issues."

The second concerns nuclear attack submarines. Now that both navies have announced that they are making significant reductions in the size of their SSN fleets toward a similar level (projected at 45-50 for the United States and 60 for Russia in 1999), the previously raised question of *a negotiated and verified reduction of SSNs* should be revisited.[52] Such an agreement would help both countries to confidently reduce their military expenditures, might prevent a future "SSN building race," and would go a long way toward preventing the proliferation of those highly offensive and environmentally dangerous weapons. Some western naval analysts and officers have even called for a ban on SSNs, but that does not seem feasible at this time.

As we approach a century in which the ocean's importance to the future of the planet is increasing, the danger of the militarization of the ocean is looming on the horizon. This is especially true in two regions where there is a serious potential for conflict: the Middle East, including the Persian Gulf, and the Western Pacific. Several countries in these regions which in the past have had only small and relatively ineffective navies are now engaged in a process of expansion and modernization.[53]

In this context, we call for *constructing a "naval technology control regime" whose purpose would be to prevent the sale or transfer of offensive or "destabilizing" naval technology to countries in regions where there is an ongoing conflict or where there is a high potential for conflict.* The purpose of such a regime would be to reduce the threat of such naval weaponry to the developed nations; to inhibit arms competition among less developed states; and to prevent the introduction of destabilizing weaponry into regional rivalries.

We have no illusions about the difficulties of achieving such a regime. After all, weapons sales remain an official policy of both governments for largely economic reasons, so there would be strong opposition to the control regime among both government and business leaders.[54] It is very difficult to distinguish between "offensive" and "defensive" naval weaponry, especially when offensive tactics appear to be the most effective form of defense in modern naval warfare.[55] In addition, many types of advanced naval technology are of a "dual-use" nature: they have legitimate civilian applications. Russia and the United States are not the only suppliers of advanced naval weaponry, so any truly effective regime would have to include all the major producers—a most difficult task. Finally, such controls would undoubtedly create resentment among the less developed nations who would see them as an attempt by the major powers to maintain superiority. Despite these difficulties, we agree that "controls on naval technology transfers are a naval arms control measure worth pursuing."[56]

What types of advanced naval technology should be included in such a regime? *First, we advocate a complete ban on the sale or transfer of nuclear-powered warships*, especially submarines. Their range, the possible link to nuclear weapons proliferation through their use of weapons-grade fuel, and the danger of environmental disaster make them a very dangerous commodity. Such a ban is feasible because there are, at present, only five countries capable of producing such vessels (the United States, Russia, the United Kingdom, France, and the P.R.C.) and it is not in their interest to see them spread.[57] Such vessels were not included in the Nuclear Nonproliferation Treaty.

It goes without saying that we support the nuclear nonproliferation treaty as it applies to naval nuclear weapons.

Complete bans on other types of naval technology are probably not feasible. Still, some systems have a greater potential offensive capability than others.

Therefore, we recommend some form of control over the transfer of the following naval technologies:

- aircraft carriers capable of launching "conventional" takeoff warplanes;
- long-range maritime strike aircraft and in-air refueling technology (e.g., U.S. A-6 Intruder, Russian Tu-22 Backfire);
- long-range conventional submarines (e.g., Russian *Kilo*, British *Upholder*), especially those equipped with the new "air independent" propulsion;
- long-range antiship cruise missiles, especially those capable of supersonic speeds and/or carrying nuclear warheads (e.g., U.S. Tomahawk, Russian AS-6);
- deep-water rising mines (e.g., U.S. Captor, Russian Cluster Bay/Gulf);
- large amphibious ships (e.g., U.S. LST, Russian *Ropucha* class).

In the process of preventing a militarization of the oceans, the U.S. and Russian navies must *eventually* include their conventional naval armaments in serious negotiations. Their direct limitation and reduction would be an effective method of strengthening security on the world ocean. These negotiations must at some point be held on a multilateral basis, with the participation of all interested states. Perhaps they could *begin* on a bilateral basis between Russia and the United States with a view to the other states joining in an agreement at a later stage.

Such negotiations might eventually include:

- reductions of the number of ships of the main classes according to the effectiveness with which they can carry out their missions;
- the prevention of naval arms buildups by restrictions on naval development programs that would still allow navies to acquire reasonable sufficiency in numbers.

As with our proposal for a Naval Technology Control Regime, we have no illusions about the difficulty of negotiating naval reductions, especially in light of the pre-World II experience. Long before we can actually negotiate naval weapons reductions, there must first be special consultations where necessary information on the current and potential structure of navies, their strategic rationales, the direction of their operational training, and the geostrategic differences in their basing could be compared. A kind of "inventory" of regional and global problems in the field of naval arms control could then be compiled. Only then would the scope, timing, and limits of future negotiations be laid down.

In contrast to the first two phases, the third stage of negotiations requires a solid scientific-methodological basis and an elaborated system of models in order to develop the best possible recommendations for the limitation of naval weapons. We have worked out a possible method, and it is described in Chapter 8.

CONCLUSION

Despite the historical, political, and technical obstacles, naval arms control can be an important step toward greater U.S.-Russian naval cooperation and even partnership. Naval arms control in the broad sense has *not* been "overtaken by events." Rather, freed from Cold War polemics, naval arms control negotiations—if naval professionals are directly involved—will help Russia and the United States leave their former naval hostility behind and chart a new course for the future. We urge both countries to seriously explore the following set of proposals we have made toward that end:

Unresolved Naval Nuclear Issues

- U.S. financial aid and technical assistance to improve Russia's ability to comply with agreements calling for the dismantling and safe disposal of naval nuclear weapons and reactors
- a verifiable bilateral agreement to destroy 50% of their stored naval tactical nuclear weapons and then invite other parties to join in a verified destruction of the entire international stockpile

Maritime Confidence-Building Measures

- a verifiable bilateral agreement for the Prevention of Incidents *Under* the Sea
- a full and formal exchange of data on the makeup, location, missions, building, and decommissioning plans for the ships and aircraft of both navies
- an increased exchange of ideas concerning strategy, doctrine, and operations through direct navy-to-navy contacts
- prenotification and observation of naval exercises

Operational Constraints

- a bilateral agreement to limit the size and activities of U.S. antisubmarine forces in designated areas near the Russian coast in such a way as to preclude effective "strategic" ASW but not hamper other "normal" naval operations, including "tactical" ASW (see the following chapter for a detailed explanation)

Negotiated Limits and Reductions of Naval Forces and Weapons

- a bilateral verifiable agreement to reduce each navy's SSN fleet to approximately equal levels, in accord with already announced unilateral reductions

- a joint effort to take the lead in establishing a multilateral Naval Technology Control Regime to prevent the sale or transfer of offensive or destabilizing naval technology to countries in regions of conflict, with emphasis on a complete ban on the sale or transfer of nuclear-powered warships, especially submarines
- a joint effort to take the lead in preparing for and taking part in eventual multilateral negotiations aimed at reducing the size of the world's navies and limiting their future building plans to a level of reasonable sufficiency.

NOTES

1. Cf. Colin S. Gray, "Arms Control Doesn't Control Arms" in Orbis, Vol. 37, No. 3 (Summer 1993), pp. 333-348; Kosta Tsipis, "Military Technological Innovation and Stability," chapter 14 in *Military Technological Innovation and Stability in a Changing World*, eds. Wim A. Smit, John Grin, and Lev Voronkov (Amsterdam: VU University Press, 1992), pp. 167-175.

2. The classic formulation of this position was contained in "Report on Naval Arms Control," submitted to the Senate Committee on Armed Services and the House Committee on Armed Services, Department of Defense, April 1991, 37 pp. In 1991 the conventional arms control cell of the Chief of Naval Operations' Strategic Concepts Group actually handed out business cards emblazoned with the slogan: "Just say No to Naval Arms Control! It's not in U.S. Interests, and *we just don't like it*." Copy in the authors' possession.

3. For example, see the statement of then Chief of Naval Operations Admiral Carlisle Trost, USN, as found in "Approaches to Naval Arms Control," Hearings before the Subcommittee on Projection Forces and Regional Defense of the Senate Armed Services Committee, 101st Congress, Second Session, May 8, 11, 1990 (Washington, D.C.: U.S. Government Printing Office, 1990), pp. 65-66: "Unfortunately, the recent history of naval arms control does not commend itself to emulation. Twice in this century, coalitions of maritime nations have been caught unprepared, and were forced to go to war against continental powers who were able to interdict the sea lines of communications. The price of that unpreparedness, *resulting in part from negotiated naval restrictions*, was paid in blood" (emphasis added; hereafter cited as SASC, "Naval Arms Control," 1990).

4. Robert Gordon Kaufman, *Arms Control during the Pre-Nuclear Era: The United States and Naval Limitations between the Two World Wars* (New York: Columbia University Press, 1990), p. 194.

5. Caroline Ziemke, "Peace without Strings? Interwar Naval Arms Control Revisited," *Washington Quarterly*, Vol. 15, No. 4 (Autumn 1992), pp. 101-102.

6. Richard C. Davis, "Future Directions for Naval Arms Control," in Lewis A. Dunn and Sharon A. Squassoni, eds., *Arms Control: What Next?* (Boulder, Colo.: Westview, 1993), p. 114, note 3.

7. For a listing of the many Soviet naval arms control proposals, see sections 840-502 and 611 in the yearly issues of the *Arms Control Reporter* (Brookline, Mass.: Institute for Defense and Disarmament Studies, 1983 ff); Ronald O'Rourke, "Naval Arms Control," Congressional Research Service Issue Brief (February 8, 1990). For a concise overview of this issue from a contemporary Russian analyst, cf. Alexei

Arbatov, "The Soviet Union, Naval Arms Control, and the Norwegian Sea," chapter 3 and appendix 3A in *Europe and Naval Arms Control in the Gorbachev Era*, eds. Andreas Furst, Volker Heise, and Steven E. Miller (New York: Oxford University Press/SIPRI, 1992), pp. 44-66.

8. Rear Admiral Valery I. Aleksin, "We Are Ready When You Are," U.S. Naval Institute *Proceedings*, Vol. 119, No. 3 (March 1993), p. 55. For another frank appraisal of Soviet naval arms control efforts, cf. Arbatov, "The Soviet Union, Naval Arms Control, and the Norwegian Sea" (above, note 7).

9. Arbatov, "The Soviet Union, Naval Arms Control and the Norwegian Sea," p. 60.

10. Cf., for example, William M. Arkin, *The Nuclear Arms Race at Sea* (Washington, D.C.: Greenpeace and the Institute for Policy Studies, 1987); Barry M. Blechman et al., *Naval Arms Control: A Strategic Assessment* (New York: St. Martin's Press, 1991); Richard Fieldhouse, ed., *Security at Sea: Naval Forces and Arms Control* (New York: SIPRI/Oxford University Press, 1990); A. Mack and P. Keal, eds., *Security & Arms Control in the North Pacific* (Sydney: Allen & Unwin, 1988); Steven E. Miller and Stephen Van Evera, eds., *Naval Strategy and National Security: An International Security Reader* (Princeton: Princeton University Press, 1988).

11. James L. Lacy, *A Different Equation: Naval Issues and Arms Control after 1991* (Alexandria, Va.: Institute for Defense Analyses Paper P-2768, December 1993), p. ii. A similar but shorter report by James J. Tritten, then on the faculty of the Naval Postgraduate School, was released in December 1992, and was reported on in the February 8-14, 1993 issue of *Defense News* on p. 38 in an article entitled "Report Stirs U.S. Navy Arms Control Issue." Whether there was any connection between that news report and the delay in releasing Lacy's report remains a matter of conjecture.

12. The texts of these agreements through 1990 can be found in Fieldhouse, ed., *Security at Sea: Naval Forces and Arms Control*, Annexe B, "Current International Agreements Relevant to Naval Forces and Arms Control," pp. 257-285.

13. Cf. *The Military Balance 1993-1994* (London: Brassey's/The International Institute for Strategic Studies. October 1993), pp. 229-243, for a summary of START I and II and other recent nuclear weapons developments.

14. *Seattle Times*, June 22, 1994, p. A1.

15. Lacy, *A Different Equation*, pp. 98-100, (emphasis added). James J. Tritten reaches similar conclusions in "A New Case for Naval Arms Control," Naval Postgraduate School Report NPS-NS-92-016, December 1992, and in "A New Look at Naval Arms Control" in *Security Dialogue*, Vol 24, No. 3 (September 1993), pp. 337-348.

16. Captain Boris Makeev took part in the 1993 U.N. Asia-Pacific Regional Disarmament Conference at Katmandu, and Dr. Meconis has participated in a series of four "Asia-Pacific Dialogues on Maritime Security and Confidence Building Measures." Progress is also occurring in the Middle East. Cf. *Context:* "Canada's Contribution to Maritime Confidence-Building in the Middle East," Canadian Department of Foreign Affairs and International Trade, Foreign Policy Communications Division, July 1994.

17. Charles Aldinger, "U.S. Will Avoid Quick Nuclear Cuts—Pentagon," Reuter, Washington, D.C., September 22, 1994.

18. For a detailed description of this situation by a retired U.S. naval officer, see Captain Peter Huchthausen, USN (Ret.), "Russian Navy in Distress," U. S. Naval Institute *Proceedings*, Vol. 119, No. 5 (May 1993), pp. 77-80. Greenpeace has estimated that a total of nearly 160 Russian nuclear submarines must eventually be disposed of. The Vol. 16, No. 3 (1995) issue of the journal *Naval Forces* contains on pp. 54-55 a news release from the Russian Navy Public Affairs Office which states that to date, over 130 nuclear-powered ships have been withdrawn from the Russian Navys inventory, but that only 42 of them have had their reactors unloaded. Existing disposal containers have been declared unsafe by Gosatomnadzor, the recently created Russian Federal nuclear oversight agency, but the Navy cannot afford the newer, safer models.

19. Huchthausen, "Russian Navy in Distress," p. 80.

20. On September 22, 1994, the Pentagon released the results of its year-long Nuclear Posture Review and announced that while the training and equipment necessary for Navy *surface* ships to deploy tactical nuclear weapons was being eliminated, nuclear attack submarines would retain the capability to launch nuclear-tipped cruise missiles. Department of Defense, *Nuclear Posture Review*, p. 21.

21. The authors are grateful to Rear Admiral J. R. Hill, RN (Ret.), for this suggestion.

22. Cf. Statement of Admiral Carlisle Trost, USN, SASC, "Naval Arms Control," 1990, pp. 63-66.

23. Commander George F. Kraus, Jr., USN (Ret.), "Russian Naval Views: Adrift in Heavy Seas," U.S. Naval Institute *Proceedings*, Vol. 120, No. 4 (April 1994), p. 119.

24. Les Aspin, *Annual Report of the Secretary of Defense to the President and the Congress* (Washington, D.C.: U.S. Government Printing Office, January 1994), pp. 76-77.

25. Aldinger, "U.S. Will Avoid Quick Nuclear Cuts—Pentagon," and "Few Changes Made in U.S. Nuclear Policy," Associated Press, Washington, D.C., September 22, 1994.

26. Cf. Robin Ranger, "Learning from the Naval Arms Control Experience," *Washington Quarterly*, Vol. 10, No. 3 (Summer 1987), pp. 49-50; Kaufman, *Arms Control during the Pre-Nuclear Era*, pp. 98-99; Stephen Roskill, *Naval Policy between the Wars, Vol. II: The Period of Reluctant Rearmament 1930-1939* (Annapolis, Md.: Naval Institute Press, 1976), p. 371; Bruce D. Berkowitz and Allan E. Goodman, *Strategic Intelligence for American National Security*, (Princeton, N.J.: Princeton University Press, 1989), pp. 99-100; Barton Whaley, *Covert German Rearmament, 1919-1939: Deception and Misperception*, (Frederick, Md.: University Press of America, 1984), pp. 91-93.

27. Cf., for example, Bruce D. Berkowitz, *Calculated Risks: A Century of Arms Control, Why It Has Failed, and How It Can Be Made to Work* (New York: Simon & Schuster, 1987). Throughout the late 1970s and 1980s, the publications of the Washington, D.C. lobbying group "The Committee on the Present Danger" provided a steady litany of verification and compliance charges in arguing against arms control with the Soviets. From the Soviet side, cf. Roland M. Timberbayev, *Problems of Verification*, Eng. ed. (Moscow: Nauka Publishers, 1984).

28. Blair L. Murray, "Trust in Tomorrow's World: Verification," chapter 8 in Dunn and Squassoni, eds., *Arms Control: What Next*, p. 144.

29. Cf. Congressional Office of Technology Assessment, *Verification Technologies: Managing Research and Development for Cooperative Arms Control Monitoring Measures*, OTA-ISC-488 (Washington, D.C.: U.S. Government Printing Office, May 1991); *Verification Technologies: Cooperative Aerial Surveillance in International Agreements*, OTA-ISC-480 (Washington, D.C.: U.S. Government Printing Office, July 1991); and *Monitoring Limits on Sea-Launched Missiles*, OTA-ISC-513 (Washington, D.C.: U.S. Government Printing Office, September 1992).

30. Cf. *Treaty between the United States of America and Union of Soviet Socialist Republics on the Elimination of Their Intermediate-Range and Shorter-Range Missiles*, signed at Washington, D.C., December 8, 1987 and entered into force June 1, 1988; *Treaty between the United States of America and Union of Soviet Socialist Republics on the Reduction and Limitation of Strategic Offensive Arms*, signed at Moscow July 30-31, 1991 and pending ratification and formal entry into force, although many provisions are already being enacted.

31. Cf. Anthony F. Wolf, "Agreement at Sea: The United States-USSR Agreement on Incidents at Sea," *Korean Journal of International Studies*, Vol. 9, No. 3 (1978), pp. 57-80; Rear Admiral Robert P. Hilton, Sr., USN, "The U.S.-Soviet Incidents at Sea Treaty," *Naval Forces*, Vol. 6, No. 1 (1985), pp. 30-37; and Sean M. Lynn-Jones, "A Quiet Success for Arms Control: Preventing Incidents at Sea," *International Security*, Vol. 9, No. 4 (Spring 1985), pp. 55-84.

32. Associated Press, Kiev, Ukraine, June 6, 1993. The total of ten collisions came from a U.S. government source who spoke on condition of anonymity. The U.S. Navy has acknowledged only the two collisions made public in 1992 and 1993.

33. Associated Press, Moscow, March 16, 1994.

34. "Russian Submarine is Spotted Off Coast," *Washington Times*, June 23, 1995, p. A7.

35. For the most detailed account to date of Cold War undersea incidents, cf. "Enemies Below," a six-part series in the *Chicago Tribune*, January 6-11, 1991.

36. Charles Aldinger, Reuter, Kiev, Ukraine, June 6, 1993, "U.S. Changes Submarine Operations for Safety." Secretary of Defense Aspin said he refused to discuss details of highly secret U.S. submarine operations with his Russian counterpart, Defense Minister Pavel Grachev.

37. Cf. the explanation offered by Sergei N. Kovalev of the Russian Academy of Sciences in "Submarine Collisions," U.S. Naval Institute *Proceedings*, Vol. 120, No. 11 (November 1994), p. 105.

38. Rear Admiral J. R. Hill, RN (Ret.), "Maritime Arms Control in Asia-Pacific Region," chapter 4 in Ross Babbage and Sam Bateman, eds., *Maritime Change: Issues for Asia* (Sydney: Allen & Unwin, 1993), pp. 45-46; David F. Winkler, "An Incidents under the Sea Agreement?," *The Naval Review*, Vol. 83, No. 2 (April 1995), pp. 110-116.

39. Aleksin, "We Are Ready When You Are," p. 56.

40. United Nations, "Transparency in Armaments," U.N. General Assembly Resolution 46/36L (New York: United Nations, December 1991).

41. For example, the Center for International Security and Arms Control at Stanford University has conducted several naval officer exchanges, as have Brown University and the Naval War College. During this project, in January 1994 Captain Makeev spoke at the U.S. Center for Naval Analyses in Alexandria, and in May and October

1994, he visited the U.S. Naval Postgraduate School in Monterey and addressed a class and the faculty on the topics of the future of the Russian Navy and naval arms control.

42. Davis, "Future Directions for Naval Arms Control," p. 110.

43. Rear Admiral J. R. Hill, letter to the authors, November 2, 1994.

44. On September 23, 1989 the United States and the Soviet Union signed a *Joint Statement concerning a Uniform Interpretation of Rules of International Law Governing Innocent Passage.*

45. Christopher Pinto, "Maritime Security and the 1982 United Nations Convention on the Law of the Sea," in Josef Goldblat, ed., *Maritime Security: The Building of Confidence* (New York: United Nations, 1992), pp. 9-53.

46. Department of State, *Limits in the Seas: United States Responses to Excessive Maritime Claims*, Publication 112 (Washington, D.C.: U.S. Government Printing Office, 1992).

47. In the Associated Press report on March 16, 1994, Admiral Igor Kasatonov, First Deputy Commander of the Russian Navy, when asked directly whether Russian submarines continued patrolling close to the shores of the United States, replied "No, they are not there." The U.S. Navy has not commented on his assertion. However, on p. 8 of its February 1995 publication *Worldwide Submarine Proliferation in the Coming Decade*, the U.S. Office of Naval Intelligence published a map titled "Russian Sub Ops Areas Past and Present," which illustrates that while in 1984 Soviet submarines did operate close to both U.S. coasts, those operations had ceased as of 1994. The reported detection of a Russian SSN following an American SSBN off the Atlantic coast in June 1995 would seem to indicate, however, that those potentially provocative operations have resumed. Cf. "Russian Submarine is Spotted Off Coast," *Washington Times*, June 23, 1995, p. A7.

48. Davis, "Future Directions for Naval Arms Control," p. 108.

49. All mention of "strategic antisubmarine warfare" has been dropped from the U.S. Navy's new strategy statements . . . *From the Sea* and *Forward . . . From the Sea*. However, the November 4, 1994 publication entitled *America and Europe: The Trans-Atlantic Alliance* issued by the Headquarters of NATO's Supreme Allied Commander Atlantic in Norfolk, Virginia continues to list "strategic antisubmarine warfare" as a "traditional mission" for which "capability" is being maintained.

50. The authors are grateful to Rear Admirals F. W. Crickard, RCN (Ret.) and J. R. Hill, RN (Ret.), and to James L. George for their critical contributions to this section. From the Russian perspective, limited operational restraints on general purpose forces remain desirable as an element of the "defense of the homeland" strategy. It is clear that limits on strategic ASW are of much greater importance from that perspective.

51. Cf. Georgy Dimitrov, "Possible New Restrictions on the Use of Naval Mines," in Goldblat, ed., *Maritime Security: The Building of Confidence*, pp. 79-90; James J. Tritten, "A New Look at Naval Arms Control," *Security Dialogue*, Vol. 24, No. 3 (September 1993), pp. 341-342.

52. Cf. James L. Lacy, "Attack Submarines: The Case for Negotiated Reductions," *Arms Control Today*, Vol. 20, No. 10 (December 1990), pp. 8-12; Ronald O'Rourke, Naval Arms Control: A Bilateral Limit on Attack Submarines? CRS Report for Congress 90-261F, May 23, 1990.

53. Cf. Ian Anthony, *The Naval Arms Trade: SIPRI Strategic Issue Papers* (New York: Oxford University Press, 1990) for an overview; for a summary of the naval arms

build-up in the Asia-Pacific region, cf. Charles A. Meconis, "Naval Arms Control in the Asia-Pacific Region after the Cold War" in Elisabeth Mann Borgese, Norton Ginsburg, and Joseph R. Morgan, eds., *Ocean Yearbook 11* (Chicago: University of Chicago Press, 1994); Michael D. Wallace and Charles A. Meconis, "New Powers, Old Patterns: Dangers of the Naval Buildup in the Asia Pacific Region," Working Paper No. 9, Institute of International Relations, University of British Columbia, March 1995; Desmond Ball, "Arms and Affluence: Military Acquisitions in the Asia-Pacific Region," *International Security*, Vol. 18, No. 3 (Winter 1993/94).

54. For a summary of recent Russian arms sales, see Michael Richardson, "Russian Arms Sales Trigger Asian Tensions," *Asia-Pacific Defence Reporter*, Vol. 21, No. 6-7 (March-April 1995), pp. 48. U.S. arms sales are regularly reported to Congress, and reported in two excellent periodicals: the *Arms Sales Monitor*, compiled and edited by Lora Lumpe and published by the Federation of American Scientists in Washington, D.C., and the *Arms Trade News*, edited by Thomas A. Cardomone, Jr., and published by the Council for a Livable World Education Fund in Washington, D.C; for an in-depth treatment of the issue of U.S. arms sales, cf. William Hartung, *And Weapons for All: How Americas Multibillion Dollar Arms Trade Warps Our Foreign Policy and Subverts Democracy at Home* (New York: HarperCollins, 1994).

55. For a discussion of this issue, see Eric Grove, "Naval Technology and Stability," in Wim A. Smit, John Grin, and Lev Voronkov, eds., *Military Technological Innovation and Stability in a Changing World* (Amsterdam: VU University Press, 1992), pp. 197-213.

56. Davis, "Future Directions for Naval Arms Control," p. 109; Tritten, "A New Look at Naval Arms Control," p. 343.

57. India and Brazil are apparently attempting to develop nuclear propulsion for submarines, but both programs are far from completion.

7

LIMITATIONS ON ANTISUBMARINE WARFARE AS A FACTOR OF STRATEGIC STABILITY

Boris N. Makeev and Charles A. Meconis

Our SSBNs will carry more of the day-to-day deterrence as we reduce our land-based missiles and strategic bomber forces. . . . We're putting more of our eggs in fewer baskets, so we must ensure that these baskets remain secure and reliable.

—Vice Admiral George W. Emery, USN

Limitations on ASW operations form an important aspect of the general problem of naval disarmament. The end of the Cold War, of East-West confrontation, and other related issues in international relations give an urgency to the inclusion of naval forces on the disarmament agenda.

Bearing in mind the difficulties and the variety of opinions on naval disarmament problems, a gradual approach is necessary. We envision three phases: (1) elaboration and reinforcement of confidence-building measures at sea; (2) limiting especially dangerous naval activities; and (3) limiting and reducing naval weapons. Today, successful negotiations are being held only in matters pertaining to the first phase. In our view, the time has come to start negotiations on the *second* phase.

We start from the premise that the optimal size of naval forces should correspond to their missions given the changed international situation that now confronts them. During the Cold War these missions were extensive, requiring enormous groups of naval forces. The range of these missions has now narrowed.

The days when the Russian Navy had the task of supporting Warsaw Pact land forces in strategic operations in the European theater obviously belong to the past. The need to carry out search operations for U.S. SSBNs in the farther reaches of the ocean has gone. The tracking of NATO naval forces in the Mediterranean and the Indian Ocean has virtually ceased.

These steps taken by Russia will, we hope, encourage U.S. naval leaders to show a more favorable attitude toward proposals to limit some types of naval activities as part of the second phase of the negotiation process. If the United States soberly evaluates the decline of the former Soviet maritime threat, it will seize a unique opportunity. While remaining a mighty seapower and maintaining its traditional control over other zones of the world ocean, the United States can reduce its defense expenditures by limiting some naval operations in areas of mutual interest with Russia. Within this context, the problem of limiting some types of antisubmarine warfare (ASW) operations should be addressed first.

ASW activities have many facets. They include virtually all the activities of navies and constitute a complex of measures directed at the detection and destruction of hostile submarines in order to prevent them from delivering missile and torpedo attacks against ships and coastal installations, and from carrying out intelligence, minelaying and other missions.

Ships and aircraft belonging to ASW forces depend on a wide network of hydro-acoustic systems, space and airborne assets, and command facilities forming a global system that monitors the submarine order of battle in wide areas of the world ocean. It is impossible to interfere with any of the links of this system without endangering the security of naval forces and the effective conduct of operations. This argument is the one mainly used by the United States whenever the limitation of ASW operations is discussed.

However, we believe that there exist in this system some links that can and should be looked upon as subjects fit for discussion at the beginning of second phase negotiations on naval disarmament. We do not have in mind ASW operations in general, but only those in certain possible SSBN patrol areas. SSBNs are an increasingly vital element of both countries' strategic deterrent force, ensuring strategic stability.

The entire question of nuclear deterrence after the Cold War is now the subject of considerable change and discussion. We offer a brief review of this topic in order to set the context for our proposal on the limitation of ASW activities against SSBNs.

NUCLEAR DETERRENCE AFTER THE COLD WAR

Nuclear-powered ballistic missile submarines (SSBNs) will take on more of a role in strategic nuclear stability as Russia and the United States implement the START I and II agreements. By the year 2003, the bulk of the strategic nuclear potential for each of these nations will be on SSBNs.[1] These SSBNs, therefore, will become the primary component of the strategic nuclear deterrent for each of their countries, capable of inflicting a powerful retaliatory strike against any would-be aggressor. At the same time, both navies are dramatically reducing the number of SSBNs in their fleets. According to the most recent official statements, by 2003 the U.S. Navy will deploy 14 SSBNs (down from 18 in 1994), while the Russian Navy will deploy 24 (down from 48 in 1994).[2]

Deterrence theory states that a nation requires a secure second-strike force to be deployed that has an assured destruction potential in the minds of any would-be aggressor. Parity in static precombat measures must be paralleled by ensuring the combat stability of the second-strike force—ensuring parity in even "worst case" dynamic scenarios. For security to be viewed as favorable by both sides, neither party should have the ability to inflict a surprise first-strike against the other in such a manner as to gain a decisive strategic advantage.

NATO and the U.S. Navy's maritime strategies of the 1980s were often criticized for their declaratory strategic antisubmarine warfare campaign against Soviet SSBNs.[3] On the one hand, the U.S. and NATO navies argued that they could sink a sufficient number of Soviet SSBNs during the conventional phase of a war to alter the nuclear "correlation of forces," thus deterring nuclear strikes. On the other hand, western navies also maintained that the level of destruction they foresaw would not be great enough to cause the Soviets to launch the nuclear missiles on these subs rather than lose them during this conventional phase of the war.

The Soviet Union also had an aggressive research and development (R&D) program for strategic ASW and a record of slow but methodical improvements in submarine technology, resulting in ever more costly improvements to submarines in a classic action-reaction spiral. In the famous 1960s book *Military Strategy*, Marshal of the Soviet Union Vasiley Danilovich Sokolovskiy discussed the concept of strategic ASW as a problem of defense in depth with the Strategic Rocket Forces (SRF) and Air Force Long-Range Aviation (LRA) striking enemy submarines in their bases, and LRA, ASW submarines, and other ASW forces being tasked with operations against enemy submarines in transit and in patrol areas.[4] The levels of deployed submarine technology never did allow the U.S.S.R. to match the United States in its aspirations, however, it caused the Soviet armed forces to adopt a *bastion defense* of SSBNs to ensure their own combat stability. It is important to note that many western naval officers and analysts also doubt the feasibility of their declared strategic ASW policy.[5] However, those doubts have not allayed Russian fears.

We will next briefly review the planned building programs for nuclear-powered attack submarines (SSNs) and consider whether such weapons systems are truly required under the new international security environment. Then we will turn to a consideration of limits on deployments of forces capable of strategic ASW. We will conclude with a consideration of verification and compliance issues associated with any arms control regime that seeks to regulate strategic ASW operations.

LIMITATIONS ON DEPLOYED HARDWARE

The question of strategic ASW as a future mission for the western and Russian fleets is clearly no longer a matter of top priority for their individual and allied defense establishments. The United States' new advanced design SSNs, the SSN-21 or *Seawolf* class, and the *New Nuclear Attack Submarine* program (NSSN, formerly *Centurion*) for a less expensive alternative, were originally designed as follow-ons to the improved SSN-688I *Los Angeles* class and generally expected to perform the strategic ASW mission. The last SSN-688I will be completed by 1996. In light of the changed international situation, the *Seawolf* class will terminate after the completion of only three units because, according to the U.S. Navy's Admiral in charge of Submarine Warfare, "it's the wrong submarine for the littorals. The *Seawolf* is not optimized for shallow-water littoral operations against diesel submarines."[6] The design of the future U.S. NSSN will focus on four post-Cold War missions: "covert intelligence collection, covert mine detection, covert insertion of special forces and their support, and antisubmarine warfare focused on diesels operating in the littoral."[7]

Newer advanced designs of Russian SSNs were once expected to perform the strategic ASW mission in addition to the related mission of protection of SSBNs within defended bastions. At present, only *Akula/Bars* class SSNs remain in production. In 1993 Admiral Felix Gromov, the Commander-in-Chief of the Russian Navy, stated that only one new class of SSNs, the *Severodinsk* class (Project 988), is being planned, and its main mission will apparently be "countering the intensive activities of foreign submarines in Russian coastal waters and even violations . . . of territorial waters."[8]

Given these developments, one can make a strong case that strategic ASW as a declaratory and programming mission for all nations should be dropped. The only real programming threat that requires attacks against "enemy" SSBNs would be a return to the worst days of the Cold War. The "reconstitution" element of the new U.S. Military Strategy takes into account a resurgent/emergent global threat (REGT).[9] A reconstitution strategy lasting eight to ten years to meet an REGT, however, does not require the reinstatement of 1980s warfighting forces, including warfighting SSNs capable of operating in enemy "home" waters. Rather, reconstitution calls for the rebuilding of forces to *deter* a global war. There are *many* options to support nuclear deterrence other than the offensive naval forces required for strategic ASW.[10]

The internationally known Russian scholar Alexei Arbatov has spoken out against Russian ASW efforts against western SSBNs:

[U]ntil such time as all nuclear weapons are eliminated under relevant agreements, the combat task of offensive and defensive strategic forces will be not to limit damage in the event of a nuclear war. . . . The strategic and military-technological reality now is the following: it is impossible to reduce one's damage in a nuclear war by hitting the aggressor's strategic forces. . . . The idea of striking back at U.S. SOFs [strategic offensive forces] is evidently strategic nonsense. . . . An even more doubtful mission is that of searching for and destroying strategic submarines of the United States, Britain, and France on the high seas.[11]

Arbatov repeated his criticisms of first strike damage limitation, strategic defensive forces, and strategic ASW for the Soviet Union in a 1990 booklet.[12]

U.S. naval analyst Richard C. Davis has suggested that "the United States could simply and quietly unilaterally cease antisubmarine warfare operations aimed at Russian SSBNs."[13] This would be an important, but insufficient, step forward.

With the Russian economy in ruin and the West providing significant aid to assist the transition to capitalism, there is no need for Russia to squander precious resources on new forces capable of protecting its own SSBNs against western ASW forces *if* there are other ways to ensure that a secure second-strike nuclear force is maintained. Why would we expect that Russia would openly build new and more capable SSNs whose major purpose was to seek out and destroy western SSBNs at the same time that the West is providing significant amounts of economic aid? The new *Severodinsk* class will inevitably incorporate improved technology, as will the U.S. NSSN. But neither design appears to emphasize strategic ASW.

Due to the changed international security environment, we should now take a fresh look at our military and naval programming goals to find more cost-effective ways to ensure the accomplishment of political tasks by military forces. Unilateral programming actions by the United States and Russia would be an excellent confidence-building measure demonstrating a shift to a new style of deterrence, one built on the threat of punishment rather than the capability of nuclear warfighting.

A significant amount of Russian literature evidence, since 1987, suggests using the U.S. McNamara-era measure of effectiveness (MOE) associated with an assumed percentage of damage afforded to the other's industry and population and an assured destruction (punishment) deterrence theory. Specifically some suggest that 400 equivalent megatons (EMT) of survivable and deliverable nuclear combat potential is appropriate for both superpowers today.[14] Other articles suggest using numbers of warheads, rather than EMT, and propose around 500-600 warheads.[15] A real minimal deterrence posture of "tens" of warheads surfaced early in the debate and gained renewed interest in 1989-90.[16] The question of a move toward "minimum" nuclear deterrence has also been debated by the United Nations Institute for Disarmament Research.[17]

On September 22, 1994, the U.S. Department of Defense announced the results of it year-long *Nuclear Posture Review*. That review focused on two main issues: (1) how to achieve the proper balance between providing leadership for further and continuing reductions in nuclear weapons while hedging against the reversal of reform in Russia; and (2) how to achieve improved safety and security for the residual force of nuclear weapons.

In addition to earlier announced measures such as taking nuclear bombers off ground alert and "detargeting" land- and sea-based nuclear missiles, the United States announced that it is placing more of its SSBNs on "modified alert," as opposed to full "alert," and that by 1997, U.S. SSBNs will be equipped with "system coded control devices [CCDs] or PALs [Permissive Action Links] by 1997."[18] These developments have long been urged by western arms control advocates—and resisted by the U.S. Navy.

It is clear that the United States is moving away from a nuclear warfighting posture, and is even going beyond a deterrence policy of mutual assured destruction (MAD) toward a "retaliation only" or "punishment" deterrence policy. U.S. Secretary of Defense William J. Perry described the change in these terms:

> I would liken MAD to two men holding revolvers and standing about ten yards away and pointing their revolvers at each other's heads. The revolvers are loaded, cocked, their fingers are on the trigger. To make matters worse, they're shouting insults at each other. That characterized MAD . . . this nuclear terror, during all periods of the Cold War. . . .
>
> Now it's time to change the way we think about nuclear weapons. . . . Therefore, the new posture which we are seeking . . . is no longer based on mutual assured destruction, no longer based on MAD. We have coined a new term for our new posture which we call mutual assured safety, or MAS.[19]

Within this context, it seems to us that state policy would demand that no capability be fielded that could undermine the other's assured second-strike capability; hence strategic ASW as a mission for one's armed forces would be in conflict with deterrence theory. Furthermore, as the number of nuclear warheads continues downward, and the associated number of SSBNs follows as we indicated above, it stands to reason that the value of each SSBN increases as the relative portion of the entire arsenal found on each submarine increases. In such a case, the affected side deploying warheads at sea will need to find a way to avoid making each SSBN a "magnet" for attack.[20]

For the immediate future, SSBNs will play a major role in both countries' nuclear forces. In the long term, there is even the possibility, albeit remote, that Russia will forego deployment of SSBNs *if* its overall number of warheads drops to "minimal" levels such as 1,000 or even 500. Eliminating the sea-based leg of the Russian triad is certainly *not* the recommendation coming either from the Russian Navy or Ministry of Defense, but neither of these institutions will make the decision. Newly confident civilian analysts may conclude that the solution to the threat posed by western ASW forces to the nuclear submarine forces of Russia can be met by simply eliminating the costly and technologically inferior submarine leg and relying instead on mobile land-based systems. Still, the cost of enlarging the Russian mobile land-based missile force may be prohibitive.

The operable policy question in this new international environment, is what can each side do to ensure that it feels secure itself without threatening the legitimate security interests by the other side?[21] Reduction in the capability to perform strategic ASW, by either unilateral programming steps taken to freeze deployed submarine technology as discussed above, or restrictions in operations, appear to be two areas for serious consideration. The first possibility would be welcome but insufficient. It is to the second possibility that this chapter will now turn.

LIMITATIONS ON STRATEGIC ASW OPERATIONS

Since Russia actively defends its SSBNs with air and naval forces, including technologically inferior SSNs, we should understand their preference for restrictions on operations rather than constraints on new submarines. One longstanding suggestion, again being advanced by some Russians, is that *all* ASW operations be *banned* in the regions of possible SSBN patrol. Indeed, Marshal of Aviation Yevgeny Ivanovich Shaposhnikov, then chief of the Commonwealth of Independent States joint military-strategic space and unified nuclear armed forces, stated that this should be a necessary precondition for Russian ratification of START II.[22]

Following the March 1993 collision between the *USS Grayling* SSN and a Russian *Delta* class SSBN, there were discussions between Presidents Bill Clinton and Boris Yeltsin in Vancouver, British Columbia, over the need to discuss restrictions on dangerous submarine operations.[23] Recent press reports indicate that the United States has ordered certain changes in the activities of its SSNs relative to Russian SSBNs.[24] If true, that is a welcome development, but further steps are needed in our view.

Most past Soviet proposals called for "ASW-free zones" in which SSBNs could be deployed without fear of surveillance. The basic problem with such proposals was that *all* ASW operations would have been forbidden within these zones. Such zones would have restricted virtually *all* warships, hydrographic vessels, and naval auxiliaries since it could be argued that even during routine transit by these ships they conduct certain (and not trivial) phases of ASW.[25] ASW-free zones would have logically restricted research as well; otherwise, a major loophole would allow treaty circumvention and noncompliance. Difficulties would also have been caused by fishing vessels and merchant ships. A total ASW-free zone would have to have been off-limits to *any* state-owned or contracted merchant or fishing vessel in order to prevent treaty circumvention.

The United States does not deploy its SSBNs in known bastions, preferring to rely on its technological superiority to provide safety in the deep open oceans. Hence, and rightly so, these past Soviet proposals for ASW-free zones were viewed in the West as being entirely one-sided and not worthy of serious consideration. Perhaps today, with the benefit of some "new thinking," a more realistic set of proposals might be created. This chapter will consider such restrictions primarily from the perspective of restrictions against the West before it discusses various *quid pro quo* alternatives.

First, the deployment of "excess" numbers of ASW forces to an area of SSBN deployments might be more easily managed than a *total* restriction on any ASW activities. For example, if Russia could convince itself that it could tolerate the loss of one or two SSBNs and still maintain an assured destruction capability, then it might tolerate the deployment of one, or maybe even two, SSNs in SSBN deployment areas where they would presumably be performing nonstrategic ASW missions. Even if a few SSNs were operating in SSBN deployment areas, it is extremely unlikely that they could singlehandedly and preemptively eliminate the Russians' protected secure strategic nuclear reserve deployed at sea.[26]

Similarly, Russia should surely not object to a single maritime patrol air-craft or a single surface ship operating in bastions, especially if they were operating without the benefit of friendly fighter aircraft. In other words, a potential disarming first-strike threat to the Russian SSBN fleet must be viewed as the political objective to be regulated, not the performance of any ASW mission.

If, for example, the West were to deploy a force sufficient to mount an offensive ASW operation (*operatsii*), then this would be an entirely different matter. Such a force would have the potential capability of destruction of a significant number of Russian SSBNs—something that does not appear to be in touch with current western efforts to help Russia's transition toward democracy and capitalism.

One could argue that an offensive ASW operation would at least require the combined arms assets of naval aviation and surface ships with advanced ASW capabilities, SSNs, the supporting shore establishment, and space. On the other hand, one could argue that the U.S. submarine force might, if deploying sufficient numbers of high technology SSNs, be capable of conducting a strategic ASW campaign without the overt assistance of surface ships and naval aviation. A restriction that might be more easily accepted by the United States would be on the deployment of forces with sufficient "strategic mass" to be capable of conducting a strategic ASW operation in waters that were known to contain Russian SSBNs.

With modern measures of effectiveness designed by their military operations research community, it might be possible to develop the probability of detection of an SSBN by various types of ASW forces. This approach was used during the Conventional Armed Forces in Europe (CFE) negotiations to equate the combat potential of various forms of tanks. MOEs designed to measure the probability of detection of a Russian SSBN could then be used to determine the amount of forces that would be capable of performing a strategic ASW operation. We offer the following example.

A very simple (and admittedly mechanistic) *algorithm for the estimation of the probability of detection* (R_{obn}) of a submarine is as follows:

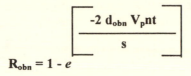

$$R_{obn} = 1 - e^{\left[\dfrac{-2\, d_{obn}\, V_p n t}{s}\right]}$$

d_{obn}	=	the range of an ASW weapons system
V_p	=	the relative velocity of the displacement of forces while searching relative to the SSBN
n	=	number of search units
t	=	time allotted to search the region
s	=	area to be searched

Source: Boris N. Makeev "Limitation of Antisubmarine Activity in the Asian-Pacific Region, as a Factor of Strategic Stability," unpublished.

A more subtle and therefore realistic search model assumes that the target is moving randomly in the deployment area, but is not taking evasive action.

$$\mathbf{Prob(t)} = 1 - e^{-2RVt/A}$$

Prob(t)	=	the probability of detection as a function of time
R	=	detection range of ASW search devices
V	=	speed of the searching attack submarine
t	=	search time
A	=	deployment zone of the SSBN

Source: Mark Sakitt, *Submarine Warfare in the Arctic: Option or Illusion?* (Center for International Security and Arms Control: Stanford University, May 1988), pp. 65-69.

We do not intend to offer a full mathematical explanation of our argument in favor of limitations on some types of strategic ASW operation here. No doubt there are several possible approaches to quantifying this issue, and the formulas listed above are meant only to be examples of possibly useful approaches. We refer interested experts to the full texts listed as sources. Still using the above as guidelines, if we assume that a normal amphibious ship has no serious ASW capability, other than visual, radar, and passive electronics support measures (ESM), we might arbitrarily assign it an ASW potential against a deployed SSBN as perhaps a 5 on a scale of 0-100. A modern SSN, on the other hand, might be rated as a 90. Using such illustrative numbers, it is possible to see that certain types of forces might be more easily subject to deployment limitations than others, either alone or in company. Using exercise data or simulations, it should be possible to quantify the level of forces normally associated with the conduct of a strategic ASW operation.

It should then be possible to allow the *rapid* (time-limited) and "innocent" transit of forces capable of a strategic ASW operation through even areas of known SSBN deployment since the ability to find SSBNs would require some considerable degree of time (t). If the United States required the transit of a force of sufficient size capable of conducting a strategic ASW operation through an SSBN patrol area, it could refrain from the conduct of coordinated and large-scale ASW activities other than those required for navigation and self-defense. Navies have a long history of adhering to "innocent passage" restrictions through the passage of other state's territorial seas.

No one should expect the Russian Navy to sit idly by and watch a large force of western ASW assets transit its sensitive ocean areas, and we should assume that the covering force would be increased or that additional SSBNs would sortie. Another obvious counteraction would be to increase temporarily the size of the SSBN deployment area, causing the area to be searched (A) to be greatly increased, thus making it impractical for the United States to find large numbers of Russian SSBNs during a rapid transit. Another possibility would be to alter the SSBN deployment areas to ones that are more easily protected.

Obviously, the probability of detection of an SSBN will depend upon the geographic and oceanographic area of deployment, the specific type of SSBN deployed, and so on, as well as various transitory factors such as the weather and mode of operation of the SSBN. These factors are extremely complicated and will be viewed by national specialists as being sensitive and not subject to release to foreign nations. Nonmilitary specialists, however, have been successful in creating much of the same information which, although not perfect, is probably good enough for negotiations.[27]

After constructing such mathematical approximations of the probability of detection of an SSBN in certain areas of the world's oceans during various climactic and oceanographic seasons by specific types of forces, we would then ascertain if those forces ought to be restricted to prevent levels that would attain certain probability of detection. Table 7.1 expresses numerical levels of fleet destruction that have been equated in the past with specific levels expressed in words and could serve as a model for the type of levels of capability that might be restricted.

Table 7.1
Levels of Fleet Destruction

Level	Percent of damage
Destruction	80-90% Sunk or Inoperable
Defeat	70% Sunk or Inoperable
Doing damage	50% Sunk or Inoperable
Substantial weakening	30% Sunk or Inoperable
Weakening	10-15% Sunk or Inoperable

Source: Captain 1st Rank (Reserves) O. Shul'man, "Wording of Combat Missions," Moscow *Morskoy Sbornik*, in Russian, No. 8 (August 1976), p. 19 (NIS-RSTP-039-76, November 1976, p. 10).

Another Russian author lists two extreme levels of destruction: (1) total catastrophe, 85-88% lost; and (2) full retention of combat capability, 9-13% lost.[28]

A more modern expression, indicating the levels of interdiction of sea lines of communication (SLOCs) by lowering the volume, is found in Table 7.2.

Table 7.2
Levels of Interdiction of Sea Lines of Communication

Level	Percent
Prevention/suppression [*nedonushcheniye*]	>80%
[Temporarily] Interrupted/frustrated [*sryv*]	60-80%
Reduction [*sokrashcheniye*]	30 to 50-60%
Impeding/Hampering [*zatrudneniye*]	25-30%

Source: Admiral of the Fleet V. Chernavin, "The Struggle on Sea Lanes of Communication: The Lessons of Wars and the Present," Moscow *Morskoy Sbornik*, in Russian, No. 1 (January 1990), p. 20 (NIC-RSTP-119-90, May 1990, p. 26 and JPRS-UMA-90-007, March 23, 1990, p. 57).

Neither Tables 7.1 nor 7.2 is meant to suggest levels of probability of detection of SSBNs that might be tolerated, but rather serve to illustrate the possibility of defining levels of destruction with specific mathematical values. Political guidance may be received that would state that it is possible to accept a modest level of risk that an SSBN would be found during peacetime. This could be translated by the military specialist to be, for example, a 30% probability of detection by a single unit as determined by the algorithms accepted during the negotiating process. The military specialists would, of course, also be using their own more accurate data to compute the probabilities and would have the options of changing SSBN deployment patterns or operations to reduce that probability.

By employing mutually agreed upon mathematical formulas, we believe it is possible to approximate the ASW forces necessary to search for SSBNs in a given region and therefore introduce a quantitative limit on antisubmarine activity in agreed regions where naval strategic forces can operate in security.

For example, the Sea of Okhotsk bordering on the Pacific is a region that may possibly be used by Russian SSBNs. Slightly less than half of that sea's total area of 1,590,000 sq. km is deep enough to enable an underwater missile launch, so the total area of deployment would be approximately 760,000 sq. km. Using one possible set of simple equations, we calculate that it would require 4 maritime patrol ASW aircraft, 10 surface ASW ships, and 9 SSNs to search the Sea of Okhotsk thoroughly. In winter, this force could be cut by half, due to the ice cover on nearly half the usable portion of the sea.[29] Again, we offer these figures as an illustration of the possibility of achieving some realistic and mutually acceptable limitations.

Thus negotiations on limiting strategic ASW activities should begin with preliminary efforts to establish regional boundaries in which anti-SSBN activities have to be restricted. The second step would be to agree upon the "strategic mass" limit of combined ASW forces allowable in the selected areas. The third step would be to delineate those ASW activities unique to an anti-SSBN campaign as distinguished from "normal" ASW operations designed to protect surface ships. An agreement would then prohibit an ASW force of sufficient "strategic mass" from engaging in anti-SSBN activities in agreed upon regions.

The political guidance on the levels of probability of detection might change, however, in time of crisis. For example, if the two military super-powers were confronting each other in some political crisis not related to the deployment of SSBNs, the Russians might wish to reduce the probability of detection to some lower level, say 10%, by a single unit. In that way, the United States would be able to send in a single unit to an SSBN deployment area without being in violation of the agreement.

The probabilities of detection by a single unit that could be tolerated would depend upon the final composition of the Russian nuclear force and the relative value of the sea-based component. The above section seeks to demonstrate that the regulation of large-scale deployments of ASW forces in SSBN deployment areas might be based upon modern MOEs in such a manner as to continue to allow ASW activities in all areas of the ocean but to prevent the deployment of forces that could undermine strategic nuclear stability.

An obvious area for further analysis is whether an ASW arms control regime is automatically eliminated during war. Many international agreements are temporarily suspended upon the formal declaration of war, but others remain in force, and some only enter into force during war. Although one might initially respond that an ASW arms control regime has no place during a war, perhaps a series of war games that tried to replicate crisis management behavior and the behavior of nations during wartime might lead to a different conclusion.

The form of an agreement should be that of a series of Navy-to-Navy contacts and confidence-building measures (CBMs) prior to the involvement of diplomats and professional arms control negotiators. The MOE for an ASW arms control regime is *not* the negotiating of an agreement or signing of a treaty "for its own sake," but the ability to modify military behavior successfully in a manner that enhances world security and does not undermine strategic nuclear stability. Once the two navies themselves are convinced that such a regime is workable, and only then, should the matter be formalized by a treaty given the advice and consent of the U.S. Senate and Russian legislature.

VERIFICATION AND COMPLIANCE

Although verification problems would abound in such an ASW arms control regime, they are probably not insurmountable. It is essential to view verification and compliance as an integral part of CBMs in which alleged noncompliance would be addressed via political mechanisms designed to handle incidents as they are occurring.

In the area of nuclear forces, the Standing Consultative Commission (SCC), was created to monitor the 1970s Strategic Arms Limitations Talks (SALT). Similar consultative commissions, such as the Special Verification Commission (SVC) and the Joint Compliance and Implementation Commission (JCIC), have been created to monitor other arms control treaties, such as the Intermediate Range Nuclear Forces (INF) Treaty and the Conventional Forces in Europe (CFE) Treaty. A similar regime, perhaps built upon the annual meetings to monitor the Incidents at Sea Agreement (INCSEA), should be created to monitor an ASW regime.

Another standard set in earlier nuclear arms control regimes was the principle of noninterference with national technical means (NTMs) of verification. The ASW arms control regime described above would not interfere with the operation of small numbers of ASW assets being used to verify compliance with the agreement. Although many western academics tend to think that NTMs is a euphemism for spaced-based or other overhead surveillance systems, NTMs have always included a sea-based component.

Just as the possession of nuclear weapons by third nations has been an obstacle to strategic nuclear and other arms control negotiations, the possession of missile-carrying submarines and ASW forces by other nations complicates proposals to restrict U.S. and Russian ASW operations. For example, would the United Kingdom or France deploy their SSBNs in the open ocean if the United States and Russia limit their submarines to safe zones? If so, the survivability of these allied submarines is more questionable since they might have to face greater numbers of Russian ASW forces directed specifically at them. Would U.S. SSBNs deployed in the open ocean be more likely to be found?

If limitations are placed on U.S. ASW forces operating in Russian ASW restricted areas, will the Russians assume that Norwegian or Japanese ASW forces would be used instead? Friends and former allies could act as "subcontractors" to ensure continued mission performance even in the face of an ASW arms control regime. Similarly, an ASW arms control regime would need to account for nations benefiting from the ASW "research" conducted by its friends or allies. Reflagging, changing the registry and flag flown by a ship owned by a nation, is an ancient maritime tradition. The United States transferred destroyers to the Royal Navy prior to its entry into World War II. When reflagging would be used to circumvent the effectiveness of an ASW arms control regime, it would make compliance extremely difficult to enforce.

These difficulties do not preclude the usefulness of a bilateral U.S.-Russian ASW agreement in our opinion. However, it is clear that any bilateral agreement involving ASW must be seen as a first step in a comprehensive regime that will eventually address all of these issues. There are too many ways of circumvention to avoid the issue of third parties. This does not mean that the United States and Russia should not enter into negotiations, but rather that they should acknowledge that the final resolution of the issue will have to be greater than just between themselves.

Even if the United States and Russia were to agree on the creation of special zones in which types of ASW operations were restricted, there will be a number of technical-legal issues regarding the law of the sea that will need to be resolved.[30] If the political will is there to create such a regime, one should anticipate that technical-legal issues can be overcome. Another issue that will need to be addressed will be the conduct of ASW operations against SSBNs that are deployed outside of the special zones. After all, there will be nothing to preclude the deployment of SSBNs on the high seas.[31]

The false alarm rate is extraordinarily high at sea. Navies normally deal with "possible" or "probable" rather than "certain" submarine contacts.[32] An ASW arms control regime would have to contain special procedures and regimes to deal with the less than "certain" contacts which, if proven valid, would verify noncompliance with rules.

The failure of the Swedish government to openly declare intrusions into its internal waters and territorial sea to be Soviet in origin suggests that it is likely that governments will demand "certain" verification of noncompliance. In other words, we may need a "smoking gun" or another "*Whiskey* on the rocks" (an actual Soviet submarine aground in Swedish waters) to "prove" that a nation is not living up to its international obligations.

Should the West wish to demonstrate that Russia is not complying with restrictions, but could do so only by exposing its own sophisticated technical or intelligence capabilities, it would have to choose between exposing the non-compliance and the related intelligence source or not publicizing the violation. The United States recently faced this dilemma and chose to expose North Korean nuclear capabilities, even though it revealed startling evidence of over-head imagery capability.[33]

Proving that a nation is not living up to its agreements is not the real issue, however; ensuring compliance is. Rather than reviewing the past Cold War record of Soviet compliance of its arms control agreements, it is time for the world to accept Russia as a new nation and grant it the benefit of the doubt until proven otherwise. In other words, we should monitor Russian behavior in post-Cold War international obligations. If there is general compliance, then we should assume that this behavior will be linked to adhering to an ASW arms control regime. Russia should expect the United States to link its continued economic and other assistance to compliance with all international agreements.

CONCLUSIONS: QUID PRO QUO?

Navies are not likely to favor eroding their power and influence in what is, until now, clearly their prerogative. If a "possible" submarine is detected off the coast of a nation, it is duly recorded and logged by military officers and intelligence professionals of relatively low rank. If asked by the government, the armed forces or intelligence services can tell their government how many "possible," "probable," or "certain" submarines are, or were, off their shores at any given time. If questioned by the public or the media, the government would use the military's input as the basis for its answer, with due caution respecting intelligence sources and methods.

If the waters off that same nation, however, were declared an ASW restricted area, as part of a formal arms control regime, then the government is more likely to take its military's or intelligence service's input and then apply both legal and political finesse to ensure that they report *no* submarines found in forbidden zones. One could even conjure up a case where a new government might attempt to discredit an arms control agreement negotiated by its predecessor, and manipulate intelligence data to demonstrate verified noncompliance. Navies cannot be expected to support any changes to the current agreements where professionals are allowed to make judgments on their own, without excessive legal or political oversight.

Perhaps the most difficult task will be to sell such ideas to the U.S. Navy when it is convinced that it has nothing to gain from changing business as usual. In order to convert the U.S. Navy, either the Russians will need to offer something that the U.S. Navy would find interesting, or the U.S. government would have to find something of value in the nonmaritime sector that would warrant a direct confrontation with the Navy worth it. This was suggested in the past when the United States said that any increased vulnerability to NATO sea lines of communication ought to be matched by a commensurate increase in Warsaw Pact land lines of communication.

If Russia is really serious about wanting to enhance the combat stability of its secure strategic nuclear reserve, it could achieve this by shifting its forces to the land in the form of mobile ICBMs, thereby eliminating the programming requirement for their own high-technology defending SSNs. This would then more easily allow the creation of an ASW arms control regime that would serve to enhance strategic nuclear stability. In fact, recent reports from Russia indicate that a combination of fiscal constraints and the impact of the START II agreement has resulted in a decision to forego construction of a new generation of SLBMs in favor of the production of the single warhead *Topol* SS-25 mobile land-based missile.[34] This in turn could lead to a cancellation or reduction of the next generation of SSBNs, currently scheduled to begin operations in the year 2003. One Russian analyst has described the future of the Russian SSBN force as being "absolutely obscure."[35]

If, as is more likely, the Russian Navy convinces its political leadership that they should keep a sea-based leg for their strategic nuclear systems, then they should be equally prepared to offer something of real value for the limitation in U.S. ASW operations. That "something" will have to be truly worth it to entice the U.S. government to take on the U.S. Navy or for the Navy to accept the restrictions themselves. Can such a "something" be found? We think so. One possibility could involve restrictions on the sale of Russian naval weapons to nations in potential regions of conflict, such as Iran, that go beyond President Yeltsin's May 1995 promise to end further sales to that country after already existing contracts are fulfilled. Yet another possibility could involve limits on future Russian SSN levels in such a way as to limit their potential threat to the small U.S. SSBN force called for in the *Nuclear Posture Review*.

In the new post-Cold War strategic context, we conclude that, despite the many obstacles, negotiations between the United States and Russia on limiting strategic ASW activities can indeed be an important step on the way to greater cooperation and perhaps even partnership between the world's two largest navies.

NOTES

1. Using static numbers of warheads, under the Strategic Arms Reduction Talks (START) II Treaty, Russia would have 55% and the United States 49% of its nuclear potential with the nuclear-powered ballistic missile submarine (SSBN) fleet. By using common assumptions about percentages of the strategic nuclear triad on alert, surviv-

ability, reliability, amounts withheld for reserve, etc., one could conclude that the secure Russian sea-based force would have 62% of its deliverable warheads and the U.S. Navy 72%.

2. Department of Defense, *Nuclear Posture Review* (Washington, D.C., September 22, 1994), p. 17; Admiral Felix Gromov, "Reforming the Russian Navy," in *Naval Forces*, Vol. 14, No. 4 (1993), p.7; *Jane's Fighting Ships, 1994-1995*.

3. For example, cf. Charles A. Meconis and Michael D. Wallace, "Naval Rivalry and Command Survivability," in Frank Langdon and Douglass Ross, eds., *Superpower Maritime Strategy in the Pacific* (London: Routledge, 1990); Mark Sakitt, *Submarine Warfare in the Arctic: Option or Illusions?* (Center for International Security and Arms Control: Stanford University, May 1988); Tom Stefanick, *Strategic Antisubmarine Warfare and Naval Strategy* (Institute for Defense and Disarmament Studies: Lexington Books, 1987).

4. Marshal of the Soviet Union Vasiley Danilovich Sokolovskiy, *Soviet Military Strategy*, ed. with analysis and commentary by Harriet Fast Scott (New York: Crane, Russak & Co., 1975), pp. 290, 302.

5. James J. Tritten, *Soviet Naval Forces and Nuclear Warfare: Weapons, Employment, and Policy* (Boulder, Colo.: Westview, June 1986), p. 282. Concerning doubts about the West's ability to mount an effective strategic ASW campaign, see the sources listed in note 3 above. The authors are grateful to Rear Admiral J. R. Hill for his reminder on this point. Letter to the authors, November 2, 1994.

6. Rear Admiral Thomas D. Ryan, USN, quoted in "Adaptable New Attack Sub Faces DAB Decision," *Navy News & Undersea Technology*, December 6, 1993, pp. 1, 7-8.

7. Rear Admiral Thomas D. Ryan, "View from the Pentagon," in Submarine *Review* (January 1994), p. 20.

8. Gromov, "Reforming the Russian Navy," p. 7. The *Severodinsk's* keel was laid down on December 21, 1993, with probable launch in 1997-98 and completion in the following year. Norman Polmar, "Republic Navies: A Continuing Interest . . . in Submarines," U.S. Naval Institute *Proceedings*, Vol. 120, No. 11 (November 1994), p. 103.

9. Patrick Tyler, "Pentagon Imagines New Enemies To Fight in Post-Cold-War Era," *New York Times*, February 17, 1992, p. 1; "Hypothetical Conflicts Foreseen by the Pentagon," *New York Times*, February 17, 1992, p. 8; Barton Gellman, "Pentagon War Scenario Spotlights Russia," *Washington Post*, February 20, 1992, p. 1; and National Defense Research Institute, *Assessing the Structure and Mix of Future Active and Reserve Forces: Final Report to the Secretary of Defense*, MR-140-1-OSD (Santa Monica: Calif.: The RAND Corporation, 1992), pp. xxiv, 105-109.

10. This basic point is developed more fully in James J. Tritten, *Our New National Security Strategy: America Promises To Come Back* (Westport, Conn.: Praeger, 1992), especially p. 150.

11. Alexei Georgiyevich Arbatov, "How Much Defense Is Sufficient?" Moscow *International Affairs*, in English, No. 4 (April 1989), pp. 34, 36, 39, 41 (this article appeared in *Mezhdunarodnaya Zhizn* in March 1989).

12. Alexei G. Arbatov, "Defense Sufficiency and Security," Moscow *Novoye v Zhizni, Nauke, Tekhnike: Seriya "Mezhdunarodnaya,"* in Russian, No. 4 (1990), (JPRS-UMA-90-008-L, June 20, 1990, pp. 14-22).

13. Captain Richard C. Davis, USN (Ret.), "Future Directions for Naval Arms Control," in Lewis A. Dunn and Sharon A. Squassoni, eds., *Arms Control: What Next?* (Boulder, Colo.: Westview, 1993), p. 108.

14. Alexei G. Arbatov, A. A. Vasilyev, and Andrey Afanasyevich Kokoshin, "Nuclear Weapons and Strategic Stability," Moscow *SSHA: Ekonomika, Politika, Ideologiya* in Russian, No. 9 (September 1987), pp. 3-13 (JPRS-USA-88-003, March 10, 1988, p. 4); Alexei G. Arbatov, "On Parity and Reasonable Sufficiency," Moscow *Mezhdunarodnaya Zhizn*, in Russian, No. 9 (September 1988), pp. 80-92 (FBIS-SOV-88-203-Annex, October 20, 1988, p. 7), reprinted in Moscow *International Affairs*, in English (October 1988), p. 83; and Alexei G. Arbatov, "Defense Sufficiency and Security," Moscow *Novoye v Zhizni, Nauke, Tekhnike: Seriya "Mezhdunarodnaya,"* in Russian, No. 4 (1990), pp. 1-64 (JPRS-UMA-90-008-L, June 20, 1990, p. 17).

15. Colonel V. Strebkov, "From the Standpoint of the New Thinking: Military Parity Yesterday and Today," Moscow *Krasnaya Zvezda*, in Russian, January 3, 1989, 1st ed., p. 3 (JPRS-UMA-89-002, January 26, 1989, p. 25); Lev Semenovich Semeyko, "Sensible Sufficiency Is a Way to Reliable Peace," Moscow *Kommunist*, in Russian, No. 7 (May 1989), pp. 112-121 (JPRS-UKO-89-013, July 24, 1989, pp. 80-81); and Vladimir Chernyshev report, Moscow TASS, in English, 1152 GMT, November 30, 1990 (FBIS-SOV-90-232, December 3, 1990, p. 3).

16. Igor Malashenko, "Parity Reassessed," Moscow *New Times*, in English, No. 47, November 30, 1987, p. 9; Colonel Yevgeny Klimchuk, "When Was Parity Established," Moscow *Argumenty i Fakty*, in Russian, No. 13, April 1-7, 1989, p. 3 (FBIS-SOV-89-067, April 10, 1989, p. 5); Colonels Vladimir Dvorkhin and Valeriy Torbin, "On Real Sufficiency of Defense—Military Specialists' Point of View," Moscow *Moscow News*, in English, No. 26, June 25, 1989, p. 6 (FBIS-SOV-89-126, July 3, 1989, p. 105); Radomir Bogdanov and Andrey Kortunov, "On the Balance of Power," Moscow *International Affairs*, in English (August 1989), pp. 3-13 (also found in JPRS-UMA-89-024, October 12, 1989, pp. 37-44); V. Dmitriyev and Colonel V. Strebkov, "Outdated Concept," Moscow *Krasnaya Zvezda*, in Russian, April 10, 1990, 1st ed., p. 3 (FBIS-SOV-90-074, April 17, 1990, p. 2); Sergey Yurakov interview with Marshal of the Soviet Union Sergey Fedorovich Akhromeyev, then chief of the U.S.S.R. Armed Forces General Staff, and academician Georgiy A. Arbatov, director of the USA and Canada Institute, broadcast on the "Serving the Fatherland" program, Moscow Television Service, in Russian, 2130 GMT, July 21, 1990 (FBIS-SOV-90-145, July 27, 1990, p. 63); and Tsutomu Saito interview with Valentin Falin, Secretary and Head of the Communist Party of the Soviet Union Central Committee's International Department, "A Discourse on the World," Tokyo *Sankei Shimbun*, in Japanese, August 18, 1990, morning ed., p. 1 (FBIS-SOV-170-A, August 31, 1990, p. 5).

17. Serge Sur, ed., *Nuclear Deterrence: Problems and Perspectives in the 1990's* (New York: United Nations, 1993, UNIDIR/93/26).

18. *Nuclear Posture Review*, p. 30.

19. William J. Perry, News Release by the Office of the Assistant Secretary of Defense for Public Affairs, September 22, 1994, pp. 1-3.

20. Indeed, the case was made in the early 1980s that if the West wanted to "push" the Soviet's nuclear deterrent to sea, it would have to accommodate restrictions on antisubmarine warfare in order to ensure the Soviets remained comfortable with their

assured second strike. See Ronald G. Purver, "The Control of Strategic Anti-submarine Warfare," *International Journal*, Vol. 38, No. 3 (Summer 1983), p. 425.

21. A major leak on the fears of top-level Communist Party (CPSU) and Soviet intelligence leaders was that provided by retired KGB (Committee on State Security) General Oleg Gordievsky: see Oleg Gordievsky, "Pershing Paranoia in the Kremlin," *The Times* (London), in English, February 27, 1990, pp. 12-13 (FBIS-SOV-90-052-A, March 16, 1990, p. 11-15); Christopher Andrew and Oleg Gordievsky, "Inside the KGB," *Time*, Vol. 136, No. 17 (October 22, 1990), pp. 78-82; and Christopher Andrew and Oleg Gordievsky, *KGB: The Inside Story* (New York: HarperCollins, 1990), pp. 582-593. The KGB's Operation RYAN, a collection effort in the early and mid-1980s to warn of a "bolt-from-the-blue" attack by the West on the U.S.S.R., was reported by Gordievsky and apparently was real. This is typical of how little the CPSU and KGB understood the United States and how dangerous it was to publish declaratory warfighting nuclear and naval strategies and to conduct certain types of aggressive deployments with naval and air forces. What the United States believed were actions taken to reinforce deterrence apparently were totally misunderstood by the other side as an actual threat to peace.

22. Akira Furumoto interview with Marshal Yevgeniy Shaposhnikov, Commander in Chief of the Joint Armed Forces of the Commonwealth of Independent States, Tokyo *Yomiuri Shimbum*, in Japanese, February 16, 1993, morning edition, p. 5 (FBIS-SOV-93-041-A, March 4, 1993, p. 1).

23. "Press Conference by President Bill Clinton and President Boris Yeltsin, Canada Place," Vancouver, British Columbia: The White House, Office of the Press Secretary, April 4, 1993, 1:45 p.m., PDT, p. 8.

24. Charles Aldinger, Reuter, Kiev, Ukraine, June 6, 1993, "U.S. Changes Submarine Operations for Safety"; Robert Burns, Associated Press, Kiev, Ukraine, June 6, 1993, "CIS-U.S.-Russia Subs"; "Sub Operations Changed," *The Monterey County Herald*, June 7, 1993, p. 2A; "Pentagon Warms to Russia," *The Washington Times*, June 7, 1993, p. A1; and "Aspin Acts To Avoid U.S.-Russian Sub Collisions," *Arms Control Today*, Vol. 23, No. 6 (July/August 1993), p. 31.

25. For example, ships transiting the ocean normally conduct visual and radar (if equipped) search—both forms of active antisubmarine warfare (ASW). Even passive search using basic electronics equipment is expected during the most routine and innocent transits, and most naval ships carry some electronic support measures (ESM) equipment. ESM, radar, and visual search are surprisingly effective and routinely used methods of ASW.

26. See Ambassador Linton F. Brooks, "Forward Submarine Operations and Strategic Stability," *The Submarine Review* (April 1993), p. 17 for a similar conclusion. See Henry Young, "Setting Goals for a Submarine Campaign," *The Submarine Review* (October 1985), p. 19-27 for a detailed analysis.

27. Perhaps the best example of this can be found in the numerous appendices to Tom Stefanick's book, *Strategic Antisubmarine Warfare and Naval Strategy*, pp. 131-365, plus the appendices to Mark Sakitt's *Submarine Warfare in the Arctic: Option or Illusion?*

28. Vadim Ledovyy interview with Captain 1st Rank (Ret.) Anatoliy Gorbachev, "An SOS from Deep Within the Fleet: The U.S.S.R. Has More Submarines But It Is

Easy To Find Them Because They Are Noisy," Moscow *Nezavisimaya Gazeta*, in Russian, November 20, 1991, p. 6 (JPRS-UMA-92-003, January 29, 1992, p. 73).

29. Boris N. Makeev, "Limitations of Antisubmarine Activity in the Asian-Pacific Region, as a Factor of Strategic Stability," 1993, unpublished.

30. R. R. Baxter, "Legal Aspects of Arms Control Measures Concerning the Missile Carrying Submarines and Anti-Submarine Warfare," in *The Future of the Sea-Based Deterrent*, eds. Kosta Tsipis, Anne H. Cahn, and Bernard T. Feld (Cambridge, Mass., MIT Press, 1973), pp. 209-232.

31. R. B. Byers, "Seapower and Arms Control: Problems and Prospects," *International Journal*, Vol. 36, No. 3 (Summer 1981), p. 514.

32. D. P. O'Connell, *The Influence of Law of Sea Power* (Annapolis, Md.: Naval Institute Press, 1975), p. 76.

33. Andrew Mack, "The Nuclear Crisis on the Korean Peninsula," *Asian Survey*, Vol. 33, No. 4 (April 1993), pp. 351-354.

34. Vladimir Belous, "Russia's Nuclear Security," *Sedonya*, February 9, 1994; Guennady Voronin, "What Kind of a Submarine Fleet Does Russia Need?" *Nezavismaya Gazeta*, December 29, 1994; Pavel Koltsov, "We are Obliged to Save the Navy," *Nezavismaya Gazeta*, March 18, 1994.

35. Alexei Zagorsky, "Russia's Naval Strategy in Northeast Asia," Paper presented to the Fourth International Seapower Symposium, Seoul, August 3-4, 1995, p. 25.

8

SCIENTIFIC AND METHODOLOGICAL PROBLEMS OF NAVAL ARMS CONTROL

Boris N. Makeev

In the preceding chapters it was argued that considerable progress is possible in the near future with regard to the first two phases of naval arms control: confidence-building measures and limits on some types of naval operations in certain ocean areas. However, if naval arms control is ever to proceed into a third phase—actual *reduction* of forces—a considerable effort will have to go into developing a mutually agreed upon methodology. This chapter proposes such a methodology. We will begin by briefly reviewing the overall context.

Disarmament is the reduction of capabilities for military confrontation of states through mutual reduction of weapons for conducting war, with the goal of reducing the threat of the outbreak of war. At the present time, major nuclear arms reductions are being carried out based on negotiations between Russia and the United States on the reduction of their level, banning production and eliminating individual types and categories of weapons, and the unilateral limiting of both nations' military budgets and military equipment development programs.

Definite achievements in the sphere of strategic nuclear forces and conventional arms reductions in Europe are well known. As for control over naval weapons, this sphere has not been encompassed by a serious negotiating process. Moreover, a number of NATO member countries, and the United States in particular, have refused to negotiate with regard to reducing naval forces and continue to substantially increase their combat capabilities in qualitative terms, despite major quantitative reductions.

One can understand the position of the West, as outlined in Chapter 2, which considers the United States an "island" state for which open sea lines of communication are vitally important and naval forces are the most important

The views expressed in this chapter are those of the author alone, and are not in any way an expression of official views of the Russian Navy or government.

component of the armed forces and an effective instrument for accomplishing missions in the sphere of U.S. interests. But it is impossible to understand the military experts, scholars, and politicians who suggest that one can conduct negotiations on arms reductions while simultaneously excluding the naval component from that process. On the contrary, it is quite obvious that, if any one of the negotiating parties attempts to fully retain or not substantially limit the naval component of their own armed forces for some reason or other, that party must limit to a greater degree *other* components of its own military potential.

A SYSTEMATIC ANALYSIS OF DISARMAMENT

In the context of the new international situation, how are we to prepare the way for eventual negotiations leading to naval arms reductions? Since such negotiations must eventually include all nations with substantial maritime interests and naval forces, how can a common ground be established? First of all, we need a comprehensive approach and systemic analysis of the disarmament process. The armed forces of each state must be viewed as a single military organism consisting of various services and combat arms that are capable of accomplishing combat missions in close coordination. We should not compare the arms of states by simply considering their individual models and systems (sometimes referred to as "bean-counting"), because of the different geostrategic conditions for their employment, basing and deployment capabilities, and also inadequate assessment of the role and significance of individual services and combat arms in various countries. We must conduct arms comparisons based on mission performance effectiveness criteria that are faced by all of the armed forces. That approach requires modeling possible combat operations between the opposing sides and determining the composition of the personnel and equipment that are required and sufficient for accomplishing probable missions with the assigned effectiveness. The essence of this methodological approach to arms reductions is demonstrated in Figures 8.1 and 8.2.

Because of the specifics of the arms and military equipment of the various armed forces, the methodology must provide for two levels of research. The *first* level assumes the evaluation of common problems and interrelationships that are characteristic for the armed forces as a whole (Fig. 8.1). At the *second* level, from the common research algorithm, there will be blocks that branch out and permit analysis and development of proposals concerning the makeup of arms of the separate services and combat arms (Fig. 8.2). Such an approach will ensure to a greater degree a clarification of their interdependence and will permit the development of the most validated criteria of defensive sufficiency and proposals for the reduction of each type and branch of forces within the framework of an agreed total military balance of forces.

Figure 8.1
Methodology of Naval Arms Control I

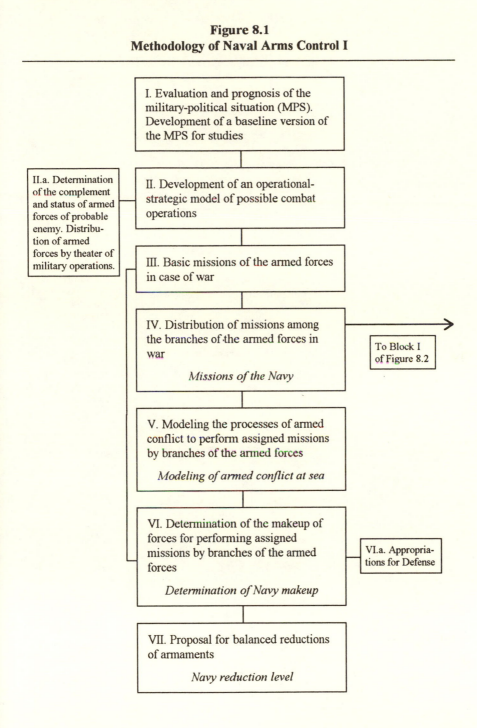

I. Evaluation and prognosis of the military-political situation (MPS). Development of a baseline version of the MPS for studies

II.a. Determination of the complement and status of armed forces of probable enemy. Distribution of armed forces by theater of military operations.

II. Development of an operational-strategic model of possible combat operations

III. Basic missions of the armed forces in case of war

IV. Distribution of missions among the branches of the armed forces in war

Missions of the Navy

To Block I of Figure 8.2

V. Modeling the processes of armed conflict to perform assigned missions by branches of the armed forces

Modeling of armed conflict at sea

VI. Determination of the makeup of forces for performing assigned missions by branches of the armed forces

Determination of Navy makeup

VI.a. Appropriations for Defense

VII. Proposal for balanced reductions of armaments

Navy reduction level

Figure 8.2
Methodology of Naval Arms Control II

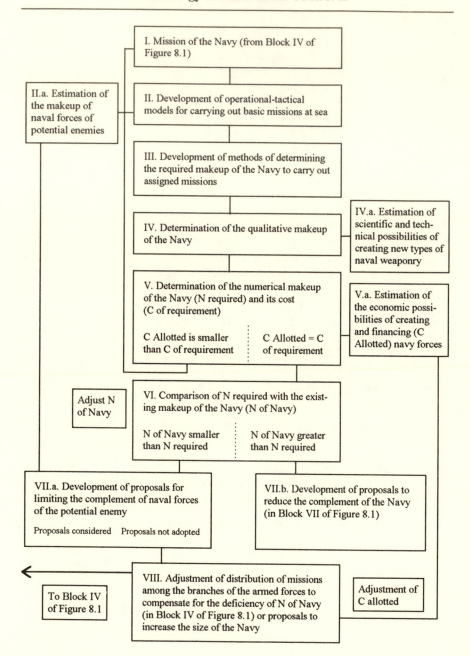

Specific research in accordance with this general methodological approach toward determining the level of sufficiency of the armed forces and the process of their reduction begins with an assessment of the military-political situation (MPS) and the development of a generalized baseline version of the situation. The military-political situation is understood to consist of the complex of conditions that determines the missions and possibilities for the deployment of armed forces. Evaluation of the MPS is conducted based upon analysis of the international relations that have developed, and also on the prediction of their future development. In the process, we can talk only with a relative degree of reliability about predictions of the military-political situation because of the inevitable uncertainty and the many variations for its development. As a result, in the event of the emergence of an armed conflict, the actual military-political situation may not coincide with what has been predicted, which can have undesirable consequences for planning the process of arms reduction and for determining the level of defensive sufficiency. Therefore, to preclude miscalculations, some measure of mutually agreed upon *balance* must lie at the foundation of the concept of arms reductions, and the recommendations that are developed must ensure the most painless adaptation of the steps being adopted to the changing situation and the possibility of their timely adjustment. Obviously the great changes in the international situation due to the end of the Cold War and the demise of the Soviet Union give a new meaning to the concept of "balance."

To achieve this, the recommendations must take into account the most dangerous situations, from among the most probable, for the country from the point of view of an armed clash. The recommendations should also be most comprehensive, that is to say, those that permit the use of armed forces in a sufficiently large range of conditions as well as realistic from the point of view of economic capabilities to support the armed forces at the level of defensive sufficiency.

We can call this generalized version that was developed based on the prediction of possible variations of the military-political situation a baseline version. It was also previously widely used by all countries during the development of their own arms programs.[1] Since validation of reduction programs is related to the validation of arms development through their similar methodology, the development of a baseline version of the military-political situation is not only required and successively justified but also tested. However, it must be used only as a basic variation for subsequent research. The operational-strategic model of possible combat operations (this model is often called a "scenario" in U.S. literature) is developed based upon it. Here, depicted in textual and graphic form, are the general conditions for the employment of the armed forces in assumed conflicts, the allocation of missions among the services of the armed forces, and the primary method to accomplish those missions, while taking into account coordination and support. Analysis of the composition and state of the armed forces of potential enemies, and also the military potential of the sides and the assessment of the objectivity and validity of the military missions declared by them at the negotiations or in official statements, is within the framework of this section of the research. The allocation of missions among the services of the armed forces in the main strategic operations is the most important stage of operational-strategic modeling.

The instability and fluidity of both international and domestic political situations in various countries requires an objective examination of all the primary goals of modern war that are vitally important for any state. In the process, we must not restrict ourselves to today's state of affairs. The goals must be examined, proceeding from the current situation and prospects for the development of the forces and equipment for conducting combat operations of states as potential participants in a military confrontation.

In our view, three main strategic missions objectively exist which each opposing side must strive to accomplish in modern war, regardless of its scale. The first is the suppression of the enemy's military-economic potential. Its priority is determined by the decisive impact of the military economy and the effective functioning of the most important military facilities on the course and outcome of the war. The second is repelling enemy aerospace attack. It is the opposite of the first mission and is important because of the effectiveness of air attack weapons and the number of nuclear assets. As a result, the threat of surprise missile-space weapons strikes will increase. Therefore, despite the well-known reduction of these offensive weapons, the development and deployment of antimissile defense systems is continuing. The third and final mission is defeat of enemy armed forces formations without which the goals of war, as a rule, cannot be attained.[2]

The fact that naval forces, being an organic component of the armed forces, participate in accomplishing practically all of the main missions of war by conducting combat operations in the sea and ocean theaters certainly does not require a separate examination. The number of missions, their size, and their level of accomplishment may be determined during the course of research while examining the operational-strategic model of war where the coordination of all the branches of the armed forces is considered. Optimal allocation of missions among them is a central problem of research at this stage of the work.

Balancing the forces *within the framework of defensive sufficiency* is conducted to define the required qualitative and quantitative composition of arms. Scientifically substantiated proposals on arms and armed forces reductions should be developed only on the basis of this research.

Work on blocks I–IV is the content of this first macro level of research, and work on blocks V–VII is the second level of research conducted according to the services of the armed forces.

Let us look at the specific content of this research using the Navy as an example (Fig. 8.2). The Navy carries out the general missions indicated above by accomplishing a number of specific partial missions in certain areas and against a specific enemy. Therefore, to determine the required composition of naval arms, we need to imagine those conditions in which the Navy's forces will operate and describe them within the framework of these operational-tactical models. In the process, they must not contain all of the details which, for instance, are discussed during the planning of an operation by staff. We require only the analog of the probable situation, which reproduces only those characteristics of the process of combat at sea on which the required composition of personnel and equipment substantially depends.

Thus the partial combat missions and the techniques for accomplishing them, which are described in the operational-tactical models, serve as the primary and initial precondition for defining needs in weapons for armed combat. Mathematical relationships between the missions and required resources are worked out within the framework of these models. Other methods of determining the required composition of the Navy are employed, for example, empirical, expert, and so on. Various factors of the combat situation on which the qualitative and quantitative composition of naval arms substantially depend are the parameters for calculations.

The selection indicators of effectiveness are the most important elements of modeling that determine the objectivity and practical acceptability of the quantitative assessments. Because of their complexity, expert assessments or other methods are used that permit us to skillfully determine the dependence of the composition of men and equipment on the volume and level of the assigned missions that are being accomplished. It is important that this work be conducted within the framework of the systems approach relying on a single algorithm. That algorithm represents a hierarchical system of models of various levels that are interrelated by inputs and outputs. They permit us to conduct the gradual optimization and balance of the composition of naval arms within the framework of defensive sufficiency and existing treaty relations.

It is advisable to conduct optimization in two stages. First of all, the qualitative character of the arms is determined, that is, what has come to be labeled the qualitative makeup, and then the required quantity of arms (the quantitative makeup). In the process, one takes into account the trends toward their development, the scientific-technical capabilities of achieving desired parameters, and also treaty restrictions in this sphere. Mathematical models and expert assessments in this case permit us to imagine the overall character of future naval systems. But the quantitative makeup of armaments is determined by the requirements of combat at sea and by the country's economic capabilities. Depending on these requirements, the qualitative character of arms is finally described at the stage of substantiating the quantitative makeup of naval arms.

Optimization of arms for the sake of their limitation within the framework of sufficiency is an interactive process (a method of continuous approximations) during the course of which a balance of the makeup of the Navy is carried out while taking into account the fact that it is a part of the armed forces, accomplishes missions under different variations of the military-political situation, and in a diverse combat situation that requires a rational combination of strike and support systems. Moreover, the volume of missions and the levels of their resolution must be coordinated with economic capabilities and treaty obligations. Coordination of the Navy's missions and the appropriations allocated for its development plays a decisive role in this process.

The required makeup of naval forces balanced in this manner is essentially the combination of those forces that are on hand (while taking into account scrapping and modernization) and new naval weapons with which the Navy will be augmented. The total balance of the increase or reduction of the Navy will depend on the decisions made in treaties, along with the indicated military requirements and economic capabilities. A general algorithm of arms reductions, that is a consequence of attaining an overall coordinated military balance, may be required at the proposal formation stage. The methodology proposed above permits us to analyze the existing composition of the existing navy (N of Navy) with the goal of assessing the level of its sufficiency, validation of the level of development of its combat arms and the plans for their future improvement, and also the threshold of permissible reduction. This analysis consists of comparing the existing and required composition of the Navy to accomplish its missions, such as repelling aggression from the sea.

If the existing navy is less than what is required, that is, if the capabilities of our navy do not meet defensive requirements, proposals are developed for the reduction of the other side's navy in the areas of the world's oceans that are under review with the submission of required validations within the framework of the proposed methodology. If the other side does not think it is possible to accept these proposals, or if they are prepared to consider them only partially, a reallocation of missions among the services of our armed forces occurs with the goal of compensating for the inadequate composition of our navy—or of its corresponding reinforcement.

This is the general concept of scientific validation of the processes for determining the level of defensive sufficiency of the armed forces as a whole and their service in particular, on which arms reduction decisions must be based. Furthermore, approaches for the acceleration and scientific validation of the advisability of negotiations of naval force limitations, first of all between the United States and Russia, exist within the framework of this concept. However, as we have argued in Chapters 6 and 7, agreements on the limitation of some types of naval activity in certain areas of the world's oceans must precede that.

We understand that attempts to balance the Russian and U.S. navies based only on their composition are fruitless at the present time. On the one hand, this has been caused by the United States' unwillingness to utilize the systems approach to the examination of its Navy's missions within the total system of its own armed forces as this concept requires and, on the other hand, by its well-known position on a different mission and role for the navies of Russia.

While not denying the fairness of certain views on this issue, however, we cannot agree with attempts to completely exclude the U.S. naval component from the overall system of arms reduction negotiations. We think that after the successful START negotiations, after the well-known initiatives on eliminating tactical nuclear weapons, including on sea-based platforms, conditions are ripe for the initiation of negotiations on limitation of the zones of some types of activity of our navies. It is also time to begin laying the groundwork for possible naval arms reductions negotiations.

CONCLUSION

This proposed methodology can be used for both bilateral and multilateral talks. It is in the interest of all parties to prevent the militarization of the world's oceans. Despite the many obstacles, the United States and Russia should take the lead in this effort by at least studying the possibility of eventual negotiations leading to naval weapons reductions. Perhaps the proposed methodology can constitute the first topic for discussion by naval experts in both countries. This would be an important first step.

NOTES

1. The most recent official U.S. attempt in this vein was the *Report on the Bottom-Up Review* by Les Aspin, U.S. Secretary of Defense, October 1993 (Washington, D.C.: Department of Defense), p. 4, fig. 3 entitled "Methodology of the Bottom-Up Review."

2. These missions are outlined in Admiral of the Fleet of the Soviet Union Sergey Georgiyevich Gorshkov, ed., *The Navy: Its Role, Prospects for Development, and Employment*, in Russian (Moscow: Voyenizdat, 1988).

9

NEW OPPORTUNITIES FOR U.S.-RUSSIAN NAVAL COOPERATION

Boris N. Makeev and Charles A. Meconis

> Cooperative measures must move away from attempts to control the actions of states to a sustained dialogue and mutual operations devised to create a common ground for peaceful relations.
> —Captains J. W. Moreland, USN, Fumio Ota, JMSDF, V. D. Pan'kov, RFN,
> *Naval Cooperation in the Pacific: Looking to the Future*

The end of the global confrontation at sea between the United States and Russia has raised the question of whether the two nations' navies will shift completely from a relationship of hostility to one of partnership. In fact, a number of successful steps in this direction have already been taken. At the multilateral level, unofficial talks among Russian, U.K., and U.S. naval officers and experts began in 1988 at Adderbury in England and have since led to official talks and even tripartite war games under the acronym RUKUS. The latest round of RUKUS talks took place in the simulation facilities at the Kuznetsov Naval Academy at St. Petersburg in April 1995. At the conclusion of the talks the three delegations signed an aide memoire in which they set out their intentions to continue the process toward developing the necessary manuals and procedures to facilitate actual operations between their fleets at sea.[1]

At the bilateral level, existing efforts at U.S.-Russian naval cooperation include:

- A visit by the U.S. Chief of Naval Operations to Russia in June 1992;
- A U.S. Navy ship visit and "Passage Exercise" (PASSEX) en route to Severomsk;
- The participation of Russian ships in the Persian Gulf for multinational operations in October 1992, January 1993, and December 1993;

- The second annual U.S.-Russian Navy Staff Talks in conjunction with the annual Incidents at Sea (INCSEA) Review in May 1993;
- A visit by Russian ships to New York City (for Fleet Week) in May 1993, and to Boston in July 1993, with accompanying PASSEXs;
- Russian participation in the BALTOPS 93 and BALTOPS 94 naval exercises, including a U.S. Navy ship visit to Baltiysk;
- The "Cooperation from the Sea" humanitarian relief exercise conducted near Vladivostok in June 1994;
- Russian-U.K.-U.S. Navy Cooperation Gaming (RUKUS 94) in May 1994;
- Reciprocal exchanges between the U.S. Naval Test Pilot School at Patuxent, Maryland and the Gromov Flight Research Institute at Zhukovsky, Russia in June and August 1994;
- An exchange of students between the U.S. Naval War College and the Kuznetsov Naval Academy in August 1994;
- A Russian visiting instructor scheduled to join the faculty at the U.S. Naval Postgraduate school in the fall 1994;
- The third annual U.S. Navy-Russian Navy Staff talks proposed for 1994.[2]

In addition to these official military-to-military naval contacts, a number of unofficial dialogues have produced a series of proposals for U.S.-Russian naval cooperation. Several meetings have been sponsored by the Center for International Security and Arms Control at Stanford University. Among their many suggestions for cooperation, they recommend that the two navies:

- Establish a joint exercise/operations team to develop joint operating procedures for bilateral or multilateral operations;
- Conduct Joint Sail Pacific. This operation is envisioned as a small-scale U.S.-Russian Navy force that would circumnavigate the Pacific Rim conducting both humanitarian and small-scale exercises with Pacific states;
- Address residual issues pertaining to UNCLOS III, such as the rules governing the demarcations of baselines and the transit rights of warships through the territorial waters of another state;
- Improve coordination of intelligence efforts, focusing on dissemination of oceanographic, hydrographic, and meteorological data;
- Develop uniform naval Standard Operating Procedures (SOPs) and Rules of Engagement (ROE);
- Coordinate mutual resupply efforts to sustain ships and aircraft at sea in the vicinity of conflict regions or during naval combat operations;
- Promulgate standard HF, VHF, and UHF frequencies for the exclusive use of naval forces.[3]

We must answer two questions before we examine ways in which even greater U.S. and Russian naval cooperation might be developed. First, are there objective reasons for such cooperation? Second, how do existing conditions effect those rationales?

Some earlier efforts to examine these questions were clearly still affected by the recent Cold War past. From the U.S. side, for example, even among its advocates, naval cooperation was seen as a possible means to "preempt Russian interest in traditional forms of naval arms control,"[4] while one of Russia's objectives was said to be "to exercise influence and leverage upon U.S. naval activism in the future, by either/both joining the United States in multilateral naval operations or/and seeing to it that a 'U.N. pennant' sits astride as a means of constraint."[5] Meanwhile, some in Russia remain worried that the United States is still attempting "to achieve military and strategic superiority through naval forces which could be used to bring political and economic pressure to bear."[6]

As we see it from the viewpoint of late 1995, opportunities for our countries' closer naval cooperation have grown as the military-political positions of each vis-à-vis the international scene began to parallel each other. Russia and the United States now face similar military threats as we enter the twenty-first century. We both "grapple with the continuation of conflicts fueled by ethnic tension, border disputes, and regional rivalries" and face "transnational threats posed by arms proliferation and international terrorism, crime, and narcotics trafficking."[7] Our responses to these threats are likely to be similar in many cases. The national interests of both countries now largely coincide in a new, multipolar world.

Those interests include: the survival of our countries as free and independent states; the promotion of our countries' economic well-being; and the construction of international relations that guarantee stability and security by promoting human rights and political freedoms through the development of democratic institutions and by promoting sustainable development in a free and open world economy.[8]

Of course, even the best of partners will have their differences, as, for example, has been the case with the United States and some of its NATO allies over the years. The United States and Russia continue to have differences in their approach to the civil war in the former Yugoslavia, and in particular to events in some of the former states of the Soviet Union in what is referred to in Russia as the "near abroad."[9]

We should also point out that the democratic liberties and institutions so characteristic of the United States are just beginning to be cultivated in Russia. But Russian national interests coincide in this respect with those of the United States through a determination to rid Russia of its totalitarian heritage and to build a new legal state modeled on western-style democracy.

Again, our problems and security options coincide as a result of these common interests. The demise of a bipolar world greatly minimizes the possibility of global armed conflict, but the possibility of increased *regional* conflict has taken its place. Potential sources of such conflicts might include: ethnic, religious, and territorial hostilities; arms proliferation; international terrorism and piracy; uncontrolled economic competition; the illegal drug trade; and human rights violations in some countries or regions.

Analysis reveals that navies have been involved in most regional crises, conflicts, and wars that have taken place during the latter half of the twentieth century.[10] The U.S. Navy constantly reiterates its long history of involvement: "Since 1945, U.S. naval forces have been involved in more than 280 crises, including 75 since 1976, and 80% of all post-World War II incidents."[11] As this is being written, international naval forces are maintaining blockades in the Adriatic and in the Persian Gulf. It is also true that the United States and Russia have been—and will remain—the great sea states of our time. Both will attempt to maintain significant naval forces consistent with their national interests, in spite of numerical reductions imposed by economic necessity.

Existing levels of cooperation between our two navies to date have largely been restricted to information exchanges, military-to-military contacts such as ship visits, joint research, and search-and-rescue operations, and a few small joint exercises, as listed above. As we see it, it is time to explore several *new* opportunities for naval operations cooperation within the context of the new multipolar world.

JOINT U.S.-RUSSIAN PARTICIPATION IN MULTILATERAL NAVAL OPERATIONS

U.S. and Russian naval forces have already operated together in the Persian Gulf to monitor Iraq's compliance with U.N. resolutions. Thus there is an important precedent for the notion that Russian and U.S. naval forces might perform joint missions to deter and retaliate against threats to regional peace and security, to enforce blockades against states that threaten regional security, to retaliate against terrorism, to rescue hostages and evacuate refugees from areas of conflict, to provide humanitarian aid to victims of regional conflicts and natural calamities, to otherwise maintain order in regions threatened by conflicts, and to protect ships from piracy and other actions that violate either nation's military and economic interests. Each of these tasks demand that military specialists, scientists, and others conduct a thorough investigation of and planning for possible joint actions.

A number of confidence-building measures will help prepare the U.S. and Russian fleets for cooperative action. We should pursue even greater exchanges of information concerning each navy's structure and composition, mission, places of deployment, and communications capabilities. Dialogues between each navy's leading specialists should take place to determine our mutual interests in given regions. Combined exercises should be planned, and preparations should be made for their execution. Each of these measures should operate from the perspective that they are to build U.S.-Russian linkages, to establish workgroups, and to promote future mutual exercises and operations.

These relationships would also promote the systematic organization of multinational naval forces for the purpose of regional peacekeeping and peace-enforcement operations. The Persian Gulf experience revealed that peace-enforcing operations entail high expenditure and demand large numbers of personnel. As the most powerful naval states, the participation of the Russian and U.S. navies can promote a more efficient organization and operation of peacekeeping and peace-enforcing naval groups. The presence of our forces in these operations tends to prevent difficulties that result from the often divergent interests of other member states' forces.

Had such measures been taken before the Persian Gulf operations, the subsequent Russian-U.S. linkages would perhaps have facilitated better organization of those efforts; better tactical and operational preparation of this multinational force; better coordination of action between different states' vessels and aircraft; and the better definition of staff requirements, the order of staff recruitment, and the order of their command.

The Issue of Command and Control

The two most difficult questions concerning the establishment and deployment of multinational naval forces are the matters of financing them and their command and control. We are not experts in financial matters, so that topic will remain outside the scope of this work.

The issue of command and control is central, and difficult. In order to operate most efficiently, multinational naval forces should do so under one command. From Russia's standpoint, it is preferable to operate under the United Nations flag, despite recent U.N. failures. Several Russian proposals along these lines have been put forward in recent years. Russian representatives at an Institute for Defense Analyses seminar in 1992 reportedly stated: "A step-by-step process is desirable. It might begin by a simple division of naval responsibilities among states, reflected in joint missions and operations. It might take the form of establishing *ad hoc* joint naval forces under U.N. and/or CSCE auspices. It might assume the status of a standing naval force under a joint U.N. command."[12]

In recent years a number of western analysts have also begun to examine (or rather, reexamine) the possibility of some sort of United Nations role in maritime peacekeeping and peace enforcement. The consensus seems to be that the idea is at least worth exploring, even though there are very many difficulties involved. For example, British analyst Michael Pugh concludes his study of this matter in the following terms:

> The obstacles to the development of multinational maritime forces are considerable. They relate to appropriate politico-military structures for different tasks,

international law, resources, interoperability, and financing. Obviously, too, the political and practical problems of reviving the [U.N.] M[ilitary] S[taff] C[ommittee] in order to re-establish a full-fledged standing U.N. naval force to engage in deterrence and peace enforcement may prove intractable. And unless there is a determined effort to find a wide consensus about the legitimating principles a breakout from traditional peacekeeping would be counter-productive. . . . [Nevertheless] for a range of multinational maritime roles, some of which lie outside traditional peacekeeping, there is scope for new thinking, flexibility, and development.[13]

It is important to recall that this notion is not really new, nor is it solely Russian in origin. In the first few years of the U.N.'s existence, a Military Staff Committee was established, as called for by the Charter, and began to plan for a standing U.N. military force.[14] By 1947 there was even something approaching a consensus on the size and nature of a U.N. naval force, which was to consist of 3 battleships, 6 carriers (4 fleet, 2 light), 12 cruisers, 33 destroyers, 64 frigates, 24 minesweepers, 14 submarines, and assault lift for 4 brigade groups (16,000 men).[15] Unfortunately, the onset of the Cold War brought this planning to a halt. The U.N. Military Staff Committee continued to exist in name, but ceased to play any meaningful role, right to the present. Now that the Cold War is over, it is time to reexamine this issue.

Recent failures by the United Nations in Somalia and the Balkans have led to growing skepticism about its effectiveness. Consequently, prospects for U.N. command of naval peacekeeping or peace-enforcement operations are dim at this time. Many naval analysts in the West doubt that there will ever come a time when such a development would be feasible, much less desirable.

Still, it might be useful to theorize about the issue. As we see it, concerning command and control in the case of multilateral maritime operations directly under the U.N. aegis, the overall structure should probably consist of a recon-stituted U.N. Military Staff Committee, as mentioned above. There would be a Commander-in-Chief of U.N. naval forces, followed by regional commanders, and so on, down to the squadron level. At the same time, squadrons and indi-vidual ships would maintain autonomy and flexibility in order to carry out far-flung regional missions. Of course, such multinational staff levels would not be constant. In our opinion, these would rise and fall depending on the task at hand. However, the top command and general structure would remain con-stant.

We envision that U.N. naval squadrons would have a requisite complement of destroyers and frigates, as well as helicopter-and-troop-bearing landing vessels, and support vessels. Asia-Pacific and Indian Ocean regional squadrons would also require contingents of aircraft.

As their missions already coincide to a considerable degree with the aim of U.N. peacekeeping forces—that of regional response and stabilization—some U.S. Forward Presence forces could be integrated into each regional squadron.

Such an integration would very likely have a positive political resonance in the regions themselves, and at the same time it could relieve financial burdens on the U.S. Navy. Such a partial integration would not prevent the U.S. Navy from taking independent action to defend U.S. national interests directly if the need arose.

In the event of an escalating regional conflict, submarine forces, minesweeping vessels, and land-based naval aviation could reinforce squadrons already in the region. Russia could be a primary source of these reinforcements. This is especially true in response to conflicts on the Eurasian continent.

Admiral Felix Gromov, Commander-in-Chief of the Russian Navy, clearly expressed his attitude toward Russia's involvement in multinational operations in "Russia at Sea," which appeared in the April 15, 1993 issue of *Rossijskaya Gazeta*. He declared that one of the Russian Navy's tasks would be "to carry out its obligations to the world community on peace-preserving missions." He also said that the Pacific Fleet's role in such operations would increase: "The Pacific Fleet on its own, or together with multinational forces, would be ready to carry out peacekeeping and other missions under the U.N. aegis." This position was recently affirmed by Admiral Valentin Y. Selivanov, Chief of the Main Naval Staff of the Russian Navy, who wrote: "Realizing the importance of enforcing law and order at sea, ensuring the safety of shipping, and expanding cooperation in the naval field, the Command of the Russian Navy is well aware of the responsibility of Russia as a major naval power, and plans its activity proceeding from this fact."[16]

The fact that the United States and Russia might take *leading* roles in recruiting for multinational naval forces does *not* mean that they would monopolize this process. United Nations squadrons would be formed from an international base with many different countries' ships and aircraft participating. The U.N. entity responsible for the organization of multinational navies would evidently appoint squadron commanders on the basis of professionalism and personal qualities, irrespective of the quantity of forces offered to the U.N. by their state.

The organizing entity above is envisioned as the Military Staff Committee operating under the direction of the U.N. Security Council. The Commander-in-Chief of U.N. naval forces and staff would function under its aegis.

We may categorize the probable activities of U.N. naval forces as those roles that monitor, deter, and restrain potential aggressors. United Nations forces fulfilling a monitoring role would seek to identify and report regional violations of international law, the violation of U.N. sanctions, use of military force at sea, terrorist acts, and piracy. Such forces should be equipped with high-speed vessels carrying military-patrol helicopters.

Deterrent forces' activities might include the monitoring of seagoing antagonists; physical intervention between such antagonists; and demonstrations of force to potential aggressors, such as the landing of troops. These and other means of force would be used in order to contain conflict in its earliest stage.

U.N. naval forces might operate jointly with multinational land forces to quickly contain, stabilize, and defuse regional conflicts. Such actions might include delivery of humanitarian aid, blockade enforcement, defense of sea navigation, and even troop landings and sea-launched missile, artillery, and aviation attacks. There are other "nontraditional" roles that could be played by U.N. naval forces, such as environmental monitoring and the enforcement of international environmental agreements at sea.

We realize that under the best of circumstances, the development of a U.N. naval force would take considerable time to work out. U.S. and Russian analysts and naval specialists must continue work to answer specific issues regarding the formation and use of such multinational peacekeeping forces.

Unfortunately, it is clear that at this time the U.S. experience in Somalia, the Balkans, and other U.N. operations has caused considerable skepticism about further U.S. involvement in operations under the U.N. aegis. After a year-long policy review, President Clinton signed Presidential Decision Directive 25 (PDD-25) entitled "U.S. Policy on Reforming Multilateral Peace Operations" on May 3, 1994. This document laid down a *very* strict set of conditions for U.S. participation in peacekeeping and peace-enforcement operations. In summary, they require that:

- Participation advances U.S. interests;
- Risks to U.S. personnel must be considered acceptable;
- Personnel, funds, and other resources are available;
- U.S. participation is deemed necessary for the operation's success;
- The role of U.S. forces is tied to clear objectives;
- An endpoint to U.S. participation can be identified;
- The U.S. public and Congress support the operation;
- Command and control arrangements are acceptable.[17]

A workshop on PDD-25 held at the U.S. National Defense University in June 1994 concluded that the directive "contains criteria for peace operations that, if strictly applied, could result in decisions to avoid U.S. participation in nearly all military operations."[18] We agree with that troubling conclusion. It is particularly disappointing that PDD-25 states that the United States "does not support a standing [U.N.] army, nor will we earmark specific U.S. military units for participation in U.N. operations." There appears to be little hope for a naval force under U.N. command at this time.

However, the current U.S. reluctance to engage in operations under the U.N. aegis does not mean that increasing U.S.-Russian naval cooperation is impossible. Now that Russia has entered into the NATO "Partnership for

Peace" agreement, Russian participation in NATO's Standing Naval Forces (STANAVFORS) in the Atlantic and the Mediterranean should become possible.

Two other critical maritime regions could well present opportunities for further cooperation: the Persian Gulf and the Western Pacific. Both regions contain sea-lanes that are vital to the global economy and therefore to international stability. At present there are no standing multilateral naval forces in either region. Both the United States and Russia maintain naval forces in those regions. We believe that both countries should take the lead in exploring the possibility of establishing standing multilateral naval forces in those regions, under an appropriate regional aegis. In Southeast Asia, for example, the Association of Southeast Asian Nations (ASEAN) has recently established a Regional Forum to address security issues. Maritime security will undoubtedly be high on the future agendas of that body, and now is the time to begin exploring the possibility of establishing a multilateral standing naval force in the region. The participation of Russian and U.S. Navy ships in such a force might help to prevent the perception of a "power vacuum" in the region, and thereby reduce the possibility of a naval arms race there.

Finally, of course, there are many bilateral forms of naval cooperation that remain to be explored, ranging from oceanic research to full-scale joint exercises. However, in terms of a genuinely *new* opportunity, we turn to the realm of strategic deterrence.

U.S.-RUSSIAN BILATERAL NAVAL STRATEGIC NUCLEAR COOPERATION

However paradoxical it may still seem at this time, we believe that *eventually*, cooperation vis-à-vis the operation of strategic nuclear-armed submarines (SSBNs) must be a significant element of future U.S. and Russian naval relations.

The irony of this situation is that we are looking to build cooperative relations with the objects of past antagonisms For over thirty years, U.S. SSBNs have been set to assault Russian territory, and Russian SSBNs have been readied to deliver nuclear blows against the United States. Yet the prevention of nuclear war was the aim of this mutual menace. These opposing forces therefore share a common objective, and opportunities thus exist for mutual cooperation. No one expects that Russia and the United States will quickly arrive at the same level of strategic cooperation that already exists between the United States and Great Britain, or even to the considerably lesser degree of cooperation that exists between the United States and France. But cooperation is now possible, and should be pursued.

In fact, the beginning of such cooperation has already occurred via the START agreements on the approximate parity of a reduced number of SSBN nuclear warheads. From our perspective, however, these agreements do not by themselves guarantee the primary aim of nuclear weapons deployment in a strategy of deterrence: the mutual ability to retaliate against nuclear attack. We consider the parity of nuclear warheads necessary but believe that parity itself is insufficient.

The next step of cooperation is dictated by the fact that strategic nuclear security demands that SSBNs remain safe within, and able to deploy their missiles from, attack positions. Strategic nuclear security therefore in turn dictates that these weapons remain able to survive antisubmarine warfare. The survival of an SSBN depends a great deal on its defensive combat capability against antisubmarine warfare forces.

The desire of each side to improve its SSBNs' defensive stability is quite understandable. Assuming this objective by both sides, perhaps the United States and Russia could coordinate efforts to assure such defensive security. This would pave the way for a gradual move from deterrence-through-mutual-assured-destruction (MAD) strategies, and even go beyond the current U.S. "mutual assured safety" nuclear posture (MAS), toward the strategic *partnership* espoused by our countries' leaders, and embodied in the first step of Russia's entry into the NATO "Partnership for Peace" agreement.[19]

For such a partnership to develop further, we must overcome the Cold War's legacy and shift our focus from the strict enumeration and evaluation of material nuclear capabilities—the so-called "bean-counting" and "war-winning" approaches of the past. Together, we must view our reduced numbers of intercontinental ballistic missiles, SSBNs, and heavy bombers *strictly* as the political means for *preventing* war, not the material means for starting or winning it. It follows that there is no reason to maintain past levels of secrecy regarding the continued development of these means. This is particularly true concerning their capabilities for defensive combat in patrol positions.

If we wish to forge a genuine strategic partnership, the situation demands greater transparency from *both* sides regarding our SSBNs' defensive stability. Such an exchange of information will not damage their combat efficiency, as some analysts believe. But it will help maintain equilibrium between strategic naval nuclear forces as a guarantee against nuclear war.

Raising our SSBNs' defensive stability demands consideration of both operational-tactical and military-technical issues. "Operational-tactical" issues refer to the concealed deployment of SSBNs, their operations within a mission area, their security with regard to antisubmarine forces, the security of their basing system, and the growth of their operational efficiency. "Military-technical" issues include the development of construction and tactical-technical elements of SSBNs: their maximum subsurface speed, maximum operational depth, stealth, countermeasures and defensive arms, electronic equipment, and so on.

Operational-Tactical Issues

Operational-tactical aspects contribute to an SSBN's combat stability by enabling its secret deployment into a given region. A detected submarine has little chance of fulfilling its mission. Successful deployment of SSBNs can be compromised by well-organized reconnaissance of their basing points, followed by searches along possible routes of travel to areas of operation and by searches in those areas proper. Therefore, mutual SSBN defensive stability could be cultivated through agreements abandoning reconnaissance of base areas. These areas are well known to both sides. We also advocate some limits on "strategic" antisubmarine searches in areas of mutual SSBN operation, under a formal treaty.

With goodwill and understanding, it would not be difficult to sign agreements limiting reconnaissance around SSBN bases. Such limitations would restrict adversarial activity within identified areas along each side's coast. These agreements would be relatively easy to observe and would not damage a navy's defensive capability outside of its strategic component.

It would be much more difficult to limit antisubmarine activity within possible SSBN operational areas. Several questions inevitably arise. How do we differentiate between antisubmarine activities that threaten SSBNs from those that do not, and how do we monitor agreements that limit the former? Will discussions to form limitations agreements actually jeopardize SSBN defensive stability as operational zones are revealed? Does Freedom of Navigation doctrine void the total exclusion of antisubmarine forces from any given SSBN area of operation under treaty and, if so, what limits shall be set on forces that can enter such a treaty zone? Is it possible to prevent the introduction of restricted forces into a treaty zone in time of crisis and, if so, is there any sense to make arrangements about the limitation of the activity of the antisubmarine forces there?

We have tried to offer thorough answers to these questions in Chapter 7 of this work and in other articles, so we will not repeat the discussion here, other than to say that we believe that a mutual agreement to limit some forms of "strategic" ASW operations is both negotiable and verifiable. Thus discussion and agreement between the United States and Russia to assure the operational-tactical defensive stability of SSBNs is timely, important, and achievable. Such agreements will be an important step to broadening our countries' cooperation at sea.

Military-Technical Issues

Military-technical issues are also central to assuring SSBNs' defensive stability. Improvements in the means of SSBN construction and modernization, and the further development of submarine technologies and weaponry proper, will continue to play an important role in nuclear deterrence.

If we consider ourselves partners moving from a relationship of mutual strategic deterrence to one of eventual strategic partnership, the exchange between our countries of such technologies and means would seem a reasonable activity. It would strengthen the overall capacities of SSBNs as nuclear deterrents. It would also eventually help build cooperative efforts to deal with third countries' possible nuclear threats.

Moreover, such cooperation may help legitimate democratic forces and institutions within Russia. Communist and Fascist factions oppose Russia's investment in these institutions and in relations with western democracies. They draw power from rhetoric that condemns the United States and other western nations as imperialist "monsters" bent on the subversion of Russian sovereignty. These factions would be dealt a heavy blow if such rhetoric was contradicted. Cooperation and information exchange with regard to SSBNs might help deal such a blow.

Such an exchange of ideas, technology, and production also presents both our countries with economic opportunities. Moreover, western analysts are well aware that in certain areas of submarine construction, Russian designs are more advanced. U.S. naval analyst Norman Polmar, for example, states that "[Russian] building techniques are sophisticated—they have long been welding titanium and HY-130 steel, which is more difficult to work with than the HY-100 steel that is giving the *Seawolf* program massive problems. Their designs are innovative; their boats' speeds and operating depths continue to surpass those of Western submarines; and, their boats' reduced signatures continue to surprise Western intelligence analysts."[20] So there would also be an element of scientific benefit.

Thus the initiation of military-technical cooperation is as necessary and timely as that of operational-tactical cooperation. This primarily entails mutual scientific and technological efforts to improve SSBNs' defensive stability, particularly with respect to their stealth and invulnerability to ASW weapons.

Russia's main efforts in this area have been toward dampening submarines' noise and other physical fields that might reveal their position underwater. Joint efforts might research optimal hull design; effective placement of rudders and other appendages; the dampening of machine and screw noises; the design of new low-noise rotor, magnetic, and waterjet engines; improved noise insulation of inner-vessel motors; and the synthesis of surface coatings to help foil hydrolocational detection.

Cooperation on signature dampening technologies for thermal, radioactive, magnetic, and gravitational fields would be limited to the exchange of theoretic information. This is due to a general lack of research in this area. Cooperation concerning advances in the field of detection devices would have to remain limited, as such projects are classified as secret by both countries.

The defensive stability of the missile submarines mainly depends in the first place on the development of their sonar, their radar, and their means of radiocommunication. Cooperation in the field of sonar might aim toward increasing the hydro-acoustic equipment's overall performance and operational range, as well as improvement in the means of object recognition, the automation of hydro-acoustic information processing, and the development of reliable submarine sound-signaling systems. This is admittedly a sensitive field, and both sides might object to full cooperation. Some western analysts note that Russia might be ahead in this area.[21]

The exchange of admissible information on research and development work concerning radiocommunications means for command and control of SSBNs on patrol could constitute a meaningful level of cooperation. Such communications means have the key role in the operations of strategic deterrence. Care would certainly have to be taken to ensure that such an information exchange would not weaken either nation's capacity to retaliate against a nuclear attack by allowing interference with VLF and ELF communications from land-based transmitters and from airborne transmitters such as the U.S. TACAMO system.

Nevertheless, we believe that the United States and Russia could cooperate to improve radioelectronic systems' capacity to receive long-wave transmissions at greater depths. Increases in such capacity would reduce the SSBNs' risk of discovery incurred as a result of forced surface or near-surface communications. We might also cooperate in the improvement of rapid-acting receivers and transmission devices associated with "burst" type broadcasting; the development of special radio buoys and antennas designed to receive and transmit after their submarine contacts' departure; and the development of radio-hydroacoustic buoys enabling communications with aircraft.

An important area of possible partnership within this area must be the development of satellite communications and other systems that increase the concealability and stability of submerged SSBNs' radio communications. Scientific-technical cooperation should look toward improvements in the field of SSBNs' performance tolerances. This work would look to develop greater operational depths and maximum speeds for submarines. Other research should focus on improvements in self-defense arms and electronic countermeasures.

An adversary's ability to detect and then successfully attack SSBNs underwater diminishes as those submarines' depth tolerances increase. Conversely, those submarines benefit from an improved capacity to detect hostile vessels. Increased speed tolerances in the same submarines—notwithstanding their negative impact on other technical defenses—improves such vessels' capacity to evade detection and subsequent pursuit by antisubmarine forces. Self-defensive arms and various countermeasures enable retaliation should a crisis arise.

Problems of metallurgy, structural mechanics, and engineering dominate attempts to increase SSBN diving tolerances. Information exchange in these areas would be very useful, particularly with reference to the application of nonmetal materials (fiberglass, plastics, etc.) in hull and associated elements' construction.

Increased speed tolerances will depend on advances in two areas: improved powerplant efficiency and improved hull hydrodynamics—the reduction of water's inertial resistance against the moving submarine. Current conventional ideas for improving hull hydrodynamics will soon be exhausted. A prospective direction for U.S.-Russian cooperation would be to engage in hydrodynamic development practically and theoretically based in *biotechnical* research. Russian biologists and hydrodynamic specialists have began research aimed at converting turbulent (vortical) waterflow on hulls' water boundary layer into laminated (stratified) flow by studying the high-speed capabilities of dolphins and other sea animals. Conversion to laminated-flow hulls would sharply reduce the amount of water resistance submarines have to compensate for.

A list of constructive and technical means to improve the defensive stability of SSBNs would not be complete without mention of defensive weapons development. Such weapons are the torpedoes and cruise missiles necessary for counterattacking hunter/killer submarines and other antisubmarine vessels.

Torpedo improvements refer to the weapons' increased capacity for effective and specialized surface and subsurface target acquisition, general guidance systems improvement, higher velocities, increases in operational depths and ranges, and reductions in such weapons' mass.

Areas needing cooperation with regard to cruise missiles include range increases in missile-torpedo trajectory, target specialization, improvement in on-board flight/trajectory control computers, development of trajectory correction systems to deal with target mobility, increases in warhead lethality, and the development of perfect self-guidance systems for antisubmarine weapons.

Even during the Cold War, there was cooperation between the United States and Russia to equip early missile-carrying submarines with antiaircraft artillery to safeguard those vessels from antisubmarine aircraft. The decision to mutually undertake this task arose in reaction to a paradoxical threat to both our nations: in a time of crisis, a lone airplane could threaten a missile submarine fulfilling its mission of global strategic deterrence, and thus initiate a nuclear tragedy.[22]

Our common efforts in all preceding areas will help increase the defensive stability of SSBNs carrying out missions of nuclear deterrence and subsequently strengthen global strategic security. Until the time comes when such weapons are no longer necessary to preserve peace, we must work to together to see that they are used only for that purpose.

CONCLUSION

U.S.-Russian cooperation at sea will strengthen the confidence our two nations have in each other, positively influence the common international situation, and serve as the mighty restraining factor against regional aggression and third countries' nuclear threats in our multipolar world. Now is the time to create and utilize new opportunities for cooperation, both in preventing regional conflicts and in preventing nuclear war.

In addition to approving of the existing proposals for U.S.-Russian naval cooperation outlined at the beginning of this chapter, we have made the following proposals toward that end.

U.S.-Russian Participation in Multilateral Naval Operations

- Conduct joint studies on the possibility of naval peacekeeping and peace-enforcement activities under U.N. command;
- Allow Russian participation in NATO's Standing Naval Forces under the Partnership for Peace relationship;
- Explore the possibility of U.S.-Russian involvement in multilateral naval forces in the Persian Gulf and the Western Pacific under an appropriate regional aegis.

U.S.-Russian Bilateral Naval Strategic Nuclear Cooperation

- The United States and Russia should go beyond the level of cooperation embodied in the START agreements and coordinate efforts to assure the defensive security of their SSBNs by:
- Negotiating limits on strategic ASW operations as outlined in Chapter 7;
- Beginning to exchange information on the operational-tactical issues concerning SSBNs including deployment, defensive security, and basing;
- Beginning to exchange information on the design and construction of SSBNs, their defensive weapons systems, both active and passive, and the communications and command and control systems.

NOTES

1. The authors are grateful to Eric Grove, Deputy Director of the Centre for Security Studies at the University of Hull for this RUKUS update in a letter on 10 May, 1995. Grove took part in the very earliest rounds of the talks at Adderbury and has remained involved throughout. He notes that the most recent tripartite war game had as its scenario joint protection, under a U.N. mandate, of a jointly owned maritime oilfield in a third party conflict. Common rules of engagement were drawn up for the combined force.

2. This list of official Navy-to-Navy contacts between the United States and Russia was provided to the authors on August 29, 1994 by Lieutenant Gary Shiffman, USN, of

the NATO, Europe, Russia Branch (N524) of the Operations, Plans, and Political-Military Affairs Directorate (N31/N52) of the Office of the U.S. Chief of Naval Operations. Further descriptions of these measures and additional unofficial efforts at U.S.-Russian naval cooperation measures and proposals can be found in the following, listed in chronological order: Captains J. W. Moreland, USN, Fumio Otya, JMSDF, and V. D. Pan'kov, RFN, *Naval Cooperation in the Pacific: Looking to the Future,* (Stanford University: Center for International Security and Arms Control, February, 1993); Admiral V. I. Aleksin, RFN, "We're Ready When You Are," U.S. Naval Institute *Proceedings*, Vol. 119, No. 3 (March 1993), pp. 54-57; Lieutenant Commander Melissa Harrington, USN, "Comments and Discussion," U.S. Naval Institute *Proceedings*, Vol. 119, No. 6 (June 1993), p. 28; Admiral Valentin Y. Selivanov, RFN, "A Navy's Job: The Role of the Russian Navy in the System of International Security and Cooperation in the Field of Naval Armaments," *Naval Forces*, Vol. 15, No. 2 (1994), pp. 22-24, 29-31; Captain 2nd Rank Alexander S. Skaridov, RFN, Commander Daniel D. Thompson, USN, and Lieutenant Commander Yang Zhiqun, PLA(N), *Asian-Pacific Maritime Security: New Possibilities for Naval Cooperation?* (Stanford University: Center for International Security and Arms Control, February 1994).

3. Moreland, Pan'kov, and Otya, *Naval Cooperation in the Pacific*, pp. 116-17; Skaridov, Thompson, and Zhiqun, *Asian-Pacific Maritime Security: New Possibilities for Naval Cooperation?*, pp. 15-22. We have listed only a small portion of the large number of suggestions in these reports. Several others have already been put into action, such as the conducting of a joint disaster relief operation in Alaska.

4. Thomas P. M. Barnett, with Floyd D. Kennedy, Jr., *Redefining U.S.-Soviet Naval Ties in the 1990s: The Opportunity for Constructive Engagement* (Alexandria, Va.: Center for Naval Analyses, November 1991), p. 5.

5. James L. Lacy, *A Different Equation: Naval Issues and Arms Control after 1991* (Alexandria, Va.: Institute for Defense Analyses, Paper P2768, December 1993), p. 104.

6. Admiral Nikolai N. Amelko (Ret.), "Naval Arms Reductions: Prospects and Difficulties," paper presented to the "Third International Conference on the Change of Soviet Military Policy and the Two Koreas: Nuclear Issues and Arms Control," Center for American and Soviet Studies, Dankook University, Seoul, Korea, November 4-5, 1991, p. 2.

7. *Director of Naval Intelligence Posture Statement 1994* (Suitland, Md: U.S. Office of Naval Intelligence, May 1994), p. 1. For a similar Russian statement, see Selivanov, "A Navy's Job," p. 22.

8. The most recent official statement of the U.S. national security strategy is *A National Security Strategy of Engagement and Enlargement* (Washington, D.C.: The White House, February 1995), 33 pp.

9. For an insightful overview of this issue from a "moderate-liberal" Russian perspective, cf. Alexei G. Arbatov, "Russia's Foreign Policy Alternatives," *International Security*, Vol. 18, No. 2 (Fall 1993), pp. 5-43. A recent highly acclaimed U.S. examination of the topic can be found in Daniel Yergin and Thane Gustafson, *Russia 2010 and What It Means for the World* (New York: Random House, 1993).

10. Cf. James Cable, *Navies in Violent Peace* (London: MacMillan, 1989); Ken Booth, *Law, Force and Diplomacy at Sea* (London: Allen & Unwin, 1985).

11. *Naval Warfare: Naval Doctrine Publication 1* (Washington, D.C.: Department of the Navy, March 28, 1994), p. 10.

12. Barbara Bicksler and James L. Lacy, *After the Fall: Russian Perspectives on Security and Arms Control* (Alexandria, Va.: Institute for Defense Analyses Document D-1141, March 1992), p. 13.

13. Michael C. Pugh, *Multinational Maritime Forces: A Breakout from Traditional Peacekeeping?* (Southampton: Mountbatten Centre for International Studies, University of Southampton, July 1992), p. 17. Other studies on the topic of a naval role for the U.N. include: Michael C. Pugh, *Maritime Peacekeeping: Scope for Deep Blue Berets?* Peace Research Centre Working Paper 119, Research School of Pacific Studies, Australian National University, 1992; Gwyn Prins, "The United Nations and Peacekeeping in the Post Cold War World: The Case of Naval Power," *Bulletin of Peace Proposals,* Vol. 22, No. 2 (June 1991), pp. 133-55; Michael Vlahos, "A Global Naval Force: Why Not?" in U.S. Naval Institute *Proceedings,* Vol. 118, No. 3 (March 1992), pp. 40-44; Charles A. Meconis and Michael Wallace, "A Modest Proposal for a U.N. Naval Peacekeeping Force," Institute for Global Security Studies Working Paper, 1991.

14. For a concise review of this early U.N. history, cf. Eric Grove, "U.N. Armed Forces and the Military Staff Committee: A Look Back," *International Security,* Vol. 17, No. 4 (Spring 1993), pp. 172-182.

15. Annex to *Overall Strength of the United Nations Armed Forces, Report by the Joint Planning (JP) Staff,* JP (47) 159, p. 6, paragraph 19.

16. Selivanov, "A Navy's Job," p. 22.

17. This summary was prepared by Dr. William H. Lewis of the Institute for National Strategic Studies at the National Defense University, and is quoted in his paper, "Presidential Decision Directive-25: Multilateral Peace Operations," *INSS Strategic Forum*, No. 3 (July 1994), p. 2.

18. Lewis, " Presidential Decision Directive-25," p. 1.

19. Paul Ames, "Russia Now Partner with Ex-foe NATO: Pact Ends Decades of Animosity," *Seattle Times,* June 22, 1994, p. A1. The term "Mutual Assured Safety" was first employed by U.S. Secretary of Defense William Perry in a press conference announcing the release of the new U.S. *Nuclear Posture Review* on September 22, 1994, p. 3.

20. Norman Polmar, "Comments and Discussion," U.S. Naval Institute *Proceedings,* Vol. 120, No. 7 (July 1994), p. 16.

21. James L. George, letter to the authors, November 14, 1994.

22. According to Dr. James J. Tritten, who researched this topic thoroughly in his book *Soviet Naval Forces and Nuclear Warfare: Weapons, Employment, and Policy* (Boulder, Colo.: Westview, 1986), there is no publicly available evidence to support this assertion by Dr. Makeev. Phone conversation with Dr. Meconis, September 8, 1994.

10

CONCLUSIONS AND PROPOSALS

Charles A. Meconis

> Sea power can no longer remain a matter of merely using and controlling the
> sea. It must also begin to include the ability to understand and protect the sea,
> and to do so for the benefit of the world at large, rather than just those who
> want to control it. Today, at the close of the twentieth century, we cannot afford
> anything less.
>
> —Luc Cuyvers, *Sea Power: A Global Journey*

The importance of the ocean to the health of our planet and those who live on
it is increasing as we approach the twenty-first century. Exploding population
and decreasing resources on land are literally pushing us into the ocean.

For the last fifty years the greatest threat to the world's oceans consisted of
the Cold War nuclear confrontation between the Soviet Union and the West.
Hundreds of nuclear-armed and propelled vessels stalked each other on and
under the world's oceans, playing cat-and-mouse to the point of collision.

That frightening situation has changed dramatically with the end of the
Cold War and the demise of the Soviet Union. Both the Russian and U.S.
navies are declining in size. If the current projections hold, by the end of the
century the U.S. Navy will decline from 452 major ships to 346 and the
Russian Navy from 522 to around 240.[1] Both navies are changing their maritime strategies in ways that downplay the declining possibility of confrontation, and facing up to the realities of the new multipolar post-Cold War world,
including declining budgets and regional adversaries. [2]

WHO CARES ANYMORE?

In an era of environmental concern, global warming, the declining seafood
catch, and the search for offshore resources have risen to the top of the ocean

agenda. Why, then, should anyone care anymore about the relationship between the U.S. and Russian navies?

The first answer is because they are there. For the foreseeable future the U.S. and Russian navies will remain the two largest and most powerful navies in the world, deploying hundreds of ships and thousands of nuclear weapons. If the peaceful and environmentally sustainable use and protection of the world's oceans is to be achieved, then those two navies must, with patience and foresight, definitively eradicate every remaining vestige of their once frightening Cold War rivalry and then proceed to become genuine partners in that task.

The second answer is that Moscow still cares. Even at the height of the old Soviet Union's naval power in the late 1980s, the U.S. Navy was a superior force. The collapse of the Soviet Union has led to a precipitous decline in Russian naval power. It is understandable that in these circumstances the Russian Federation is anxious to establish a new and friendly relationship with its powerful former adversary.

The third answer is that the world still cares. The Russian Navy may be largely confined to its bases these days, but Norway and Japan have not forgotten that it exists. In areas such as the Persian Gulf and Southeast Asia, the absence of either or both navies is simultaneously desired by some and feared by others. Now that the U.N. Law of the Sea has entered into effect, many of the world's nations with maritime interests are concerned about the militarization and the "Balkanization" of the ocean, and the world's two largest navies are an integral part of the big picture.

NAVAL ARMS CONTROL FOR ITS OWN SAKE?

For all these reasons, we believe that it is important for Russia and the United States to make the most of a number of new opportunities for U.S.-Russian naval cooperation. First we must seize the current opportunity to remove the last few Cold War "icebergs" still drifting in the world's oceans. In other words, we must engage in naval arms control. The very term "naval arms control" is controversial in the West. Throughout the Cold War, the U.S. Navy maintained a highly visible "Just Say No" attitude toward naval arms agreements with the Soviet Union,[3] and the demise of the U.S.S.R. is seen by some as evidence of the wisdom of that policy—and the end of further talk on the subject. Naval arms control is, in this view, simply another item in a long list of dubious political processes that have been "overtaken by events." If by "naval arms control" one means only formal, bilateral, negotiated agreements between the United States and the "Soviet Union" resulting in unfavorably lopsided major ship reductions or unrealistic operational restraints that affect one party unfairly—the U.S. Navy's preferred Cold War definition—then of course it is dead, along with the Soviet Union and the Cold War itself.

However, the issue of preventing or containing maritime conflict in the post-Cold War era is not dead. We are convinced that naval arms control in the *broad* sense can play an important role in that effort—and in creating a framework for U.S.-Russian naval cooperation and possibly even partnership.

We define "naval arms control" as any action, agreement, or statement, whether unilateral, bilateral, or multilateral in form, that reveals, restricts, restrains, or reduces the operations, capability, composition, structure, or size of any nation's naval forces for the purposes of preventing conflict, reducing damage should conflict occur, and reducing the cost of procuring and maintaining naval forces. By "naval" forces is meant both sea-based forces and those land-based forces that have sufficient reach to significantly affect naval activities, for example, strike aircraft and antiship missiles.

We envision a three-stage process in which the two navies and their governments agree first to a series of maritime confidence-building measures, second to certain carefully considered operational restraints, and finally, to reductions in naval weapons that will have to involve other major naval powers. In advocating this process, we have tried to face up to the many objections to naval arms control set forth during the Cold War.

The *Ghosts of Naval Arms Control Past* objection includes the controversial results of the major naval arms control agreements forged between the two world wars. We reject the contention that those agreements were total failures. They contributed to strengthening the U.S.-U.K. alliance, provided frameworks for mutual reductions when those were inevitable, and prevented the spending of considerable money on weapons systems that would have been obsolete by the time World War II began.

The *Island Nation vs. Continental Power Asymmetry* objection held that the United States was so much more dependent on maritime security than the Soviet Union that naval arms control was by definition disadvantageous to the West. This objection has truly been "overtaken by events." The democratic Russian Federation no longer seeks global parity in naval forces as a means of offsetting its weakness, nor is there any need for the United States to rapidly reinforce Europe given the withdrawal of Russian forces from eastern Europe. Both countries—and navies—have adopted new security strategies that call for a reassessment of recent naval arms control proposals.

Cold War era doubts about *Verification and Compliance* have also declined in salience. While neither of these issues can be overlooked, the combination of new technologies and Russia's new political openness toward on-site inspections, and so on, have gone a long way toward solving these problems. In the naval realm in particular, naval professionals on both sides have been extremely successful in implementing the Prevention of Incidents at Sea (INCSEA) Agreement.

We are not advocating naval "arms control for its own sake." The most typical argument against arms control in general has been that it is unattainable when needed and unnecessary when attainable. We stand that axiom on its head and maintain that because naval arms control is not now "needed," it is attainable. Then, should it *become* needed, (e.g., should U.S.-Russian relations deteriorate in the future), it will be in place. During the worst moments of the resurgence of the Cold War in the early 1980s, U.S. and Russian naval officers continued to meet under the INCSEA agreement and kept a vital communications link open when almost all others had shut down.

In dealing with this controversial issue, we have not agreed in all respects. From a Russian perspective, for example, restraints on general purpose operational-level naval deployments in what they consider "sensitive" open ocean areas (e.g., the Barents Sea) are desirable. From the standpoint of many naval analysts and practitioners in the West, they are objectionable on both principled and pragmatic grounds and are thus unattainable.

From the U.S. standpoint, Russian naval arms sales are often provocative, and severe restrictions on them are desirable. From the Russian perspective, such sales are a dire economic necessity at this time, and U.S. attempts to restrict them are interpreted by some as an attempt to secure and even increase the large U.S. lead in arms sales.

Having said that, we have reached a very large measure of agreement, if not consensus. Together we propose the following naval arms control measures.

Unresolved Naval Nuclear Issues

- U.S. financial aid and technical assistance to improve Russia's ability to comply with agreements calling for the dismantling and safe disposal of naval nuclear weapons and reactors;
- A verifiable bilateral agreement to destroy 50% of both nations' stored naval tactical nuclear weapons and then invite other parties to join in a verified destruction of the entire international stockpile.

Maritime Confidence-Building Measures

- A verifiable bilateral agreement for the Prevention of Incidents *under* the Sea;
- A full and formal exchange of data on the makeup, location, missions, building, and decommissioning plans for the ships and aircraft of both navies;
- An increased exchange of ideas concerning strategy, doctrine, and operations through direct navy-to-navy contacts;
- Prenotification and observation of naval exercises.

Operational Constraints

- A bilateral agreement to limit the size and activities of U.S. antisubmarine forces in designated areas near the Russian coast in such a way as to preclude effective "strategic" ASW but not hamper other "normal" naval operations, including "tactical" ASW (see Chapter 7 for a detailed explanation).

Negotiated Limits and Reductions of Naval Forces and Weapons

- A bilateral verifiable agreement to reduce each navy's SSN fleet to approximately equal levels, in accord with already announced unilateral reductions;
- A joint effort to take the lead in establishing a multilateral Naval Technology Control Regime to prevent the sale or transfer of offensive or destabilizing naval technology to countries in regions of conflict, with emphasis on a complete ban on the sale or transfer of nuclear-powered warships, especially submarines;
- A joint effort to take the lead in preparing for and taking part in eventual multilateral negotiations aimed at reducing the size of the world's navies and limiting their future building plans to a level of reasonable sufficiency.

Some will conclude that we are trying to resurrect deservedly dead issues. That is not the case. For example, during the Cold War the Soviet Union repeatedly put forth proposals for a *complete ban* on all U.S. ASW activities in the ocean areas employed by their ballistic missile submarines (SSBNs). We have devised a new approach toward enhancing nuclear stability by calling for restrictions on only certain quantifiable ASW force levels (amounting to a "strategic mass"), engaged in specific types of activities clearly linked to conducting a search-and-destroy campaign against SSBNs in specified zones. Furthermore, we recognize that a different *quid pro quo* will have to be found in order to gain acceptance of this proposal by the United States, and offer some suggestions.

In addition, we have developed some completely new proposals. Despite the economic incentives in both countries for exporting weapons, we advocate a mutual ban on exporting "destabilizing" naval weapons to third parties in regions of conflict. Long-range naval strike weapons such as submarines (especially but not only nuclear craft), aircraft carriers, maritime strike aircraft, cruise missiles, and so on, in the hands of actual or potential regional adversaries pose a serious threat to international stability in the post-Cold War world, and the short-term economic advantages of, for example, selling Russian *Kilo* submarines to Iran or U.S.-assembled Type 209 submarines to Egypt are not worth the risk.

We also realize that some western naval experts would prefer to dismiss the entire naval arms control agenda as a Cold War relic and jump straight to a cooperative posture. That is not a realistic position, however, because for Russia the Cold War "leftovers" retain a great deal of significance, particularly in light of the internal political situation. Russian ultranationalists and old-line Communists continue to make considerable propaganda hay out of the "naval superiority of the United States" and its refusal to engage in "naval arms control." It is with this in mind that we have put forth our naval arms control proposals.

Navies do not make national, much less global, policy. But when it comes to formulating maritime policy, who knows the ocean better than professional sailors? The *ultimate* task of navies, as with every military force, is to fight and win wars. But their *first* task is to prevent war, and that task remains critical in the volatile world we now face. Navies are not, per se, environmental or police agencies. But who else has the necessary trained personnel and sophisticated equipment to perform those functions beyond coastal areas? Whether the task is constructing a holistic approach to a policy of sea power, or preventing and containing regional conflict, or policing, monitoring, and protecting the ocean environment, navies have a crucial role to play for the foreseeable future.

Once the Cold War leftovers have been dealt with, as the two largest and most powerful navies in the world, the naval forces of the United States and Russia have both the responsibility and the opportunity to take the lead in constructing a regime of *cooperative security* at sea.

TOWARD U.S.-RUSSIAN NAVAL PARTNERSHIP

A number of small but important steps toward U.S.-Russian naval cooperation have already been taken or planned, as listed in Chapter 9. In that chapter we also summarized a number of further proposals for cooperation made in unofficial forums.

We support all of these proposals. However, we feel that the time is to ripe to take even bolder steps in the direction of partnership. Therefore we call upon the two navies and our governments to implement the following measures.

U.S.-Russian Participation in Multilateral Naval Operations

- Conduct joint studies on the possibility of naval peacekeeping and peace-enforcement activities under U.N. command;
- Allow Russian participation in NATO's Standing Naval Forces under the Partnership for Peace relationship;

- Explore the possibility of U.S.-Russian involvement in multilateral naval forces in the Persian Gulf and the Western Pacific under an appropriate regional aegis.

U.S.-Russian Bilateral Naval Strategic Nuclear Cooperation

- The United States and Russia should go beyond the level of cooperation embodied in the START agreements and coordinate efforts to assure the defensive security of their SSBNs by:
- Negotiating limits on strategic ASW operations as outlined in Chapter 7;
- Beginning to exchange information on the operational-tactical issues concerning SSBNs including deployment, defensive security, and basing;
- Beginning to exchange information on the design and construction of SSBNs, their defensive weapons systems, both active and passive, and the communications and command and control systems.

Regional conflict is now the greatest military danger facing both countries. Both navies have an interest in preventing and, if necessary, containing such conflicts. This is why we have called for several forms of naval cooperation to address that risk.

We must begin to explore ways in which the U.S. and Russian navies can operate together with the navies of other nations to prevent regional conflict. Multinational naval cooperation is a vital means toward achieving a peaceful international environment. The exact form of that cooperation is very much open to question. From Russia's perspective (and that of some western analysts), the United Nations is the best aegis for such naval cooperation. At best, this is a very long-term solution, given the many questions concerning the U.N.'s ability, financial and otherwise, to play such a role following its recent failures in Somalia and the Balkans. In the near to midterm, however, now that Russia is a member of the NATO "Partnership for Peace" agreement, it should be possible, under at least some circumstances, for Russian and U.S. naval forces to operate together in either of NATO's Standing Naval Forces. Outside of the NATO arena, we argue that Russia and the United States should take the lead in exploring the creation of multinational standing naval forces in such vital regions as the Persian Gulf and the Western Pacific in order to act as a stabilizing factor in those volatile regions.

We believe that the Russian and U.S. navies can operate together to study and protect the ocean environment and to act together to control such illegal activity as piracy and terrorism at sea.

Finally, we have been so bold as to propose that Russia and the United States explore the possibility of moving toward strategic nuclear partnership with regard to SSBNs, both in operational and technical matters, in a manner similar to the current partnership between the United States and Great Britain.

Some will dismiss this as fantasy. We acknowledge that it is a visionary proposal, but we mean it seriously for the long-term future. Of course, the continued reduction of nuclear weapons is in everyone's interest, especially in light of the dangers of nuclear proliferation. But as long as U.S. and Russian sea-based nuclear weapons remain in service as an element of deterrence, cooperation is a far better context than confrontation for their continued operations.

WHAT'S IN IT FOR THE UNITED STATES?

One final and most serious question mark casts a long shadow on this enterprise from a U.S. perspective: what's in it for us? After all, at this time the Russian Navy is largely confined to port and the U.S. Navy has its hands full with regional flare-ups and a declining budget. The most obvious objection to our agenda from a U.S. perspective concerns the future of Russia as a democratic nation with a responsible foreign policy and a truly "defensive" military strategy. Given the enormous political changes of the last five years, only a fool would attempt to "predict" Russia's future. Of this, however, we are certain: the very *process* of working together on this agenda for naval cooperation *in itself* will strengthen the hand of those in Russia who believe in democracy and cooperative security, and that is very much in the interests of the United States. It is true that Russians will decide the future of Russia. By adopting our agenda, it is our conviction that the United States and its Navy can make a positive contribution to Russia's future with very little risk to U.S. national interests at this point in history.

From a U.S. perspective, this agenda also constitutes a hedge against the failure of reform in Russia. *Now* is the time to "lock in" under verifiable agreements such critical elements of both countries' military drawdowns as the removal and destruction of naval tactical nuclear weapons and the reduction of both nations' nuclear attack submarine fleets. *Now* is the time to broaden and deepen ways to prevent and defuse dangerous incidents over, on, and *under* the sea. *Now* is the time to strengthen the communications links between naval professionals that can withstand the roller-coaster of politics.

Not to do so is, in our view, to run the risk of the two navies and their governments drifting back into a stance of suspicion, if not hostility, at considerable economic and political cost.

The United States Navy and the Navy of the Russian Federation have a unique opportunity at this point in history to cooperate in building a realm of genuine maritime security as we enter what some are already calling "The Ocean Century." We urge naval leaders and diplomats in both countries to take up this challenge with courage and careful thought.

NOTES

1. *Jane's Fighting Ships 1994-95*; *Combat Fleets of the World 1993*; IISS, *The Military Balance 1994-95*; Les Aspin, *Report on the Bottom-up Review* (Washington, D.C.: Department of Defense, October 1993); "Russia's Future Navy Plan," *Naval Forces*, Vol. 14, No. 6 (1993), pp. 6-7; interviews with Captain 1st Rank Boris N. Makeev (Ret.), Washington, D.C., January 17-24, 1994 and Monterey, Calif., May 10-17, 1994; "Russia Dumping 3 Carriers," *Seattle Post Intelligencer*, February 15, 1994; Dr. Scott C. Truver, "Tomorrow's Fleet: Effective Force or 'Rotten Timber'"? Center for Security Strategies and Operations Critical Issues Paper, April 1994; "Navy Cuts Fleet to 331 Ships," Reuter, February 24, 1994; "How Many Ships?" by John Diamond, Associated Press, February 25, 1994; Department of Defense, *Nuclear Posture Review*, September 22, 1994, p. 17; Norman Polmar, "Republic Navies: A Continuing Interest . . . in Submarines," U.S. Naval Institute *Proceedings*, Vol. 124, No. 11 (November 1994), p. 103.

2. Cf. Department of the Navy, . . . *From the Sea: Preparing the Naval Service for the 21st Century* (Washington, D.C., September 1992); *Forward . . . From the Sea* (Washington, D.C., November 1994); Admiral Felix Gromov, RFN, "Reforming the Russian Navy," in *Naval Forces*, Vol. 14, No. 4 (1993), pp. 6-12; Admiral Valentin Y. Selivanov, RFN, "A Navy's Job," in *Naval Forces*, Vol. 15, No. 2 (1994), pp. 22-31.

3. The classic formulation of this position was contained in "Report on Naval Arms Control," submitted to the Senate Committee on Armed Services and the House Committee on Armed Services, Department of Defense, April 1991, 37 pp. In 1991 the conventional arms control cell of the Chief of Naval Operations' Strategic Concepts Group actually handed out business cards emblazoned with the slogan: "Just say No to Naval Arms Control! It's not in U.S. Interests, and *we just don't like it*." Copy in the authors' possession.

SELECTED BIBLIOGRAPHY

Aldinger, Charles. "U.S. Will Avoid Quick Nuclear Cuts—Pentagon." Reuter, Washington, D.C., September 22, 1994.

Aleksin, Rear Admiral Valery I., RFN. "We Are Ready When You Are." U.S. Naval Institute *Proceedings*. Vol. 119, No. 3 (March 1993).

Amelko, Admiral Nikolai N. (Ret.). "Naval Arms Reductions: Prospects and Difficulties." Paper presented to the "Third International Conference on the Change of Soviet Military Policy and the Two Koreas: Nuclear Issues and Arms Control." Center for American and Soviet Studies, Dankook University, Seoul, Korea, November 4-5, 1991.

Ames, Paul. "Russia Now Partner with Ex-foe NATO: Pact Ends Decades of Animosity." *Seattle Times*, June 22, 1994.

Andrew, Christopher, and Oleg Gordievsky. "Inside the KGB." *Time*. Vol. 136, No. 17 (October 22, 1990).

————. *KGB: The Inside Story.* New York: HarperCollins, 1990.

Anthony, Ian. *The Naval Arms Trade: SIPRI Strategic Issues Paper.* New York: Oxford University Press/SIPRI, 1990.

Arbatov, Alexei. "Russia's Foreign Policy Alternatives." *International Security.* Vol. 18, No. 2 (Fall 1993).

————. "The Soviet Union, Naval Arms Control, and the Norwegian Sea." Chapter 3 in Andreas Furst, Volker Heise, and Steven E. Miller, eds., *Europe and Naval Arms Control in the Gorbachev Era.* New York: Oxford University Press/SIPRI, 1992.

Arkin, William M. *The Nuclear Arms Race at Sea.* Washington, D.C.: Greenpeace and the Institute for Policy Studies, Neptune Papers No. 1, October 1987.

Aspin, Les. *Annual Report to the President and the Congress, 1994.* Washington, D.C.: Department of Defense, January 1994.

————. *Report on the Bottom-Up Review.* Washington, D.C.: Department of Defense, October 1993.

"Aspin Acts To Avoid U.S.-Russian Sub Collisions." *Arms Control Today.* Vol. 23, No. 6 (July-August 1993).

Associated Press. "Navy Taking Short-range N-weapons off Ships." February 24, 1992.

Atkins, Arthur G. "Budget Cuts, Troop Withdrawals Shake, Reshape Russian Military." *Arms Control Today.* Vol. 24, No. 3 (April 1994).

Ball, Desmond. "Arms and Affluence: Military Acquisitions in the Asia-Pacific Region." *International Security.* Vol. 18, No. 3 (Winter 1993/94).

———. *Building Blocks for Regional Security: An Australian Perspective on Confidence and Security Building Measures (CSBMs) in the Asia-Pacific Region.* Canberra: Strategic and Defence Studies Centre, Australian National University, 1991.

Barnett, Thomas P. M., with Floyd D. Kennedy, Jr. *Redefining U.S.-Soviet Naval Ties in the 1990s: The Opportunity for Constructive Engagement.* Alexandria, Va.: Center for Naval Analyses, November 1991.

Bateman, Commodore Sam, RAN, and Commander Dick Sherwood, RAN, eds., *Strategic Change and Naval Roles: Issues for a Medium Naval Power.* Canberra Papers on Strategy and Defence No. 102. Canberra: Strategic and Defence Studies Centre, Australian National University, 1993.

Baxter, R. B. "Legal Aspects of Arms Control Measures Concerning the Missile Carrying Submarines and Anti-Submarine Warfare." in Kosta Tsipis, et al., eds., *The Future of the Sea-based Deterrent.* Cambridge, Mass.: MIT Press, 1973.

Belous, Vladimir. "Russia's Nuclear Security." *Sedonya.* February 9, 1994.

Berkowitz, Bruce D., and Allan E. Goodman. *Calculated Risks: A Century of Arms Control, Why It Has Failed, and How It Can Be Made To Work.* New York: Simon & Schuster, 1987.

———. *Strategic Intelligence for American National Security.* Princeton, N.J.: Princeton University Press, 1989.

Bicksler, Barbara, and James L. Lacy. *After the Fall: Russian Perspectives on Security and Arms Control.* Alexandria, Va.: Institute for Defense Analyses Document D-1141, March 1992.

Blechman, Barry M., et. al. *Naval Arms Control: A Strategic Assessment.* New York: St. Martin's Press, 1991.

Boorda, Admiral J. M., USN. "Loyal Partner—NATO's Forces in Support of the United Nations." *NATO's Sixteen Nations.* Vol. 39, No. 1 (1994).

———. "The Southern Region—U.S. Forces in Action." *NATO's Sixteen Nations.* Vol. 38, No. 2 (1993).

Booth, Ken. *Law, Force, and Diplomacy at Sea.* London: Allen & Unwin, 1985.

———. *Navies and Foreign Policy.* London: Croom Helm, 1977.

Breemer, Jan. "Naval Strategy is Dead." U.S. Naval Institute *Proceedings.* Vol. 120, No. 2 (February 1994).

Brooks, Ambassador Linton F. "Forward Submarine Operations and Strategic Stability." *The Submarine Review* (October 1985).

Browning, Lynnley. "Russia To Join Western Ships in Naval Maneuvers." Reuter, March 17, 1994.

Cable, James. *Navies in Violent Peace.* London: MacMillan, 1989.

Cardamone, Thomas A., Jr. *Arms Trade News.* Washington, D.C.: Council for a Livable World Education Fund. Published monthly.

Clinton, President Bill. *A National Security Strategy of Engagement and Enlargement.* Washington, D.C.: The White House, February 1995.

————. "Reforming Multilateral Peace Operations: Presidential Decision Directive 25." Washington, D.C.: The White House, May 3, 1994.

Congressional Office of Technology Assessment. *Monitoring Limits on Sea-Launched Missiles.* OTA-ISC-513. Washington, D.C.: U.S. Government Printing Office, September 1992.

————. *Verification Technologies: Cooperative Aerial Surveillance in International Agreements.* OTA-ISC-480. Washington, D.C.: U.S. Government Printing Office, July 1991.

————. *Verification Technologies: Managing Research and Development for Cooperative Arms Control Monitoring Measures.* OTA-ISC-488. Washington, D.C.: U.S. Government Printing Office, May 1991.

Corbett, Julian S. *Some Principles of Maritime Strategy* (1911), Annapolis, Md.: Naval Institute Press, 1972.

Corrigan, Gerald M. "A Sound Investment Reconsidered: The Future of the U.S. Navy's Undersea Surveillance System." *Naval Forces.* Vol. 14, No. 6 (1993).

Crickard, Rear Admiral Fred W., RCN (Ret.), and Gregory L. Witol. "Seapower and Reservation for Peaceful Purposes." Paper prepared for *Pacem in Maribus XXII,* Annual Conference of the International Ocean Institute, Madras, India, December 4-8, 1994.

Cushman, Lieutenant General John H., U.S. Army (Ret.). "Maneuver from the Sea." U.S. Naval Institute *Proceedings.* Vol. 119, No. 4 (April 1993).

Dalton, The Honorable John H., Secretary of the Navy, Admiral Frank B. Kelso II, USN, Chief of Naval Operations, and General Carl E. Mundy, Jr., USMC, Commandant of the Marine Corps. *"Revolutionizing Our Naval Forces": Department of the Navy 1994 Posture Statement on the Fiscal Year 1995 Budget of the United States Navy and the United States Marine Corps.* Washington, D.C.: Department of the Navy, 1994.

Davis, Malcolm R. "Russia's Big Arms Sales Drive." *Asia-Pacific Defence Reporter.* Vol. 21, No. 2-3 (August-September 1994).

Davis, Richard C. "Future Directions for Naval Arms Control." Chapter 6 in Lewis A. Dunn and Sharon A. Squassoni, eds., *Arms Control: What Next?* Boulder, Colo.: Westview, 1993.

De Camp, Major William T. III, USMC, and Major Kenneth F. McKenzie, Jr., USMC. "A Hollow Force?" U.S. Naval Institute *Proceedings.* Vol. 119, No. 6 (June 1993).

Department of Defense. *Nuclear Posture Review.* Washington, D.C.: Department of Defense, September 22, 1994.

————. "Press Conference with Secretary of Defense William J. Perry, General Shalikashvili, Chairman, JCS, Deputy Secretary of Defense John Deutch, Mr. Kenneth H. Bacon, ATSD-PA. Thursday, September 22, 1994." Washington, D.C.: Department of Defense, September 22, 1994.

————. "Remarks Prepared for Delivery by Secretary of Defense William J. Perry to the Henry L. Stimson Center, 20 September, 1994." Washington, D.C.: Department of Defense New Release, September 20, 1994.

————. "Report on Naval Arms Control." Submitted to the Senate Committee on Armed Services and the House Committee on Armed Services, Washington, D.C.: Department of Defense, April 1991.

Department of State. *Limits in the Seas: United States Responses to Excessive Maritime Claims.* Publication 112. Washington, D.C.: U.S. Government Printing Office, 1992.

Department of the Navy. *Antisubmarine Warfare: Meeting the Challenge.* Washington, D.C.: Office of the Chief of Naval Operations, April 1990.

——. *Forward . . . From the Sea.* Washington, D.C. Department of the Navy, November 1994.

——. *. . . From the Sea: Preparing the Naval Services for the 21st Century, A New Direction for the Naval Service.* Washington, D.C.: Department of the Navy, September 1992.

——. *Naval Warfare: Naval Doctrine Publication 1.* Washington, D.C.: Department of the Navy, March 28, 1994.

——. "Power From the Sea." Unpublished draft, August 27, 1994.

Dimitrov, Georgy. "Possible New Restrictions on the Use of Naval Mines." Chapter 5 in Josef Goldblat, ed. *Maritime Security: The Building of Confidence.* UNIDIR Doc. 92/89. New York: United Nations, 1992.

Drew, Christopher, Michael Millenson, and Robert Becker. "Enemies Below." Six-part series in the *Chicago Tribune*, January 6-11, 1991.

Dur, Rear Admiral Philip A., USN. "Presence: Forward, Ready, Engaged." U.S. Naval Institute *Proceedings.* Vol. 120, No. 6 (June 1994).

Edney, Admiral Leon, USN. "Future Alliance Maritime Posture." *NATO's Sixteen Nations.* Vol. 37, No. 1 (1992).

Fedorchak, Captain Scott A., U.S. Army. "It Must Be Joint." U.S. Naval Institute *Proceedings.* Vol. 119, No. 6 (June 1993).

Fieldhouse, Richard, ed. *Security at Sea: Naval Forces and Arms Control.* New York: SIPRI/Oxford University Press, 1990.

Friedman, Norman. *The U.S. Maritime Strategy.* London: Jane's, 1988.

Garrett, Lawrence H. III, Secretary of the Navy, Admiral Frank B. Kelso II, Chief of Naval Operations, and General A. M. Gray, Commandant of the Marine Corps. "The Way Ahead." U.S. Naval Institute *Proceedings.* Vol. 117, No. 4 (April 1991).

George, James L. "Finally, A 'Forward' Naval Strategy." *Naval Forces.* Vol. 16, No. 3 (1995).

——. *The U.S. Navy in the 1990s: Alternatives for Action.* Annapolis, Md.: Naval Institute Press, 1992.

Goldblat, Josef, ed. *Maritime Security: The Building of Confidence.* UNIDIR Doc. 92/89. New York: United Nations, 1992.

Gordievsky, Oleg. "Pershing Paranoia in the Kremlin." *The Times* (London), February 27, 1990.

Gordon, Michael R. "U.S. Is Considering Aiming Its Missiles Away from Russia." *New York Times,* December 6, 1993.

Gray, Colin S. "Arms Control Doesn't Control Arms." *Orbis.* Vol. 37, No. 3 (Summer 1993).

Greenhouse, Steven. "U.S. Cuts Nuclear Arsenal, Hoping Russia Will Follow." *New York Times,* September 23, 1994.

Gromov, Admiral Felix, RFN. "Reforming the Russian Navy." *Naval Forces.* Vol. 14, No. 4 (1993).

Grove, Eric. *Battle for the Fiørds: NATO's Forward Maritime Strategy in Action.* Annapolis, Md.: Naval Institute Press, 1991.

———. "Naval Technology and Stability." Chapter 16 in Wim A. Smit, John Grin, and Lev Voronkov, eds., *Military Technological Innovation and Stability in a Changing World.* Amsterdam: VU University Press, 1992.

———. "U.N. Armed Forces and the Military Staff Committee: A Look Back." *International Security.* Vol. 17, No. 4 (Spring 1993).

Handler, Joshua, and William Arkin. *Nuclear Warships and Naval Nuclear Weapons 1990: A Complete Inventory.* Washington, D.C.: Greenpeace, 1990.

Hanley, Dr. John T. "Implications of the Changing Nature of Conflict for the Submarine Force." *Naval War College Review.* Vol. 46, No. 4 (Autumn 1993).

Harrington, Lieutenant Commander Melissa, USN. "Comments and Discussion." U.S. Naval Institute *Proceedings.* Vol. 119, No. 6 (June 1993).

Hartmann, Frederick H. *Naval Renaissance: The U.S. Navy in the 1980s.* Annapolis, Md.: Naval Institute Press, 1990.

Hartung, William. *And Weapons for All: How America's Multibillion-Dollar Arms Trade Warps Our Foreign Policy and Subverts Democracy at Home.* New York: HarperCollins, 1994.

Hay, Bud, and Captain Bob Gile, USNR (Ret.). *Global War Game: The First Five Years.* Newport, R.I.: Naval War College, n.d., ca. 1984.

Hill, Rear Admiral J. R., RSN (Ret.). *Arms Control at Sea.* Annapolis, Md.: Naval Institute Press, 1989.

———. "Maritime Arms Control in the Asia-Pacific Region." Chapter 4 in Ross Babbage and Sam Bateman, eds., *Maritime Change: Issues for Asia.* Sydney: Allen & Unwin, 1993.

Hilton, Rear Admiral Robert P., Sr., USN. "The U.S.-Soviet Incidents at Sea Treaty." *Naval Forces.* Vol. 6, No. 1 (1985).

Hodgson, Bryan. "Kamchatka: Russia's Land of Fire and Ice." *National Geographic.* Vol. 185, No. 4 (April 1994).

Holbrooke, Richard. "Japan and the United States: Unending the Unequal Partnership." *Foreign Affairs.* Vol. 70, No. 5 (Winter 1991-92).

Huchthausen, Captain Peter, USN (Ret.). "Russian Navy in Distress." U.S. Naval Institute *Proceedings.* Vol. 119, No. 5 (May 1993).

International Institute for Strategic Studies. *The Military Balance 1993-1994.* London: Brassey's/IISS, October 1993.

Isby, David. "The Targeting of Former Soviet Ballistic Missiles." *Jane's Intelligence Review* (November 1993).

Joint Chiefs of Staff. *National Military Strategy of the United States of America: A Strategy of Flexible and Selective Engagement.* Washington, D.C.: The Pentagon, February 1995.

Joint Statement Concerning a Uniform Interpretation of Rules of International Law Governing Innocent Passage. Signed by the United States of America and the Union of Soviet Socialist Republics, September 23, 1989.

Katana, Commander Tom, USN. " . . . From the Sea: SEALS to the Carriers." U.S. Naval Institute *Proceedings.* Vol. 119, No. 6 (June 1993).

Kaufman, Robert Gordon. *Arms Control during the Pre-Nuclear Era: The United States and Naval Limitations between the Two World Wars.* New York: Columbia University Press, 1990.

Kelso, Admiral Frank B. II. "Charting a Course for the Future." *Seapower.* Vol. 34, No. 4 (April 1991).

————, and General Carl E. Mundy, Jr., U.S. Marine Corps. "The Naval Service Is Joint." U.S. Naval Institute *Proceedings.* Vol. 119, No. 5 (May 1993).

Kerr, Pauline. *Eyeball to Eyeball: U.S. & Soviet Naval & Air Operations in the North Pacific, 1981-1990.* Canberra: Peace Research Centre, Australian National University, 1991.

Koltsov, Pavel. "We are Obliged to Save the Navy." *Nezavismaya Gazeta.* March 18, 1994.

Kortunov, Sergei. "A Russian Perspective on Naval Arms Control and CSBMs." Chapter 7 in Andrew Mack, ed., *A Peaceful Ocean? Maritime Security in the Pacific in the Post-Cold War Era.* Sydney: Allen & Unwin, 1993.

Kraska, Lieutenant (JG) James, USNR. "Gatekeepers of the Gulf." U.S. Naval Institute *Proceedings.* Vol. 120, No. 3 (March 1994).

Kraus, Commander George F., Jr., USN (Ret.). "Russian Naval Views: Adrift in Heavy Seas." U.S. Naval Institute *Proceedings.* Vol. 120, No. 4 (April 1994).

Kristensen, Hans M., William M. Arkin, and Joshua Handler. *Aircraft Carriers: The Limits of Nuclear Power.* Washington, D.C.: Greenpeace, June 1994.

Lacy, James L. *A Different Equation: Naval Issues and Arms Control after 1991.* Alexandria, Va.: Institute for Defense Analyses Paper P-2768, released December 1993.

Lancaster, John, and Barton Gellman. "National Security Strategy Paper Arouses Pentagon, State Department Debate." *Washington Post,* March 3, 1994.

Lehman, John. *Command of the Seas: Building the 600 Ship Navy.* New York: Scribner's, 1988.

Lewis, Dr. William H. "Presidential Decision Directive-25: Multilateral Peace Operations." *INSS Strategic Forum.* No. 3 (July 1994).

Love, Robert W. *History of the U.S. Navy, Volume One: 1775-1941.* Harrisburg, Pa.: Stackpole Books, 1992.

Lumpe, Lora, ed. *Arms Sales Monitor.* Washington, D.C.: Federation of American Scientists, published monthly.

Lynn-Jones, Sean M. "Agreements To Prevent Incidents at Sea and Dangerous Military Activities: Potential Applications in the Asia-Pacific Region." Chapter 4 in Andrew Mack, ed., *A Peaceful Ocean?* Sydney: Allen & Unwin, 1993.

————. "A Quiet Success for Arms Control: Preventing Incidents at Sea." *International Security.* Vol. 9, No. 4 (Spring 1985).

Mack, Andrew, ed. *A Peaceful Ocean? Maritime Security in the Pacific in the Post-Cold War Era.* Sydney: Allen & Unwin, 1993.

————, and Paul Keal, eds. *Security & Arms Control in the North Pacific.* Sydney: Allen & Unwin, 1988.

Makeev, Captain 1st Rank Boris (Ret). "Naval Aspects of National Security and Confidence-Building Measures in the Asia-Pacific Region." Paper presented to the United Nations Workshop on Confidence Building Measures, Katmandu, January 1993.

————, et al. *The Navy: Its Role, Prospects for Development, and Employment.* In Russian. Moscow: Voyenizdat, 1988.

————. "Questions of Theory: Naval Arms Limitations and Defensive Sufficiency." In Russian. *Morsky Sbornik,* No. 1 (January 1993).

Meconis, Charles A. "Naval Arms Control in the Asia-Pacific Region after the Cold War." In Elisabeth Mann Borgese, Norton Ginsburg, and Joseph R. Morgan, eds., *Ocean Yearbook 11* Chicago: University of Chicago Press, 1994.

————, ed. "Asia-Pacific Dialogue on Maritime Security and Confidence-Building Measures." Transcript of Proceedings held on September 11-13, 1992. Seattle: Institute for Global Security Studies, 1993.

————, and Michael D. Wallace. "A Modest Proposal for a UN Naval Peacekeeping Force." Seattle: Institute for Global Security Studies Working Paper, 1991.

————, and Michael D. Wallace. "Naval Rivalry and Command Survivability." Chapter 7 in Frank Langdon, and Douglass Ross, eds., *Superpower Maritime Strategy in the Pacific.* London: Routledge, 1990.

Miller, Admiral Paul David, USN. "Adapting Alliance Forces To Meet Needs." *NATO's Sixteen Nations.* Vol. 39, No. 1 (1994).

Miller, Steven E., and Stephen Van Evera, eds. *Naval Strategy and National Security: An International Security Reader.* Princeton, N.J.: Princeton University Press, 1988.

Moreland, Captain J. W., USN, Captain Fumio Otya, JMSDF, and Captain V. D. Pan'kov, RFN. *Naval Cooperation in the Pacific: Looking to the Future.* Center for International Security and Arms Control: Stanford University, February 1993.

Mott, Commander C. P., USN. "Naval Forces after . . . *From the Sea.*" U.S. Naval Institute *Proceedings.* Vol. 119, No. 9 (September 1993).

Mundy, General Carl E., Jr., USMC. "Getting It Right . . . *From the Sea.*" U.S. Naval Institute *Proceedings.* Vol. 120, No. 1 (January 1994).

Murray, Blair L. "Trust in Tomorrow's World: Verification." Chapter 8 in Lewis A. Dunn, and Sharon Squassoni, eds., *Arms Control: What's Next?* Boulder, Colo.: Westview, 1993.

Nickerson, Collin. "Fast, Well-armed Pirates Terrorize Modern Shippers." *Boston Globe,* May 11, 1993.

Office of Naval Intelligence. *Director of Naval Intelligence Posture Statement 1994.* Suitland, Md.: Office of Naval Intelligence, 1994.

————. *Worldwide Submarine Proliferation in the Coming Decade.* Suitland, Md.: Office of Naval Intelligence, 1995.

Oliver, Rear Admiral Daniel T., USN. "A Force Molecule." U.S. Naval Institute *Proceedings.* Vol. 119, No. 6 (June 1993).

Owens, Admiral William O. *High Seas: The Naval Passage to an Uncharted World.* Annapolis, MD: Naval Institute Press, 1995.

Peppe, Lieutenant Commander P. Kevin, USN. "Submarines in the Littorals." U.S. Naval Institute *Proceedings.* Vol. 119, No. 7 (July 1993).

Perla, Peter. *The Art of Wargaming.* Annapolis, Md.: Naval Institute Press, 1990.

Pierce, Commander Terry C. "Not a CVN Gator." U.S. Naval Institute *Proceedings.* Vol. 119, No. 6 (June 1993).

Polmar, Norman. "Comments and Discussion." U.S. Naval Institute *Proceedings*. Vol. 120, No. 7 (July 1994).

Potorov, Captain 1st Rank Viktor, RFN, "National Interests, National Security, and the Russian Navy." *Naval War College Review*. Vol. 47, No. 4 (Autumn 1994).

Preston, Antony. "Russia's Future Navy Plan." *Naval Forces*. Vol. 14. No. 6 (1993).

Prins, Gwyn, and Robbie Stamp. *Top Guns and Toxic Whales: The Environment & Global Security*. London: Earthscan Publications, 1991.

————. "The United Nations and Peacekeeping in the Post-Cold-War World: The Case of Naval Power." *Bulletin of Peace Proposals*. Vol. 22, No. 2 (June 1991).

Pugh, Michael C. *Maritime Peacekeeping: Scope for Deep Blue Berets?* Canberra: Peace Research Centre, Australian National University, 1992.

————. *Multinational Maritime Forces: A Breakout from Traditional Peacekeeping?* Southampton: Mountbatten Centre for International Studies, University of Southampton, July 1992.

Purver, Ron. "The Control of Strategic Anti-Submarine Warfare." *International Journal*. Vol. 38, No. 3 (Summer 1983).

Ranger, Robin. "Learning from the Naval Arms Control Experience." *Washington Quarterly*. Vol. 10, No. 3 (Summer 1987).

Robinson, Dr. Ross. "The Changing Patterns of Commercial Shipping and Port Concentration in Asia." Chapter 6 in Ross Babbage, and Sam Bateman, eds., *Maritime Change: Issues for Asia*. Sydney: Allen & Unwin, 1993.

Roskill, Stephen. *Naval Policy between the Wars, Vol. II: The Period of Reluctant Rearmament 1930-1939*. Annapolis, Md.: Naval Institute Press, 1976.

Ryan, Rear Admiral Thomas D. "View from the Pentagon." *Submarine Review* (January 1994).

Sakitt, Mark. *Submarine Warfare in the Arctic: Option or Illusion?* Center for International Security and Arms Control: Stanford University, 1988.

Schafer, Susan M. "Bumped Sub." Associated Press, February 28, 1992.

Schmemann, Serge. "Moscow Outlines 'Doctrine' for Its Military of the Future." *New York Times*, November 3, 1993.

Selivanov, Admiral Valentin Y., RFN. "The Baltic Fleet—Safeguarding National Interests." *Naval Forces*. Vol. 16, No. 3 (1995).

————. "A Navy's Job: The Role of the Russian Navy in the System of International Security and Cooperation in the Field of Naval Armaments." *Naval Forces*. Vol. 15, No. 2 (1994).

Shen, Yi-Hua. "The Disarmament of Naval Forces in the North Pacific." *The Korean Journal of International Studies*. Vol. 24, No. 4 (Winter 1993).

Siegel, Adam B. "'Just Say No!' The U.S. Navy and Arms Control: A Misguided Policy?" *Naval War College Review*. Vol. 43, No. 1 (Winter 1990).

Skaridov, Captain 2nd Rank Alexander S., RFN, Commander Daniel D. Thompson, USN, and Lieutenant Commander Yang Zhiqun, PLA(N). *Asian-Pacific Maritime Security: New Possibilities for Naval Cooperation?* Center for International Security and Arms Control: Stanford University, February, 1994.

Smith, Captain Edward A., Jr., U.S. Navy. "What . . . *From the Sea* Didn't Say." *Naval War College Review*. Vol. 48, No. 1 (Winter 1995).

Sokolovsky, Marshal of the Soviet Union Vasiley Danilovich. *Soviet Military Strategy*. New York: Crane, Russak & Co., 1975.

Statistical Abstract of the U.S. 1993: National Data Book. Washington, D.C.: U.S. Department of Commerce, 1994.

Stefanick, Tom. *Strategic Antisubmarine Warfare and Naval Strategy*. Institute for Defense and Disarmament Studies: Lexington Books, 1987.

Strategic Arms Reduction Treaty II. Signed by the United States and Russia, January 3, 1993.

Sur, Serge, ed. *Nuclear Deterrence: Problems and Perspectives in the 1990s*. UNIDIR Doc. 93/26. New York: United Nations, 1993.

Swartz, Captain Peter M., USN, and Jan S. Breemer, with James J. Tritten. "The Maritime Strategy Debates: A Guide to the Renaissance of U.S. Naval Strategic Thinking in the 1980s." Monterey, Calif.: Naval Postgraduate School Report NPS-56-89-019, September 30, 1989.

Timberbayev, Roland M. *Problems of Verification*. Moscow: Nauka Publishers, English edition, 1984.

Torremans, Guy A. H. "NATO's New Standing Naval Force Mediterranean." *Naval Forces*. Vol. 14, No. 3 (1993).

Treaty between the United States of America and Union of Soviet Socialist Republics on the Elimination of Their Intermediate-Range and Shorter-Range Missiles. Signed at Washington, D.C., December 8, 1987.

Treaty between the United States of America and Union of Soviet Socialist Republics on the Reduction and Limitation of Strategic Offensive Arms. Signed at Moscow, July 30-31, 1991.

Tritten, James J. *A New Case for Naval Arms Control*. Monterey, Calif.: Naval Postgraduate School Report NPS-NS-92-016, December 1992.

————. "A New Look at Naval Arms Control." *Security Dialogue*. Vol. 24, No. 3 (September 1993).

————. *Our New National Security Strategy: America Promises To Come Back*. Westport, Conn.: Praeger, 1992.

————. *Soviet Naval Forces and Nuclear Warfare: Weapons, Employment, and Policy*. Boulder, Colo.: Westview Press, 1986.

Trost, Admiral Carlisle, Chief of Naval Operations. "Approaches to Naval Arms Control." Hearings before the Subcommittee on Projection Forces and Regional Defense of the Senate Armed Services Committee, 101st Congress, Second Session, May 8, 11, 1990. Washington, D.C.: U.S. Government Printing Office, 1990.

Truver, Scott C. "Tomorrow's Fleet: Effective Force or 'Rotten Timber?'" Arlington, Va.: Center for Security Strategies and Operations, Techmatics Inc., April 1994.

Tsipis, Kosta. "Military Technological Innovation and Stability." Chapter 14 in Wim A. Smit, John Grin, and Lev Voronkov, eds., *Military Technological Innovation and Stability in a Changing World*. Amsterdam: VU University Press, 1992.

Tuzmukhamedov, Bakhtiyar. "'Sailor-Made' Confidence-Building Measures." Chapter 4 in Josef Goldblat, ed., *Maritime Security: The Building of Confidence*. UNIDIR Doc. 92/89. New York: United Nations, 1992.

United Nations. *The Naval Arms Race.* U.N. Study Series 16, U.N. Doc. A/40/535. New York: United Nations, 1992.

————. Annex to *Overall Strength of the United Nations Armed Forces, Report by the Joint Planning (JP) Staff.* JP (47), United Nations, December 23, 1947.

U.S. General Accounting Office. *Navy Carrier Battlegroups: The Structure and Affordability of the Future Force: A Report to Congress.* Washington, D.C.: U.S. General Accounting Office (GAO/NSIAD-93-74), February 1993.

U.S. Waterborne Exports & General Imports. Washington, D.C.: U.S. Bureau of the Census, TM985, updated monthly.

Van Ettinger, Jan. "Oceans, Climate Change, and Energy." in Elisabeth Mann Borgese, Norton Ginsburg, and Joseph R. Morgan, eds., *Ocean Yearbook 10.* Chicago: University of Chicago Press, 1993.

Vlahos, Michael. "A Global Naval Force: Why Not?" U.S. Naval Institute *Proceedings.* Vol. 118, No. 3 (March 1992).

Voronin, Guennady. "What Kind of a Submarine Fleet Does Russia Need?" *Nezavismaya Gazeta.* December 29, 1994.

Wallace, Michael D., and Charles A. Meconis. "New Powers, Old Patterns: Dangers of the Naval Buildup in the Asia Pacific Region." Working Paper No. 9, Institute of International Relations, University of British Columbia, March 1995.

————. "Submarine Proliferation and Regional Conflict." *The Journal of Peace Research.* Vol. 32, No. 1 (1995).

Watkins, Admiral James D., USN. "The Maritime Strategy." Supplement to U.S. Naval Institute *Proceedings,* Vol. 112, No. 1 (January 1986).

Weber, Peter. "Safeguarding the Oceans." Chapter 3 in Lester R. Brown, et al., *State of the World 1994.* New York: W. W. Norton, 1994.

Weeks, Dr. Stanley B. "Crafting a New Maritime Strategy." U.S. Naval Institute *Proceedings.* Vol. 117, No. 1 (January 1992).

————. "Measures to Prevent Major Incidents at Sea." Chapter 3 in Josef Goldblat, ed., *Maritime Security: The Building of Confidence.* UNIDIR Doc. 92/89. New York: United Nations, 1992.

Whaley, Barton. *Covert German Rearmament, 1919-1939: Deception and Misperception.* Frederick, Md.: University Press of America, 1984.

White House, The. *A National Security Strategy of Engagement and Enlargement.* Washington, D.C.: The White House, July 1994.

————. *National Security Strategy of the United States 1993.* Washington, D.C.: U.S. Government Printing Office, 1993.

————. "Press Conference by President Bill Clinton and President Boris Yeltsin, Canada Place." Washington, D.C.: The White House, April 4, 1993.

Winkler, Lieutenant David F., USNR, "An Incidents Under the Sea Agreement?" *The Naval Review.* Vol. 83, No. 2 (April 1995).

Winnefeld, Commander James A., Jr., USN. "Staying the Course." U.S. Naval Institute *Proceedings.* Vol. 120, No. 5 (May 1994).

Wolf, Anthony F. "Agreement at Sea: The United States-U.S.S.R. Agreement on Incidents at Sea." *Korean Journal of International Studies.* Vol. 9, No. 3 (Summer 1978).

Yergin, Daniel, and Thane Gustafson. *Russia 2010 and What It Means for the World.* New York: Random House, 1993.

Young, Henry. "Setting Goals for a Submarine Campaign." *The Submarine Review.* (October 1985).

Zagorsky, Alexei. "Russia's Naval Strategy in Northeast Asia." Paper presented to the Fourth International Seapower Symposium, Seoul, August 3-4, 1995.

Ziemke, Caroline. "Peace Without Strings? Interwar Naval Arms Control Revisited." *Washington Quarterly.* Vol. 15, No. 4 (Autumn 1992).

INDEX